Praise for *What Are You Going to Do?*

I've had the privilege of traveling with Compassion and know firsthand the tremendous work they do, but I didn't know the amazing story of their founder, Everett Swanson. How incredible to read about one man taking a bold step, his vision for children in need, and the result that is this marvelous organization. This is a must-read for anyone looking for an inspiring story of faith and encouragement.

MICHAEL W. SMITH, Grammy Award–winning Christian artist; bestselling author; actor

"What are you going to do?" Wow! These simple but powerful words heard by Everett Swanson have transformed so many lives around the world. I have had the honor to partner with Compassion for over thirty years. I have traveled and seen the incredible work that began with those powerful words. The church is the community, and this story shows how Everett embodied that in his work and vision. As I sit and think about these words and the work of Compassion, how fantastic at this point in life to know the most important thing is to invest in the people coming along behind us, and this story is a read that inspires just that.

AMY GRANT, Grammy Award–winning singer and songwriter

When God asks you a question, you should seriously consider your answer. Everett Swanson's world was rocked when he came face-to-face with one of the harshest realities of war: orphaned children left to fend for themselves in the streets and back alleys. But his biggest shock came when God asked him, "What are you going to do?" Swanson's response is shared in this courageous journey of a brokenhearted pastor whose compassion, sacrifice, and faithfulness against impossible challenges sparked one of the largest and most respected child ministries in the world, Compassion International. That response has literally transformed the lives of millions of children over the last seven decades. But beware, you will be challenged to answer that same question: "What are you going to do?"

WESS STAFFORD, President Emeritus, Compassion International; author of *Too Small to Ignore* and *Just a Minute*

Most have heard of the amazing work that Compassion is doing all across the globe, but few know the riveting true story of its founder, Everett Swanson. During the height of the Korean War, on a fateful winter day in war-torn Seoul, Everett encountered a street orphan who would not only change the trajectory of his own life, but also the millions of children who would come to experience the life-saving love and support of this wonderful organization. This story will captivate you, surprise you, and dare you to be a better human.

BRENT MCCORKLE, writer/director of *Jesus Revolution* and *I Can Only Imagine*

This book is a testimony to how God leads Compassion through Pastor Swanson, and God's endless love and mercy in Korea. I was delighted by how other powerful and moving Korean stories are woven into Pastor Swanson's story.

JUSTIN SUH, head of Compassion Korea

On the pages that follow, you'll read how a small, dusty, Illinois farm and the war-torn streets of South Korea, more than six thousand miles away, shaped a man's heart in a way that would change the lives of millions over the next several decades. Reverend Everett Swanson unexpectedly became a world-changer. And I'm so glad his story is finally being told. His life serves as a testimony of what can happen when God calls and an obedient heart answers. You will be challenged as you read. You will be inspired. But most of all, I pray you will be moved—moved with compassion to make a difference in the lives of others.

SANTIAGO "JIMMY" MELLADO, president and CEO, Compassion International

I set this book down asking myself if I was living the risk that godly obedience requires. When the voice of the Holy Spirit tugged, Everett Swanson pulled on his muddied Midwestern farm boots and followed. I think we need more Swansons who look into the empty eyes of the forgotten and marginalized, then wrestle with the question, "What am I going to do?" If you are ready to put a mirror to your faith and a challenge to your heart, grab a cup of coffee and dive into this immersive story of grit, heartache, and hope.

TIM JOHNSON, Freedom Pastor, Crosspointe Church, Tyler, TX

Few Christian nonprofits have had a global impact like Compassion International. I have been on the ground with Compassion in desperate places and seen their impact firsthand. Practically all of us know of their mission and work—but few know the full story behind this power organization. Eric Wilson and Matt Bronleewe share the riveting story of Everett Swanson and the founding of Compassion International. Wilson and Bronleewe transport us into the devastation of the Korean war to feel the chill of abandoned children, and confront us with the gnawing question: "What are you going to do?" We travel the country with Everett and his wife, Miriam, as they try to convince a nation of churchgoers to show compassion (which in Latin, Wilson and Bronleewe explain, means, to *suffer with*) to the orphan and the hurting. Everett's story reminds us that what is missing most in our practice of faith today is not a willingness to believe, it's a willingness to *do*. This is one of the greatest challenges to Christ followers today: Will you leave the comfort of your sanctuary and the safety of your subdivision to suffer with the least and the last? What are you going to do?

PALMER CHINCHEN, author of *True Religion*, *Barefoot Tribe*, and *Justice Calling*; Compassion International college speaker

When I was a young believer, I read so many biographies of the Christian "greats" that I eventually became discouraged, thinking I could never do such things. So, I wasn't initially thrilled at the prospect of reading this story about Everett Swanson, despite my great respect for the work of Compassion International. I am so glad I did. Here is the story of a man, an ordinary guy, who simply did his best to follow Jesus and share God's love. And look what has happened! Consider the tremendous good that has come to the world, not because of a superstar minister or incredible personality. Rather, it's because of someone simply saying "yes" to the opportunities that presented themselves, ultimately just saying "yes" to God. You know what? That's something I can do. That's something anyone can do. This book has given me fresh hope and vision for doing that very same thing for as long as I live.

JOSHUA WYMORE, missionary with Ireland and Beyond

This wonderful book is a testament to the indomitable spirit of Christian mission—from humble beginnings to monumental global impact. Yet, it doesn't shy away from revealing the sacrifices that big dreams demand, both from the founder of Compassion International and his loved ones. Far from a rose-tinted perspective, this is a raw and genuine portrayal of commitment in the face of overwhelming odds. Personally, we so loved reading the history of an organization we've respected and supported for 35+ years. Clearly, it's a story of calling, of the overwhelming weight of possibilities, and of the gradual unveiling of life's grand designs. But most importantly, it's a story about answering that all-important question, *What Are You Going to Do?* with the broken world you face daily. That's the question we are newly inspired to answer through our life together.

ANDI ASHWORTH & CHARLIE PEACOCK, coauthors of *Why Everything That Doesn't Matter, Matters So Much*

Our family began supporting Compassion over thirty years ago. Though we have had the privilege of visiting our sponsored children in India and Rwanda, I knew nothing about Compassion's history except that they began in Korea after the war. I opened *What Are You Going to Do?* with excitement and remained gripped until the last page. It's not only an inspiring story, but the authors present the material in a way that I'm sure will leave each reader challenged as well as touched.

JUDITH GALBLUM PEX, author of *Walk the Land, A People Tall and Smooth*, and *To Belong*

This is the true story Everett Swanson, founder of Compassion International, vividly told as only Wilson and Bronleewe can. From humble farm to war-torn Korea to the genesis of Compassion International, *What Are You Going to Do?* speaks to Swanson's faith and calling to lessen the suffering of others, and his incredible legacy that has served millions of children. Inspirational, evocative, and important, it will leave readers asking: "What Am I Going to Do?"

TOSCA LEE, *New York Times* bestselling author

Surprising, inspiring, motivating—here's the untold, uplifting account of the origin of Compassion International. You'll emerge encouraged and challenged by this story of serving Jesus by serving those in need. Take it to heart and share it with others!

LEE STROBEL, bestselling author, founder of the Center for Evangelism and Applied Apologetics at Colorado Christian University

This is a story that needs to be told. As a Compassion advocate for over twenty years, I cannot recommend this book enough. I dare you to read Everett's story and try to walk away unchanged. This book will leave you challenged by the echoing reverberation of one simple question in wake of a life well lived: "Now, what am I going to do?"

MIKE DONEHEY, lead singer of Tenth Avenue North

The story of Compassion is an inspiring account of God weaving His plans through the faithful life of Everett Swanson. Told from the unique vantage point of Matt Bronleewe and Eric Wilson, this is a book well worth becoming a priority read for any Christian.

KEITH & KRISTYN GETTY, artists and hymnwriters

A sterling example of what one individual can do to make a huge difference in the world if they believe in and listen to God. Even when the challenge weighs them down. Everett Swanson answered the call and left the rest to desire and faith. Can one person change the world? They can if they are willing to answer this question: "What are you going to do?" I highly recommend you not only read this book, but also use it to guide you to your answer to this question.

STEVEN YOUNG, founder, Home Street Home Ministries; author of *From Chains to Change*

Most people see a need and find someone else to champion the cause. Not Everett Swanson. He changed the world by saying, "If not me, who else?" A brilliant life and story that forces us to answer the question about our own lives when we encounter the poor and the needy: "What are you going to do?"

LUKE SMALLBONE, For King and Country

How One Simple Question Transformed Lives Around the World

What are you going to do?

The Inspiring Story of
Everett Swanson and the
Founding of **COMPASSION
INTERNATIONAL**

ERIC WILSON AND MATT BRONLEEWE

MOODY PUBLISHERS
CHICAGO

Edited by Kevin Mungons
Interior design: Puckett Smartt
Cover design: Erik M. Peterson
Cover graphic of map copyright © 2023 by Porcupen/Adobe Stock (188538845). All rights reserved.
Cover photo courtesy of Compassion International
Author photo, Wilson: Carolyn Rose Wilson
Author photo, Bronleewe: Sara Kiesling

Library of Congress Cataloging-in-Publication Data

Names: Wilson, Eric Peter, author. | Bronleewe, Matt, author.
Title: What are you going to do? : how one simple question transformed
    lives around the world: the inspiring story of Everett Swanson and the
    founding of Compassion International / by Eric Wilson and Matt
    Bronleewe.
Description: Chicago : Moody Publishers, 2024. | Includes bibliographical
    references. | Summary: "The inspiring true story of Everett Swanson.
    Swanson's heart broke when he stumbled upon starving orphans. He asked
    himself, "What are you going to do?" His answer led to the organization
    known today as Compassion International. Everyone-young and old-should
    know this amazing story of faith, courage, and compassion"-- Provided by
    publisher.
Identifiers: LCCN 2023025363 (print) | LCCN 2023025364 (ebook) | ISBN
    9780802432919 (paperback) | ISBN 9780802471826 (ebook)
Subjects: LCSH: Compassion International--History. | Church
    charities--Developing countries--History. | Evangelicalism--United
    States--History. | Humanitarianism--Religious aspects--Christianity.
Classification: LCC HN980 .W54 2024 (print) | LCC HN980 (ebook) | DDC
    361.7/5091724--dc23/eng/20231011
LC record available at https://lccn.loc.gov/2023025363
LC ebook record available at https://lccn.loc.gov/2023025364

"What Are You Going to Do?"

Dedicated to all those who have responded
to the question in times past, those who respond today,
and those who will respond in future generations.
Your answers matter.

Junyoung Jang,
our Korean researcher on this project, answered the question
in sacrificial fashion during the years of COVID-19.
She went to great lengths to gather stories from those who worked
and lived in Compassion orphanages during the Korean War.
Without her patience, wisdom, and cultural sensitivity, it is doubtful
these pages would have been completed with anything close to the
intrigue, grit, and veracity that she and her interviewees provided.
In a very real sense, Junyoung Jang is a coauthor of this book.

TABLE OF CONTENTS

What Are You Going to Do? uses representative dialogue, without quotation marks, to indicate the authors' creative license in setting historical scenes that are well sourced from historical events. This dialogue was approved for contextual accuracy by Swanson family members and Compassion International. Some names were also changed for legal and privacy purposes.

Though Koreans traditionally give their family name first, followed by given name, many English-speaking Koreans recognize the Western format, which we have adopted here in consultation with our Korean ministry partners.

Part 1

Fall 1952
Seoul, South Korea

"If it is distant from your eyes,
it also becomes distant from your mind and heart."
— *Korean Proverb*

REV. EVERETT F. SWANSON cannot escape the devastation. If he covers his ears, the concussion of mortar shells still buffets his chest. If he covers his eyes, the smell of death in wooden carts still fills his nostrils. He doesn't even think to cover his mouth, because he has no words to describe the horror all around.

Lord, have mercy.

Everett finishes a silent prayer and continues his walk between the bombed and bullet-scarred buildings of Seoul. Though a brisk morning wind sweeps down from the mountains, at least the sun is out. For this, he is thankful, and he tucks his coat under his arm.

It is his second trip to South Korea, this time by invitation of Chaplain Hyung-do Kim, a lanky fellow, chief chaplain at the Ministry of National Defense. Everett has preached to thousands of Korean officers in training, prayed with amputees in army hospitals, and surveyed the front lines where soldiers pace beside barbed wire.

Such a rugged, bountiful country.

And now the Korean War is tearing it apart.

Everett combs back thinning black hair and waits on a corner in the downtown district as a convoy rumbles past. The trucks stir up dust and diesel fumes, forcing him to wipe at his glasses.

13

Everywhere he looks, he sees a situation more desperate than a year ago. One of Korea's oldest names, *Chosŏn*, can be translated as "morning calm," yet its long history is one of conflict. Envied for its teeming rivers, fertile rice paddies, and strategic location, it is currently in a tug-of-war between America, China, and Russia. Refugees are pouring in from the north. Not so long ago, they experienced mighty revival, and now their cities have been leveled by US napalm and bombs. They come here with nothing but the clothes on their backs. The elderly hobble among them. Rich and poor, it doesn't matter, they live in shanties along the river.

At the street corner, Everett feels a sudden tug at his elbow. Before he can register what is happening, his coat is pried loose from under his arm. He turns and spots a Korean boy darting away.

Oh no, you don't!

Everett is nearly thirty-nine, not as light on his feet as he used to be, but still strong from his farm-boy roots. He has baled hay, mucked stalls, and filled pig troughs with slop. He's not about to let some youth get away with petty theft. By the time he takes off in pursuit, the kid is a half-block ahead, weaving between young ladies in black skirts and an older gentleman in a traditional horsehair hat. The traffic cop in the intersection pays no mind, stiffly pointing vehicles this way and that.

Everett's feet pound the dirt. He will catch this rascal.

The kid bumps into a street vendor, nearly trips, then keeps going. The vendor shouts at him. These beggar boys, as they are called, are a regular nuisance, parading defiantly in their tattered cotton pants while looking for opportunities to pester and steal.

Why not just ask for the coat? Everett might've handed it to him.

No, this thievery cannot be allowed. This ruffian can't grow up believing this is the answer. Such tactics won't win him any friends and will only make life harder in the long run. These are lessons Everett teaches his own children back home.

He pumps his arms faster. He is gaining on the beggar boy.

The kid races around a corner.

Everett makes a hard turn, regains his footing, and picks up speed. He can almost reach the boy's bony shoulder. Another three or four steps and the culprit will be in his grasp.

At the last second, the boy veers into an alleyway.

Everett shoots on by, skids to a halt, then backtracks. The alley is narrow, dark, and smelly. There is no sign of the thief. There's also no outlet. The dirty-faced urchin must be hiding here, probably only feet away.

Give me back my coat, Everett calls out, and I won't turn you in.

Silence.

Letting his eyes adjust, he hovers at the mouth of the alley. He is a pastor. All he had hoped for this morning was to enjoy a walk before praying with wounded, downtrodden soldiers. That is his job. He doesn't have time for beggar-boy games.

He spots his coat in the shadows, wadded atop a heap of garbage. As he snatches at it, the pile of rags comes alive. Startled, he takes a step back, then notices a dozen faces peering up at him, orphans with almond-shaped eyes over sniffling button noses.

Everett's heart seizes in his chest and his indignation melts away.

How long have they been here? When was their last meal?

He moves forward, arms extended in concern. These kids are so young. Having lost their fathers or mothers, they are survivors. They shy away from him. He knows on a deep level this isn't right.

Everett believes communism must be defeated, but these children shouldn't be forced to pay the price. Already, South Koreans have been cut off from relatives in the northern provinces, and North Koreans will view America as an enemy for decades to come. Now these little ones have been stripped of everything. They are so much more than beggar boys and girls. They are created in God's image.

Overwhelmed with compassion, Everett wants to draw them into an embrace. Perhaps he should pray with them. Have they ever heard the name of Jesus?

Their unblinking eyes stare into his.

Lord, what am I thinking?

Sure, Everett is a pastor, but these kids need practical help. They are so gaunt, their trousers held up with frayed, knotted ropes. Their limbs are shivering, their teeth chattering. If his own sons and daughter were hungry, he wouldn't just rattle off a quick prayer and hand them a Bible lesson, would he? Has he become that callous?

Wait here, Everett tells the huddled children, hoping they understand.

Leaving his coat behind, he hurries to a shop on the main thoroughfare and buys bowls of steaming soup. Trying not to spill, he delivers them back to the alleyway and sets them into outstretched hands.

What now? Where can he take these boys and girls?

Everett knows of US Army units who have "adopted" local orphans, providing them with food, clothing, and toys. While American soldiers have shocked many Koreans with their swearing, drinking, and gambling, they have also won some over with their generosity. What will happen, though, when the troops are shipped home?

He isn't sure what to do.

As he wanders back to his lodgings, he notices other kids in the streets. They lurk between buildings, under horse carts. Many carry tin pails and beg for food. Some bear the scars of napalm. Everett, while documenting homeless families along the river and women washing garments in the icy shallows, has somehow failed to notice the sheer number of these orphans. There must be thousands, even tens of thousands, here in Seoul alone.

Night falls, but Everett can barely sleep.

Will the Land of the Morning Calm ever be calm again?

* * *

The next morning, temperatures plummet. It is deathly cold. Everett sees his own breath as he steps outside, and the chill burrows into his bones. Ignoring his discomfort, he returns to the alley with food and hot tea.

As he draws near, a South Korean army truck pulls in front of him and squeals to a stop. Soldiers hop down and poke at a heap of rags. When nothing moves, they scoop up the pile and toss it into the back of the vehicle. They pull up to the next alley and repeat the process. This time, Everett's attention is drawn to a thin, lifeless arm jutting from the rags. Children have frozen to death overnight.

Dear God, no!

Everett vows then and there to do something. His options are limited, though, and he has only two days before his return to the States. He returns to the alley, and also shares his concerns with local aid workers, but he feels helpless.

On the date of Everett's departure, a fellow minister of the gospel, a Korean pastor, stops him at the airport. The man looks him straight in the eye and issues a challenge: "Mr. Swanson, you have seen these tremendous needs and opportunities. You have seen all these children. So tell me . . . What are you going to do?"

Suddenly, this is the most pressing question in the world.

Everett drops into his window seat on Pan Am Airlines and that question churns through his head. As the propellers begin to turn—*throppity-throppity*—he reminds himself he is no position to do anything. He has no funds. No backing. Who is he but a poor preacher with a family of his own to feed?

The plane accelerates down the runway, climbs into the sky, then levels out for its journey across the Pacific. With each *throppp-throppp-throppp* of the propellers, those six little words spin again through Everett's thoughts:

What are you going to do?

Throppp-throppp-throppp . . .

What are you going to do?

For years the people of Korea have had their hearts broken by hardship and tragedy, and now his own heart is breaking too.

What are you going to do?

Chapter 1

A NOBODY

In the bitter winter of 1913, the American Midwest braced for yet another storm. Dubbed the White Hurricane, the late-November weather system wreaked havoc across the Great Lakes, capsized vessels in 80 mph winds, and knocked out vital lines of communication. Waves battered and obliterated a Chicago seawall along the shores of Lake Michigan.

Sixty miles due west stood the township of Sycamore, Illinois. The residents didn't yet have home radios or TVs, and in the weeks following, they relied on the *Chicago Tribune* or local *Daily Chronicle* for updates as they handled the damage with stoic resolve.

On December 13, Emil Swanson paced his farmhouse floor with thumbs hooked into his suspenders. Though he knew he still had fences to mend, his mind was on more pressing matters.

His wife was in labor. It had been hours now. Groans carried through the walls from the other room and candlelight flickered weakly beneath the door.

Dear God, how much longer? Is everything all right?

Emil loved his wife dearly. He had immigrated from Sweden at age fifteen, learned English at a nearby schoolhouse, then married Emma Johnson, a fellow Swede. After losing their first child in infancy, Emma had birthed three healthy sons. This morning, their boys had wanted to know if they'd be getting another brother this time, or a baby sister, and Emil couldn't provide an answer. God alone knew the details of this child knit together in the womb.

A cry pierced the air, loud enough to stop Emil's pacing. It rose in pitch, then fell away. Running a hand over his head, he breathed his wife's name and waited.

At last, he heard an infant's wail.

Once allowed into the room, Emil found Emma upright in bed and sporting a weary grin. The swaddled form at her bosom had ten tiny fingers and a head of black hair. Emil searched his wife's eyes for the answer to a nine-month mystery.

A boy, she told him. Meet Everett Francis Swanson.

He beamed. *Oh, thank You, Lord. You are good!*

Early in marriage, the Swansons had decided against a life in Chicago. They wanted to raise a family away from big-city temptations, focused instead on integrity and hard work. Emil knew he would still have to get up early tomorrow to milk the cows and address the storm damage. This was how things worked in the Swanson household, and their newborn would help with the chores as soon as he could walk.

He was a nobody. A regular farm boy. An immigrant's son.

He had none of the Rockefellers' fame or wealth, none of the Vanderbilts' earthly prestige. Why, he'd be lucky if he fit into his brothers' hand-me-downs.

No one could have guessed he would impact millions of lives around the world.

While even Emil and Emma couldn't foresee where their fourth son's life would take him, they did believe God had a divine plan for the boy. Following Proverbs 22:6, they dedicated him to the Lord as they had with each of their kids and agreed to "train up a child in the way he should go."

* * *

Everett was six months old when the assassination of a duke in eastern Europe triggered World War I. Along the Western Front, pimple-faced soldiers rolled out razor wire and dug trenches to hold back the Germans. Both sides hurtled grenades and fired howitzers, while tanks, planes, and U-boats dealt their own deadly blows.

In April 1917, America finally joined the war, and President Woodrow Wilson implemented the Selective Service Act, drafting millions of men into service. The United States, many believed, was in a struggle of freedom versus tyranny, democracy versus imperialism, good versus evil. Army recruitment materials depicted Germans as apes, carrying off helpless maidens. Boy Scouts sold bonds to fund the war. Women were encouraged to work in munitions factories, while kids in backyards play-acted with stick rifles. They saw themselves as heroes, one and all.

For most Americans, pastors included, stoking fervor for God and country went hand in hand. Killing was more palatable when seen as holy war.

The Swansons viewed it differently.

As loyal citizens, Father and Mother were grateful for their liberties and stood by their president's decision, but they did not take lightly the loss of life. Even though DeKalb County had been named after a Revolutionary War hero, it was sobering to imagine their own youngsters facing enemy bullets and flamethrowers. The Bible the Swansons read daily to their children spoke of God's love for all humanity. He cared as much for soldiers born in Berlin as for those born in Chicago or Sycamore.

* * *

As World War I ground toward a conclusion, the Swansons did their best to scrape by. With the addition of baby Rose, Mother now had seven mouths to feed. She was grateful for Emil's job as a tenant farmer.

Highly regarded in the community, he was a good judge of draft horses and earned a small profit by working the dairies and cornfields. Of course, tenant farming was a fickle business. Bad weather, inferior seed, and unethical landowners often made things difficult if not impossible.

Oh my, Mother said, the daylight's almost gone.

She changed little Rose and put her down for a rest, then moved into the kitchen to prepare a meal for her boys. Her swollen belly pressed against her apron as she drew her hair into a bun. She itched at her tummy, then noticed five-year-old Everett in the doorway.

Baby number six, she told him. You have a brother or sister on the way.

Everett absorbed this stoically. Though he was a child of few words, he had plenty of strength and stamina, topped off with a bit of mischief. He stomped around in oversized boots and hefted milk containers half his height. He trudged through the fields like his father, chopping at pesky thistles. When the older boys wrestled in the evenings, he didn't hesitate to throw himself into the fray.

Mother tussled his hair. Everett, she said, go fetch us some corn and start shucking. It's nearly time for supper.

He nodded and marched off.

She sighed and wondered, as all mothers do, what her young son's future might hold. Some parents pushed their kids toward high-end salaries and acclaim. She was more concerned about personal character. Ray, her oldest, was already impressing his teachers with his sharp mind, and Les and Lawrence were gentle, good-hearted boys. They'd do well, she had no doubt.

What about Everett, though? He was harder to figure.

The boy would be starting school in another year, and while staying quiet would be no problem for him, sitting still would pose a challenge. Where would he put all that energy? Perhaps he'd grow to work the soil like his father, tilling, planting, and harvesting for hour upon hour without complaint.

Oh, enough of her musings. She had mouths to feed.

May the Lord do with her son as He so willed.

Chapter 2

TIME TO GROW

Everett's feet were rooted like stumps to the floorboards. Standing in the store aisle, he stared at the Rawlings baseball mitt on the shelf and wondered how much it cost.

C'mon, his brother Lawrence said. The clerk won't bite.

Why can't you just ask him for me?

'Cause you gotta do it yourself.

Everett's legs refused to budge. He touched the mitt's stitching and breathed in the scent of leather. He had friends who owned gloves and he wanted one badly, but he couldn't bring himself to make a basic inquiry. What if his crooked teeth showed? What if he stood there, mouth hanging open, and not a word came out?

He thought of a section Father liked to quote from Proverbs 17:28: "Even a fool is counted wise when he holds his peace."

Lawrence clapped a hand over his shoulder. For cryin' out loud, how're you going to make it in school if you can't even talk to your teacher?

Everett wondered the same thing.

Almost six years old, he had spent most of his days on the farm picking berries, baling hay, climbing trees, and going fishing. He tried to do all the things his big brothers did and looked forward to the day Father would let him borrow the shotgun to deal with rodents in the crops. He also latched onto his oldest brother, Ray, eager to absorb his knowledge in budding film technology. A camera allowed Everett to get close to a subject without drawing attention to himself.

Despite his active body and mind, Everett was still too shy to open his mouth. He figured it was best to be counted wise. Words, to him, were like coins to be saved—and he was saving up for something worthwhile.

* * *

Sometime in 1919 or 1920, the Swanson family of eight piled into the car with all their luggage and drove over two thousand miles west, from Sycamore to Seattle. Washington's waterfalls and snow-cloaked mountains left them in awe, as did the stories of gold prospectors and lumberjacks. The land was unspoiled, untamed. Father said they would make a better living here as they attended a church up on Queen Anne Hill.

It was school that worried Everett. He'd be entering first grade.

How far would he have to walk to class? Would he like his teacher? If she gave him loads of homework, would he still have to milk ten cows twice a day?

Before he and his brothers could head for the schoolhouse, Mother lined them up by birth order for a photograph—Ray, Les, Lawrence, Everett, Rose, and little Robert. Feeling bashful, Everett tugged at his tweed cap, pretty sure this was his first photo ever.

The camera flashed, and he blinked against the magnesium flare. Maybe, he mused, he should grow up to be a photographer. While hiding behind the lens, he could even earn enough money to buy a baseball mitt. Last summer he'd seen orchestra bands and Red Cross banquets celebrating the soldiers who returned from the war. Wouldn't it be great if he could bring such things to life through a camera?

Time to get going, Everett's mother told him. Don't want to be late on your very first day, do you?

Everett turned to catch up with his brothers.

Whoa, hold on, Mother said, snatching the cap from his head. You look like a little urchin, hair going every which way.

He squirmed in her grip.

Father grinned over a cup of black coffee, his boots already muddy from his morning tasks. Poor kid's going to go bald if you keep that up, Emma.

Please don't encourage him.

Father's voice turned stern. All right, son, hold still for Mother.

The second the comb stopped raking through Everett's hair, he squashed the cap back over his head and darted up the path toward school.

Did Everett first hear of the Korean peninsula in that tiny Seattle classroom? Or perhaps from a visiting missionary at a service on Queen Anne Hill? He himself never specified when God planted this seed in his heart. Like most Americans, he knew very little about that ancient land. Korea was clouded in mystery, just a faraway spot on the map.

The seed needed time to grow.

Chapter 3

JUST ONE GLIMPSE

All right, I know it's our last week in Seattle, Father said. That doesn't change the fact it's Easter Sunday and we are going to church as a family. Everyone into the car.

It was April 1, 1923, but as far as Everett was concerned, there would be no pranks played today. Despite their family's planting of gardens, tending of orchards, and raising of cows, they'd been unable to make ends meet. After much deliberation, Father and Mother had decided it would be best to return to tenant farming in Sycamore. There, at least, corn and dairy products were hot commodities. In the town itself, the Borden's Condensed Milk plant relied daily on fresh local milk.

Are you ready to celebrate Christ's resurrection? Father called from behind the wheel.

He is risen, Mother answered.

He is risen, indeed!

Everett groaned, which earned him a sharp look. He slumped into the back, squeezing between Les and Robert. None of this seemed fair. Who said they had to move again? Why did he have to leave his friends before fourth grade was even over?

They rumbled up Queen Anne Hill to the big red church. Flowers budded along the walkway and a Swedish flag flew overhead.

The Swedish Baptist General Conference had its roots in pietism. The movement emphasized personal transformation, biblical doctrine, and a desire for holy living. It wasn't enough to just study and pray. Faith should be put into action. Believers were to deal kindly with unbelievers instead of avoiding them, and they were to show special concern for orphans and widows.

At the curb, Everett and his siblings spilled from the car for inspection. Father checked for loose shoelaces and untucked shirts.

Les, he said, your tie's knotted all wrong. And Rose, darling, your bow's about to fall out of your hair.

Oh, leave them be, Mother said, nudging her husband. You tease me about the way I fuss over the children before school. Well you, dear, are just as bad.

Orderliness is important, he responded. This is God's house.

Everett wasn't sure yet what he thought about God—not that his parents knew this. He and his siblings were expected to be at church every time the doors opened and always in proper attire. Even if appearance didn't guarantee godliness, it was supposed to establish a sense of reverence. And were there any people more reverent than his parents? Father taught Sunday school and served as a deacon, while Mother filled in as an organist. Faith affected every part of their lives.

Father and Mother's dedication was equally evident at home. More than once, Everett heard his parents crying out to God for lost souls. For them, there was no greater joy than to hear of a person who converted.

Which meant converting souls must be the greatest calling of all.

There was little chance, though, of Everett becoming a preacher. While his brother Ray wanted to work with evangelistic films, and Les and Lawrence planned to be ministers of the gospel, Everett preferred pulling on boots and tromping through the barnyard over wearing a tie and sitting motionless in a pew. Unsure of his own beliefs, he was too small to be a preacher, too afraid to speak up.

Of course, this was all about to change.

* * *

The morning's sermon began with a story about a sycamore tree. The story was found in Luke 19:2–6: "Now behold, there was a man named Zacchaeus who was a tax collector, and he was rich. And he sought to see who Jesus was, but could not because of the crowd, for he was of short stature."

Nine-year-old Everett could relate. He wasn't sure he knew who Jesus was, and right now he couldn't even see over the heads in the row in front of him.

"So he ran ahead and climbed up into a sycamore tree."

Sycamore. This caught Everett's attention. Just like their hometown.

Whether he liked it or not, he'd soon be back in Illinois amongst the trees that hugged the Kishwaukee River. A Native American tribe had once lived there, hewing dugouts and weaving baskets from bark. The Potawatomi gave the waterway its name, meaning "river of the sycamores."

Why did Zacchaeus climb the tree? the pastor asked his congregation. Zacchaeus was an unpopular man, a tax collector, but none of that stopped him from trying to see Jesus as He passed by. He didn't care how foolish he looked, so long as he could catch just one glimpse of the Lord.

Amen, someone muttered.

Everett wondered if he would ever be brave enough to look foolish. He pulled a leg under himself to sit higher and get a better view of the pulpit. Down the row, his father shot him a look and motioned for him to stay still.

The pastor returned to the text in Luke. "And when Jesus came to the place, He looked up and saw him, and said to him, 'Zacchaeus, make haste and come down, for today I must stay at your house.' So he made haste and came down, and received Him joyfully."

Everett's interest in this message was growing. He pictured Jesus with a playful smile and Zacchaeus with a look of surprise. Jesus didn't just call attention to the short guy in the tree but wanted to spend time with him.

"And Jesus said to him, 'Today salvation has come to this house'" (v. 9). Was this what it meant to be saved? Everett wondered. To see Jesus and to be seen by Him? To invite Him in with joy?

His heart shifted in his chest, and he planted both hands on the pew to further elevate himself. He sensed his father throwing him another reproachful look, but he was too intent on the pastor's story to glance away. Never had the Scriptures seemed so relevant. He didn't want to miss a word. If there were a tree in the middle of the aisle, he would have climbed it himself.

Father cleared his throat, a sure sign he was losing patience.

Everett didn't even turn. Not now. This Easter morn, his eyes were on a Jesus who seemed more real, more present, than ever. His ears perked up as the pastor inquired if there were any present today who needed their own glimpse of the Savior? Was there anyone like Zacchaeus who wished to see and be seen?

When Everett stopped his bouncing, Father sighed in relief.

Now don't be shy, the pastor said. Respond boldly to the Spirit's nudging.

Unable to contain himself, Everett shot his hand into the air.

You there, young man. Hallelujah! Do you truly want to see Jesus and know His goodness for yourself? Do you understand the price paid upon the cross at Calvary? Do you repent this day of your sins?

Nodding, Everett felt tears well in his eyes.

Do you want Jesus to forgive and save your soul?

Yes!

Then today is your day of salvation. The pastor quoted from Luke 15:10: "There is joy in the presence of the angels of God over one sinner who repents."

Churchgoers rejoiced over Everett's decision and suddenly his parents were at his side, their eyes bright and wet in the sun-dappled sanctuary. He knew they had prayed for this moment since he was born—and now he was born again, part of their spiritual family. His sense of God's mercy was overwhelming.

Father chuckled. Oh, what a fool I was, son. And on April first, of all days. I thought you had to use the washroom, moving around in your seat as you were.

They all laughed.

Everett would remember this date for the rest of his life. "The moment I opened my heart's door to Jesus Christ," he later wrote, "I had a new responsibility to God to whom I now felt morally accountable; to Jesus Christ for He redeemed me with His precious blood; to the Holy Spirit who convicted and regenerated me; and to my fellow men everywhere for Christ had said, 'Ye are my witnesses, Go ye.'"

As a witness, Everett Swanson could no longer stay silent.

He finally had something worth talking about.

Chapter 4

DEFENSELESS

The flame in him did not die. If anything, Everett found his zeal for God burning brighter as he reached his early teens. He turned youth group testimonies into mini-sermons. He minced no words and spoke plainly from God's Word.

Resettled with his family in Sycamore Township, Everett often passed the Soldier's Monument that rose fifty feet above the courthouse lawn. A plaque at its base commemorated Civil War veterans who had "fought to preserve the Union, that the nation shall under God have a new birth of freedom."

While he felt a new freedom and respected Abraham Lincoln's ideals—a statue of the former president even guarded the high school's halls—his own loyalties were to the King of kings, the commander of the heavenly host.

Would a good soldier cower in a bunker and stay quiet? Would he pull away from the fight?

Absolutely not.

With hair slicked back, Everett marched from class to class at Sycamore High carrying his leatherbound Bible. If one of his teachers made a statement that seemed to oppose Scripture, he asked for the privilege of refuting it.

Everett's own brothers were impressed as he joined a gospel team, traveling to speak at the county jail, the sanatorium, the old folks' home, the local churches, and even on street corners. He overcame his shyness to face the crowds, and lives were changed as a result.

What made him such a fervent young man?

Money was never his goal. The Swansons were a frugal bunch, and aside from an occasional update to his wardrobe, he didn't spend much on himself.

Proving himself to his parents wasn't much of a factor either. They trusted and committed their kids to God's keeping, giving them plenty of personal liberty as they reached their mid-teens. Everett knew he had their full support.

Forgetting past sins may have fanned the white-hot fervency of some ministers but for Everett there weren't any deep dark secrets. As other boys his age chased girls, played sports, and worked on cars, he tilled the fields, sang in the school choir, and later participated in Future Farmers of America. Though he wasn't immune to temptation, he rarely had time for trouble.

Trouble was all around, though. It was in the news, in front-porch conversations, and in the streets only sixty miles east of Sycamore.

In 1929, Prohibition still held sway over Chicago, with bootleggers, speakeasies, and moonshine making headlines. Corruption and greed ran rampant. On February 14, Al "Scarface" Capone's men entered a garage on the city's North Side and used tommy guns to mow down seven rival mobsters. No arrests were ever made, and Capone became the area's undisputed crime lord.

Months later, on Wall Street, the hype of the Roaring Twenties came to a crashing halt on Black Monday as the market suffered its steepest decline ever. Panic set in. Private lives and public companies fell to shambles. By year's end, investors lost an estimated $40 billion. Dozens of related suicides took place, with some plunging from bridges or buildings, and others choosing to eat a bullet.

It was the start of the Great Depression.

While witnessing these results of a lawless age, Everett received his lifelong call to the ministry. As stated in 1 Peter 3:15, a Christian should "always be ready to give a defense to everyone who asks you a reason for the hope that is in you." He believed now more than ever that it was his duty to be a defender of the faith.

His message was simple: Jesus offers love and forgiveness, free of charge, for people everywhere—and all He asks in return is your life.

As battle lines were drawn between darkness and light, Everett was ready to say whatever he needed to say and go wherever he needed to go. There were no excuses. Hadn't Jesus instructed His disciples to spread into all the world and preach the gospel? Nearly two thousand years later, this world was more accessible than at any other time in history.

* * *

As Everett celebrated his sixteenth birthday in the winter of 1929, his older brothers were taking strides in their own vocations. Ray was in Seattle, and in years to come would work with Moody Bible Institute in science and film. Les was a gentle soul in the hard world of local loan collections, where he managed to inject godly wisdom and hope. Lawrence was dedicated to full-time ministry, with his eyes on a Midwest pastorate.

I need a paying job, Everett told his parents.

Oh, don't you have enough on your plate already? Mother said.

How am I supposed to travel and evangelize without a car?

You can go by bus or train, Father pointed out. Automobiles are a luxury.

Everett tried to contain his frustration. Things are changing, he said. These days, girls hardly even pay attention to a guy without a car.

Alright, son, is it a car or a girl you're after?

A job, he said hurriedly. I need a paycheck.

His mother squeezed his hand. Yes, you do, she said, eyes twinkling.

Armed with his parents' immigrant work ethic, Everett took a weekend shift at Turner Brass Works on the south end of town. In rows of barracks, employees created a variety of brass goods—nameplates, arc lamps, and gas lanterns—and provided light to countless homes and businesses. Decades later, Turner Brass would even make relay torches for the Los Angeles Olympics.

As satisfying as he found hard work, Everett wanted to provide spiritual light. Earlier that year, he and the students of Sycamore High had listened to the US president give his inaugural address over the radio. This was a first, and Everett wondered how he might use similar technology to share God's Word.

Eager to harness the potential in these new commodities, Everett would first need to deal with the various temptations each one presented. Like most teenage boys, he dreamed of driving his own automobile, but didn't realize until he climbed behind the wheel that he was a bona fide lead foot.

Oh, how he loved speed. The faster the better!

With an arm out the window, he wore a wide grin and let his fingers ride the wind. Was there any greater thrill than the roar of an engine and the blur of a curvy road? The joy of the moment erased any sense of wrongdoing.

Best be careful, Father warned him. Our police force just added an officer on motorcycle.

It's your safety that most concerns me, Mother said.

While Everett did his best to heed his parents, he drove as though nothing could hurt him. Lost in the moment, he often forgot where he was going. School, chores, work, none of it mattered when the air was whipping through his hair. His high school yearbook, *The Oracle*, even made a point of mentioning: "Everett Swanson's excuses for morning tardiness are willed to Weslie Lindstrom."

Despite the excuses and tardiness, Everett walked his high school halls with purpose. He was a junior now, with sinewy arms and sturdy shoulders. He loped past the boys in their letterman sweaters, his blue eyes fixed straight ahead and his Bible firmly in hand—until the day a girl with auburn hair stepped into view.

Her name was Miriam Edwards.

And the defender found himself defenseless.

Chapter 5

THE SPARK

There was no avoiding her. Each day at school, Everett encountered Miriam on the front steps, in the cafeteria, and during choir practice. They even sang together at the DeKalb Music Festival. He was almost seventeen and she was fifteen. Short and petite, she liked wearing nice shoes. She had smooth clear skin and an eye for fashion, and when she brushed by him in the halls, he tried hard to look away.

Lord, how he needed guidance.

Each night, he knelt beside his bed and asked for wisdom and strength. He awoke sometimes with his knees still on the floor and his head on the mattress. He'd never been in love before and wasn't sure how to handle this.

What should I do? he asked his sister, Rose. Do I say hello, just nod, or act like I don't even notice her?

Rose was a romantic, a literary soul. Just follow your heart, she said.

He wasn't convinced by her advice. Didn't Scripture warn that the heart was deceptively wicked? And what if Miriam was a distraction from his calling?

The Depression was worsening across the country and many people were in need. Companies were shutting down, workers were waiting in long lines for food, and crime and poverty were potent realities. Everywhere Everett looked, he saw both practical and spiritual work to be done. Could he really make a difference? Could a young man make a truly lasting impact?

Yes. He wanted to believe so.

He found inspiration in DeKalb County stories of those who had done good for others. In the 1800s, a man named David West had worked for the Underground Railroad, using a special false-bottomed buggy to ferry African Americans to freedom in Canada. Then came the orphan trains, organized by one Charles Loring Brace. He transported thousands of orphans away from the pollution of crowded East Coast cities, and though not all the children were treated as they deserved, many arrived at a local train station and were placed in loving homes.

Everett also found inspiration from his family roots. In 1891, Dr. O. L. Swanson had helped start a church in Sycamore while still a seminary student. Two years later he traveled to Assam, India, where he did extended work as a missionary.

From West to Brace to Swanson, each had followed a calling.

Though now certain of his own calling, Everett wondered if it was best to marry or to instead dedicate himself solely to the Lord's work. Of course, his own parents had married young. And didn't 1 Timothy 3:2 specify that a bishop or pastor "must be blameless, the husband of one wife"? Many of today's ministers had spouses. Billy Sunday, the pro-baseball-player-turned-evangelist, had a wife who kept on preaching even after he died.

If Everett was honest with himself, his desire was to find a bride as well. Yes, he wanted a woman to share life with.

How would Miriam feel about it, though?

You oughta ask her to a movie, Rose suggested. I hear *The Kiss* is playing down at Fargo Theater, and my friends, they all say Greta Garbo is fabulous.

With my work schedule, I'm not sure I could go.

Sure. But if Miriam says yes, at least you'll know she's interested.

* * *

Interested or not, Miriam refused to be rushed. A petite Norwegian with a backbone of steel, she admired women such as Madame Curie and Helena Dolder. Dolder had recently run for sheriff of DeKalb County and won by a landslide.

Imagine that!

Miriam and her family lived in Sycamore, in a three-story house built by their father. The oldest of nine children, Miriam assisted her mom in the kitchen, watched after her siblings, fed the chickens, and tended their small garden.

When it came to her faith, she kept that private. Her father, a bullheaded Norski, knew the Bible inside and out, but often ranted about greedy ministers and the passing of the offering plate. On the occasions her mother took their family to church, her father refused to go. Instead, he played cards with his kids on the weekdays, then drank heavily on the weekends. Once liquor hit his system, he was not a nice man. Sharp words were his weapons of choice, though his fists had been known to draw blood.

Miriam's mother endured it all quietly, sweet as could be. After the heartache of multiple miscarriages, she doted on her surviving children, even as she struggled with depression. Whenever she felt ignored, she stood at the bottom of the stairs and sang out, "Nobody likes me, everybody hates me, I guess I'll go eat worms."

For obvious reasons, Miriam wasn't in any hurry to marry or have kids.

This didn't mean she was unaware of Everett Swanson, with his black hair, hawk-like nose, and deep-set eyes. He had a good sense of humor and an easy laugh. His uneven smile lent him a touch of charm.

By the time Miriam was a junior and Everett a senior, the two were often seen together. They attended the late-autumn corn pageant and cheered for their football team during the winter game against DeKalb. Miriam listened to Everett's stories of golfing with his classmates during Senior Week, and he applauded her role in a glee club production of *Once in a Blue Moon*.

Lawrence kidded them about their clear attraction to one another. Well, look at you, he said to Everett. Aren't you energetic in your courting of Miriam?

Everett turned red and didn't speak a word.

Miriam pretended she hadn't heard.

She did finally agree to go bowling with him, and they might have roller-skated too, had he not viewed it as dancing on wheels. Dancing was dangerously close to being a sin. Instead, he strolled with her past the downtown shops, bought her treats from the popcorn stand, and shared a fountain soda with her at Barker and Sullivan.

Yes, he had feelings for her. That was plain to see.

She still had reservations, though. And when it came to love, she certainly believed in having a vote.

Saying yes to a life with Everett Swanson would be agreeing to a life-style unlike any she ever envisioned. He wanted to serve God by traveling the country and conducting evangelistic meetings. This was all well and good, but it required serious deliberation on her part. If married, they would never be affluent—that much was a given—and they would face her father's contempt for any man who called himself a preacher.

Her biggest concern was an even weightier one: What if she some-how came between Everett and God's calling?

Miriam had watched others tie the knot, then let their dreams and passions fade away. Life took its toll, as she'd seen with her own parents. Getting married and bringing children into days as dark as these seemed ill-advised, at best. Then again, what better way to fight the darkness? A godly family would truly be a testimony.

Despite her list of reservations, Miriam did trust and respect Everett. Few men in town could match his character. He worked hard like her father, without exhibiting any of her old man's cruelty. More importantly, he treated her as an equal. He never pushed her verbally, physically, or emotionally.

The other night, Everett had even called her the love of his life.

She wasn't sure how to respond. Could she say she loved him back? Was she ready for a lifelong relationship? Was she ready to cast her vote?

She looked away and said nothing, quietly blinking back tears.

* * *

By 1931, the Depression pervaded everything. Millions were unemployed and a number of local banks closed their doors. With Everett nearing graduation, Father and Mother encouraged him to pursue a degree at Bethel College, but he couldn't imagine making that kind of commitment.

This world was so quickly falling apart. Jesus might return any day.

Instead, using money saved from working the assembly line at Turner Brass, and from selling Watkins seasonings door to door, Everett purchased a canvas revival tent. Though nothing like the three-poled monstrosity Billy Sunday used to reach the masses, it was a start.

On graduation day in early June, Everett lined up with his classmates in his tassel and gown. The class motto they had chosen was Not the Sunset but the Dawn. It pointed to beginnings and beauty, to a new day ahead.

He glanced over the crowd. His parents were near the front, glowing with pride. And there was Miriam, a few rows back, simply watching him.

What was going on behind those beautiful eyes?

Considering the somber era in which they lived, Everett heard fellow graduates express fears about what lay ahead. Despite their hopeful class motto, many of them saw this day of celebration more as a day of reckoning. One of the yearbook writers even described the seniors as martyrs walking down to get their diplomas.

For Everett, martyrdom was more than a metaphor. Answering the call of God might cost him not just a shot at love but his very life.

Was this being dramatic? Maybe so, but the facts were undeniable.

He had grown up thinking only the early church and Middle Ages produced martyrs, but in recent decades God's people had paid the ultimate price on nearly every continent. From Congo to Mexico to Ukraine, the list of martyrs grew. In Seoul, Korea, during the 1860s, a ruler posted an edict that led to thousands of Christians dying by guillotine along the banks of the Han River. The stories of Christian martyrs were in books, magazines, newspapers.

Could he face that sort of death? Everett asked himself. Could he marry a woman, then subject her to a life of ridicule, danger, and hardship?

He sought Miriam's face in the crowd, but she was reading her program.

As the ceremony concluded, a final charge was given to the graduates and later printed for all to read. With thoughts running every which way, he barely noted the words that hinted so strongly at his own future:

Class of 1931
Have the courage not only to rise above the sordid but to strive for and keep a lofty ideal. If you would be indispensable to your community go on developing appreciations: for the kindness of others; for honorable dealing; for beauty in sound, form, and color, and for the Author of it all.

Everett had already set out to be *indispensable* to his community. Events would later lead him from his rural upbringing to gutted villages overseas, where he would show *kindness* in the face of brutality and *honorable dealing* with foreign officials. In fact, his simple, naive trust in others would result in remarkable successes—and in personal heartbreak as well.

Throughout his life, he would also shoot film by his own hand, utilizing *beauty in sound, form, and color* to introduce people to thousands of orphans and to the remarkable men and women who served them.

Truly, *the Author of it all* had a plan.

Right now, though, Everett knew none of this.

Graduation ended with whoops and cheers and caps tossed high into the air. Everett hollered too. He was done with school, done with homework. The future lay before him. He already had a job, a car, a tent, and a calling.

But what about someone to have and to hold?

From the crowd, Miriam's eyes found his. A smile tugged at her lips, and she held his gaze. There was a glimmer there—a spark, a fire! She'd never let her guard down before, never let him see straight into her thoughts. Considering her abusive home life, he had found this understandable. Now, though, she was confirming something special between them, a bond that went beyond words.

His chest swelled and he was unable to hide a goofy grin.

It was only a matter of time now. Good things came to those who waited.

* * *

On December 16, 1934, after dating for several years, Everett took Miriam as his lawfully wedded bride. She was the love of his life. He'd just turned twenty-one and her twentieth birthday was a month away. Standing before friends and family in a Sycamore sanctuary, the young Mr. and Mrs. Swanson sealed their vows with a kiss.

Overjoyed, Everett felt like a man ready to take on the world.

Part 2

Spring 1953
Daegu, South Korea

"Waiting for the earth to spin, for streaks of light
to brighten the eastern sky, in that quiet moment there is a calmness
that makes Korea the most beautiful country in the world."
—*Tucker Elliot*

GI-SOOK LOVES HER COUNTRY, so rugged and noble, yet everywhere she looks she sees horrendous conditions. Men live in shanties along the Nakdong River. Boys in rags dart through the markets, stealing food. Girls sell themselves outside the Daegu train station to pay for their younger siblings' next meals.

Gi-sook wants to cry just thinking of it. At eighteen years old, she's one of the lucky ones. She still has her parents, her brothers, and a roof over her head.

All thanks, of course, to her father's traditional teapot.

Her thoughts race back to a bitter winter.

* * *

In the deathly cold of November 1950, Gi-sook and her father flee their home and cross the river in Pyongyang. He is a businessman, a greedy capitalist in the communists' eyes, and if he stays in North Korea he will be killed. Beneath his coat, he carries a teapot containing all his wealth in gold, melted down.

Gi-sook and her father head south on foot past factories, farms, and villages destroyed by American B-29 Superfortresses. Their hands are frozen, their bones brittle, by the time they reach the border four weeks later.

This is the critical moment.

Papers, the guards demand, shifting the rifles on their shoulders.

Gi-sook and her father comply. She has heard of despicable things done by soldiers to young women, and she's dressed herself in motherly garb to avoid their attention. She burrows her chin into her torn padded coat with its tufts of cotton poking through. Exhausted as she is, it's not hard to act the part of an older woman. She is shivering uncontrollably, her cheeks scraped raw by the harsh winds.

You cannot pass, a guard snaps at her. We need further proof of identity.

Gi-sook shudders. She can't walk back to Pyongyang alone. What will she eat? Where will she sleep? In 1945, Russians and Americans split the Korean peninsula, separating friends and families, and now both sides are at war. The Russians and Chinese are aiding North Korea, while the Americans are backing South Korea. Hundreds of thousands are dead, innocent civilians among them.

No, she thinks. *If I go back, I will surely die.*

Her father drops to his knees before the guards, begging them to let his daughter through. They stare down at him without a shred of mercy. If she doesn't intervene, she suspects he might be beaten, even killed. His teapot will be discovered, their fortune taken away.

At this moment, Gi-sook believes all hope is lost. Though a devout aunt regularly invited her to church back in Pyongyang, Gi-sook has no faith of her own. She only went at Christmastime and barely knows a song or two.

Is God even real? Is it too late to pray to Him now?

An old church tune pops into her head. She has no idea what prompts it, but she's always loved the words to "Joy to the World."

May I sing a worship song? she asks the border guards.

Startled, one points his rifle at her. Are you a Christian? If so, go ahead.

She isn't, but she does.

The words flow over her parched lips and her voice gains strength. The guards listen without interruption, their faces blank. As she finishes, they simply step aside and let her and her father walk unhindered through the checkpoint.

Gi-sook and her father reach Seoul the next day, then ride for hours by truck over hard, uneven roads. As they move southeast, the temperatures warm and people walk around without socks—a sure way of getting frostbite in the north. This single observation convinces her things will be different here.

When at last they arrive in Daegu, they feel protected. The city is surrounded by mountains and its very name means "large hill." This natural stronghold helps create the Busan Perimeter, guarded by UN troops. Even so, Gi-sook and her father are two drops in a flood of refugees. Food is scarce. Tens of thousands are penniless. Disease and starvation are evident on every corner.

They have their teapot, though. They have their gold.

With her father's smuggled treasure, they buy a home in Daegu and the rest of their family eventually joins them from North Korea. Her parents spend the next few years working hard and saving to afford university educations for their children.

We will do more than survive, her father insists. We will thrive.

But how can I thrive, Gi-sook wonders, *when others are still suffering?* In these years since their escape, she has become deeply dissatisfied. Every day she sees orphans and young prostitutes wandering these dirty streets. Did she get past those border guards just to live a life of ease?

She is invited one afternoon to meet with a Christian elder at nearby Juamsan Mountain. There, during a prayer meeting, she witnesses God's work among humble men and women. Daegu has become the Jerusalem of Korea, a place of great spiritual awakening. The joy Gi-sook experiences here is indescribable. Feeling loved and accepted, she decides to follow Christ, and from this moment on she practically lives on the mountain.

Her parents visit her many times. You must come home with us, they insist. What has happened to you?

I can't go back to a normal life, she responds. I mean no disrespect.

You are our daughter, Gi-sook. You deserve much better. Don't let yourself become too crazy for this Jesus.

She knows her parents' intentions are good. She is meant for something more, though. To love God is to love others. To follow Jesus is to carry a cross. After all the grace He has shown her, she wants to offer His grace to others. Already, her heart aches for those displaced by this senseless war. They have nowhere to go, no homes, no education.

Gi-sook asks herself: *What are you going to do?*

For days on end, those six little words peck at her—*tap, tap, tap.* There must be a way she can help. If she doesn't, who will?

What are you going to do?

After checking into various options, she sets up a tent near an army base. She invites orphaned children and the young women from the train station, then instructs them in the basics of reading, math, and science. They aren't always easy to work with. They are hungry and unwashed. They're eager to learn, though, and keep coming each day.

Slowly, her efforts earn her parents' respect.

Take this, her father says, slipping her some money from his savvy business dealings. It is noble what you are doing, Gi-sook, but look at your brothers now heading off to university in Seoul. You, too, could earn a degree and a good wage.

Everything that makes me happy is right here, Father.

What about marriage? Promise me you won't marry one of the Christian men up on this mountain. If you do, you'll be poor the rest of your days.

Even the straw shoe has a mate, she says, quoting a Korean proverb.

Maybe so, Gi-sook, but two straw shoes cannot hold up for long. Please, not one of those Christians. It will be a difficult path and I will never agree to it. I will not.

She sees the anguish in her father's eyes. Even at this moment, her stomach is hollow with hunger and his concern for her is genuine. This is her final chance to turn back and embrace the lavish life he wants for her.

Tap-tap-tap . . .

What are you going to do?

Gi-sook sets her chin. Father, you are a man of honor, but I must obey my Father in heaven, regardless of the consequences. If He wishes for me to marry, then He will bring to me the right man when it is time. Even then, I will expand my facilities and keep serving others.

Just like that you have made your decision?

She nods. This is what I must do.

Chapter 6

NO GUARANTEES

As 1935 swung around, Everett and Miriam Swanson began building their new life together. Despite some early conflicts, they were truly committed to each other. The romance between them would draw comments for years to come, and the mutual sparkle in their eyes would persist to the very end.

Now was just the beginning, though.

And they had work to do.

When he was single, Everett had embarked on his solo tent ministry while an estimated 15 million Americans were out of work. He had sought out communities in need of revival, as despondent men and women stood in breadlines and nearly half the nation's banking institutions closed their doors. It was an era depicted in Steinbeck's *The Grapes of Wrath*, with entire families on the brink of starvation. Even as he wrestled with discouragement, he reminded himself of the apostle Paul's words in 1 Timothy 4:12: "Let no one despise your youth, but be an example to the believers in word, in conduct, in love."

Yes, he could do that.

Speaking directly, living uprightly, and showing love.

Now Everett was ready to hit the road again, this time with his new bride, on a vagabond, nationwide, evangelistic tour. Family members gathered round, watching as he tucked Miriam's suitcase beside the gospel tent in the back. He closed the trunk, dusted off his hands, then held the door open for his wife.

A fool's errand, her father grumbled. My daughter deserves better.

Though Everett had his parents' support, he couldn't just brush off his father-in-law's concerns. In the country's current state, traveling was a risky proposition, with gas prices sky-high and DeKalb County roads still years from being paved. Wouldn't it make more sense for the newlyweds to be moving into a home and picking out items at Johnson's Furniture Mart?

Things are bad, Everett responded aloud to his father-in-law. No arguing that. More than ever, though, people need hope, and we cannot ignore this opportunity.

What about Miriam? She's the one you ought to be thinking of.

I'll do my best for her, sir. But it's the Lord who is our provider.

Tell that to the millions of folks without jobs. Oklahoma's had temperatures over 115 degrees. Parts of Kansas were buried by dust storms. This nonsense of yours, don't you think it can wait?

Everett and Miriam did not think so.

Over the next eighteen months, the Swansons barnstormed from state to state, wherever the Spirit led. They had no itinerary, no income, and no guarantees. If invited, they stayed in pastors' or parishioners' homes. If offered meals, they partook with gratitude. They relied solely on generosity and freewill offerings while visiting schools, auditoriums, churches, and community halls. Billed as the Singing Evangelist, Everett sang gospel tunes and Miriam joined him in duet. They ended every gathering with an altar call and a joyful rendition of "Hallelujah Meeting."

Was it easy? Far from it.

Driving hundreds of hours over rutted roads in a car without air-conditioning could test any relationship, and Everett's penchant for speed didn't help. Miriam's struggles with the road atlas created a whole other set of challenges, and occasional breakdowns, flat tires, and thunderstorms only added to the frustrations.

Through it all, the bride and groom experienced some wonderful moments together. They bonded as ministry partners, singing songs for weary souls and praying for those seeking salvation.

Then in 1936, spring fever hit. Miriam was quick to recognize the symptoms, but she wasn't certain her husband did.

Do you notice anything different about me? she asked him.

Is it your hair? Everett ventured. What're you telling me?

Smiling, she smoothed her blouse over her belly. Soon enough, she hinted, there won't be any hiding it.

Hold on, now. Are you saying . . . ?

Oh, do I really have to spell it out for you?

He raised his arms. Well, hallelujah! God is good.

She laughed. Hands on the wheel, Everett. Eyes on the road.

Despite their excitement, a subsequent medical checkup revealed that Miriam's pregnancy could face serious complications, and they decided she would return to her parents' home in Sycamore as she nurtured this little one in her womb.

Only for a short while, she assured Everett. I'll be on bed rest. You carry right along with your preaching. I know you and you'll grow restless otherwise.

But your father. You're sure you'll be alright?

His bark's worse than his bite. Anyway, Miriam added with a nudge, it's his "good-for-nothing" son-in-law he has issues with. I'll be fine. Write down some baby names and we'll talk them over when you return.

Something biblical would be my preference.

That'll be just fine, Everett. Make a list.

* * *

Names were important in Korea as well. A name had value and worth. Respect for one's culture and heritage were deeply ingrained, with fathers wearing outfits rich in tradition and meaning, and mothers passing down kimchi recipes as prized family secrets. The Land of the Morning Calm was proud, self-sufficient, and saw no need for help from foreign traders and missionaries.

Then, in 1910, the Japanese annexed Korea without the consent of its leaders. Japan tried to make the territory its own, destroying cultural landmarks, uprooting native trees, and ravaging the land. Korean children were forbidden to speak their own language in school, and Korean men were forced into manual labor. In the years that followed, thousands of females were forced into service as "comfort women" to slake the lust of the occupying troops.

Those brave Koreans who dared to resist found themselves in Seoul's infamous Seodaemun Prison, and when nationwide protests broke out in 1919, Japanese troops stormed in to arrest tens of thousands, burn down churches full of people, and kill over 7,000 demonstrators.

Korea waited for the United States to honor a treaty and intervene.

The great democracies did nothing.

Later that year, when President Woodrow Wilson received the

Nobel Peace Prize, Koreans bristled at the obvious Western apathy. Was there anywhere they could turn? Anyone they could trust?

In 1932, Korean resistance fighters tried to draw international attention, with one man tossing a grenade into the Japanese emperor's horse carriage. A few months after this failed attempt, another fighter managed to kill Japanese dignitaries with a bomb disguised as a water bottle. Both assassins paid with their lives.

The colonizers, in years to come, would even institute a policy known as *soshi-kaimei*, pressuring Koreans to exchange the power and meaning of their traditional names for Japanese ones. Some went along with this to avoid trouble. Many refused.

These troubles were mostly overlooked in Western news sources.

For Everett and Miriam, choosing their firstborn's name was a freedom they took for granted. Everett was determined to honor God as a father. A father should provide and protect, guide and instruct. These were huge responsibilities. More than anything, he wanted to follow his own parents' example and "train up a child in the way he should go."

Lord, he prayed, *may I be up to the task.*

He had only his own child in mind, unaware he would eventually be trusted with thousands of them.

Chapter 7

TAKING A TOLL

The Swansons became a family of three on February 15, 1937. Adolf Hitler was exerting power in Europe, Franklin D. Roosevelt was celebrating reelection, and *Gone with the Wind* was still riding high on the bestseller list, but Miriam's sole focus was on giving birth to a child. When the hours-long ordeal ended, her husband was invited into the hospital room.

A boy, she told him. Meet David Everett Swanson.

Everett beamed. Thank You, Lord! You are good.

In Hebrew, *David* meant "beloved," and this healthy, blond-haired newborn was truly that. To Everett and Miriam, he was a belated Valentine's gift.

The next week, as frost glistened on the silos and cornfields, Everett carried in pails of milk to help Father and Mother on their tenant farm. Age had slowed both his parents a bit, and he loved them with all his heart. Despite the wind knifing at his bare skin, he welcomed this physical labor after many long months on the road.

Indoors, Miriam nursed their infant. Everett was glad to be home with his bride after a season of ministry. As indicated in 1 Corinthians 7:5, it was not good for a husband and wife to be apart for too long, "except with consent for a time, that you may give yourselves to fasting and prayer."

Your lips are blue, Everett's mother pointed out as he arrived indoors.

I'm alright, Mother.

She handed him hot coffee in exchange for the milk pails. You ought to take better care of yourself. You now have a newborn to think of.

And I'm a grown man, he reminded her.

It can't be helped, she said with a shrug. I'll never stop being your mother.

When Everett heard David's cries, he stepped into the sitting room and found his wife rocking their little one by the fire. Miriam adjusted the baby's knitted cap and positioned him over her shoulder. Everett stepped closer, his smile radiant as he slipped a finger into his son's tiny, curled fist, and gave his firstborn child a nickname.

How are you, little Daver? Are you warm enough? Have you been fed?

Miriam shot Everett a look, and he felt ashamed of his earlier annoyance with Mother. She was right. It couldn't be helped. This parental love was boundless, swelling his chest and flooding his thoughts.

Oh, what glorious love the heavenly Father must have for His children! Who could fathom the depths of it?

He took David into his arms and cradled him. Like his own father before him, he prayed for his son—for his salvation, purpose, and future.

* * *

By summertime, the Swansons were back on the road, evangelists on a mission. They traversed the country and delighted in their squealing, wide-eyed boy. David, without a choice in the matter, was now part of their gospel trio.

Everett turned down the radio and glanced over. How's he feeling?

His tummy's still upset, Miriam replied, as she adjusted the baby blanket over her shoulder. You know, he might feel better if his father slowed down just a bit.

Everett eased his foot off the gas. There were no speed limits along this stretch of rural road, but Miriam's tone was a law unto itself. He turned back up the showtunes playing on the radio and glided past a sign for Wichita.

During the Depression, few places were harder hit than Kansas. Dust storms became frequent as drought turned rich farmland into loose topsoil. Monstrous billows raged across the plains, shutting down schools and leaving ghost towns in their wake. Even so, the locals laughed at misfortune, claiming the dust was so thick that the crows flew backwards just to keep the dirt out of their eyes.

Pressing on, Everett and Miriam found solace and even some Kansas-style humor in the lyrics of a popular hymn by John Newton:

With Christ in the vessel
I can smile at the storm

Despite courageous smiles, they were still impacted by the weather. A pastor made note of this in a letter of recommendation from southeastern Kansas:

> Everett Swanson has closed a revival campaign with us, and while sickness and bad weather has hindered the progress of our meeting, yet much and lasting good has been wrought in the church and the community.

In November, the secretary-treasurer of an oil and gas company typed his own endorsement of the young pastor:

> Everett Swanson conducted a union evangelistic meeting in Chetopa with marked success. He is a fearless and faithful preacher of the whole gospel, and is cordially recommended to any church.

Despite Miriam's unflagging support, Everett wondered if all this travel was good for her and their newborn. Shifting sleeping arrangements and inconsistent meals were taking a toll, and he had to consider the needs of his family.

Was it time to settle down? Perhaps his father-in-law was right.

But settling down sounded so . . . confining.

Everett was well aware of the apostle Paul's warning in 1 Timothy 5:8 that if someone doesn't provide for the members of their own household, they are denying the faith. Taking care of loved ones was a divine directive, and ignoring the obligations of marriage and parenthood wouldn't make those obligations disappear.

I am called to go, though. Not to stay.

This was also an injunction from God's Word.

In the back, on Miriam's lap, David was turning fussy. The car was warm, the air dry and dusty, and Everett could see little legs kicking in his mirror.

You'll be alright, Daver. Not too much farther, I promise.

Staring out the window, Miriam seemed unconvinced.

Chapter 8

VERY LITTLE HOPE

Still intent on the task before him, Everett trekked with his wife and one-year-old son across the Great Plains, over the Rockies, and into Canada. It was doable, just the three of them, ministering wherever a tank of gas led. Miriam fell into a routine and little David learned to sleep with the purring of the engine.

We're adjusting, Everett thought. *No need to settle down just yet.*

In 1938, the Singing Evangelist conducted gospel meetings in Vancouver, British Columbia. Using the minimal cash on hand, he handled car and tent repairs, acquired food and lodging, and tried to make his wife and son comfortable. Miriam sang with him at the pulpit whenever she could, but the pressing realities of infant feedings, naps, and cloth diapers often hindered her. Gathering David into her arms, she pressed her lips together and slipped dutifully outside.

One evening, Everett couldn't wait to share a bit of good news. Our meetings here have been extended another two weeks. Isn't it incredible, Miriam? The Lord's hand is blessing our efforts.

Two weeks, hmm? Sounds like quite a challenge.

We're tired, sure. But we'll manage. We always do, don't we? As followers of Christ, we are called to be living sacrifices.

Manage? Miriam turned, her eyes staring into his. Yes, I suppose we will.

His throat tightened. I've upset you, haven't I?

Am I one to ever complain? No, I knew full well the life I'd be entering into with you. She frowned, then shook her head. I'm just wondering what will happen as our family expands. Will I have to go live with my parents like last time? Will we ever find a place of our own?

Miriam, you know we don't have money for a down payment on a—

You and me, Everett, that's one thing. We can live on the road, ignoring my father's ridicule. We've done it off and on since saying "I do." Things're changing, though, and it's time we start praying for God to open a door.

He always does.

Well, He better hurry, since you and I are having another baby.

Forgetting the worries of the moment, Everett stepped back, raised his arms, and whooped with excitement. Their trio would soon be a quartet.

His wife smiled at his response, then shrugged and looked away.

He tried to imagine this from her point of view—the four of them on the road, in unfamiliar beds, in the canvas revival tent. He thought of the cold nights and hot days, the soggy diapers and teething cries. Miriam was right, of course. Something needed to change.

And preferably before the due date.

In an effort to plant some roots, Everett accepted an appointment with the Christian Business Men's Committee. CBMC had a mission to reach men in the marketplace, equipping them spiritually to make a difference at home and work. Everett, in his new role, would receive regular paychecks as he preached at meetings across Washington State.

It's an answer to our prayers, Miriam rejoiced, one hand on her belly.

Certainly is, Everett agreed.

Nevertheless, as he broke down their tent and bagged up the poles and stakes, a wave of melancholy swept over him. So many spontaneous moments and memories. So many powerful times of praise. So many adventures.

It felt as though his calling was slipping away.

* * *

Despite his initial resistance, Everett enjoyed his time with CBMC. It not only alleviated family and financial burdens, but also reminded him of his childhood love for the Pacific Northwest. The rivers were mighty, and the fishing was good. The natural splendor shouted of God's wonder-working power.

Why ever, he wondered, had his parents decided to leave here?

He still held fond memories of his family's stint in Seattle. His oldest brother, Ray, remained in the area, presenting science films for Moody Bible Institute. Everett even picked up a few pointers from Ray about the camera's potential in ministry, using the *beauty in sound, form, and color* mentioned years earlier at his high school graduation.

One day while wrapping up a campaign, Everett received a request to preach at a church north of Seattle. It was a dying congregation, without a full-time pastor.

Did you say yes? Miriam asked.

It'll be a pretty drive. Lots of logging and fishing country up there.

A family outing sounds nice enough. She stepped closer and tugged at his shirt. But you, mister, are not going anywhere until I wash and iron this thing.

They drove the following Sunday to Mount Vernon, a town huddled between the Cascade Range and the Pacific Ocean. Old mill equipment rusted in the mist off the Skagit River, and buildings in need of paint looked feeble compared to towering, snow-clad Mount Baker.

The congregation at Emmanuel Baptist Church was even less impressive, made up of a despairing few who showed little enthusiasm. As the music died away and congregants eyed him coolly, Everett occupied the pulpit. He wore slicked-back hair, a patterned tie, and the clean shirt beneath his jacket. Thanks to Miriam, he looked presentable, despite the funereal mood.

I am here today, he told them, to preach the Word of the Lord.

And that is what he did, with warmth, passion—and very little hope of a response. When Miriam's alto voice joined his tenor for a final song, he was pleasantly surprised to see a few others singing along. He spotted flickers of life in their eyes. Had they been moved by the sermon and music?

The church board, soon after, offered Everett his first pastorate.

Would it mean a salary? Miriam asked him later in private. Is there a parsonage? This could be the answer to our prayers, don't you think?

He nodded, though his eyes were lowered.

What're you worried about? The timing can't be mere coincidence.

There's hardly anyone here, Miriam. It's out in the boondocks, and the ones we saw this morning, they were barely alive.

Since when have death and despair stood in your way?

Everett still wasn't convinced. His CBMC commitments had him already tied to a schedule, and this assignment would further bind him to one spot. Gone would be the rambling faith of the past five years. Gone would be the stimulation of new listeners and locations. It was selfish, he realized, but he was almost twenty-five now and it seemed he was losing his freedoms for good.

And what if these good people of Mount Vernon didn't like him?

What if he wasn't up to the challenge of long-term discipleship?

It was one thing to please a crowd for a meeting or two, and quite another to engage them month after month. For years he had answered the evangelistic call—the highest calling, in his parents' eyes—and he gravely questioned if a pastorate was the right way to go. Would he look back on such a decision with regret?

Of course, there were also his babies to think of.

Being a father was his first priority.

Yes, he told the church board at last. Yes, I will do it.

Though he delivered his decision with a smile, he would always remember it as one of the greatest battles of his life, deciding to leave his beloved work as an evangelist to focus instead on this out-of-the-way, broken-down church.

* * *

For Everett and Miriam, the area's similarities to their own hometown must have seemed providential. Perhaps the *Author of it all* had an actual hand in this.

Skagit County's history, like that of DeKalb County, could be traced back thousands of years to Native Americans who lived along its waterways. Settlers had entered the valley in the 1800s, and Mount Vernon was founded in 1877. The community had a distinct Scandinavian influence. Sixty miles north of Seattle, it was the same distance as Sycamore from Chicago. And, like Sycamore, it was named the county seat.

Full of expectancy, Everett, Miriam, and David occupied their first family home, a pretty little parsonage. The arrival of a Swedish pastor and his Norwegian wife did not go unnoticed—in a town this size, nothing did—and some showed up at Sunday service just to see what all the fuss was about.

As a benefit of this new role, Everett also received his official ordination.

Meet Rev. Everett F. Swanson.

According to a fellow minister, Everett covered nearly every home in the town and warmly invited people to church. Working-class people who could sniff out the slightest whiff of arrogance or hypocrisy recognized him as one of their own. They were lumberjacks, dairy farmers, commercial fishermen, and sailors, and they noticed he didn't mind their muddy boots, barnyard odors, or grimy handshakes.

In his pulpit, Everett was never stingy with time or money. He welcomed speakers from other ministries and denominations and gladly took freewill offerings for them. He believed Christians were all part of a larger family and should be taught to give generously. He knew from his own farm upbringing that if a cow was not milked, she would eventually go dry.

As Emmanuel Baptist grew, so did the Swanson household.

Sharon was born in May 1938, a happy baby with a sunny disposition that matched her parents' in this new location.

Jonathan arrived in September 1940. Called Jack by those who knew him, he had a sly grin, a mischievous streak, and a sweet devotion to his mother.

Paul entered the world in December of 1941. A good-hearted tyke, with a sensitive nature.

World War II was raging on faraway continents, but here in Washington State things were mostly calm. The family of six enjoyed the routines of school, playtime, meals around the dinner table, and prayers before bed. Being in ministry was far from lucrative, yet God was faithful, and their basic needs were always met.

Then the war came knocking at America's door.

Chapter 9

WORRIES OF WAR

On Sunday, December 7, 1941, Japanese planes attacked Pearl Harbor at dawn. Launched from aircraft carriers, they came by the hundreds, skimming the waves and strafing the US naval base asleep on Honolulu's fringe.

For nearly two hours bombs rained down and torpedoes exploded. Smoke and flame engulfed the harbor.

The surprised Americans fought back valiantly and fired over a quarter million rounds of ammunition, but their losses were extensive. The Imperial Japanese destroyed six US ships and 169 military aircraft. They wounded over a thousand troops and killed over 2,400 men and women, nearly half of them on the sinking USS *Arizona*.

A young man from Sycamore, Private Russell Deffenbaugh, was found with his finger still clenched around the trigger of an anti-aircraft gun. He had shot down at least one enemy plane, and for his valor he received a posthumous Purple Heart.

Another fellow, an air force officer named Elmer Rund, miraculously survived the ambush and vowed his life to God. Though Elmer Rund soon betrayed this vow, he and Everett Swanson would meet ten years later and become fast friends.

As the wreckage in Pearl Harbor smoldered, President Franklin D. Roosevelt ended two years of neutrality and thrust the country into World War II. Weeks later, he ordered the forced relocation of 112,000 Japanese Americans from their homes to remote internment camps. This decision effectively turned thousands of loyal US citizens into prisoners of war.

* * *

It was nearing Christmas in Skagit Valley, where Everett and Miriam shared the same concerns as every other Mount Vernon citizen.

What did this war mean for their homes? For their families?

Were they safe here on the Pacific Rim?

With persistent rumors of Japanese submarines, blackout orders were given, streetlights were turned off at prescheduled times, and cars were fitted with hooded headlights to avoid being targeted by enemy bombers. Nearly every town conducted drills led by volunteer air-raid wardens.

Miriam's worries deepened when her younger brother was drafted to serve overseas, and she and Everett realized they would be raising their toddlers amidst a global conflict much like the one they themselves had lived through as children.

Would humanity ever learn? Would history ever stop repeating itself?

World War I, dubiously called the War to End All Wars, had failed to end much of anything.

Thirteen days after Pearl Harbor, the nation was rocked again when a Japanese sub torpedoed and sank a tanker off the coast of northern California. Another tanker was attacked three days later, but all of its crew survived. A freighter hit five miles offshore from Los Angeles limped into harbor on Christmas Eve, thankfully without one casualty.

Everett heard these reports over the radio the same as everyone else. He also read the newspapers and knew how fragile life seemed to many in his congregation. Speaking to them from the Bible, he gave reassurances and called upon his listeners to pray and be certain their souls were right with God.

"War is always a terrible thing," he would preach in years to come. "And peace will not come by the nations of the UN or by war, but only when the Prince of Peace—Jesus Christ—returns to earth to rule in righteousness."

There were, of course, some bright spots during this period, including the friendship of a sailor called Sarge. The man's chiseled face and gruff tone couldn't hide his big heart. He played with the kids, ribbed the adults, and kept things light.

Sarge, like Elmer Rund, would later play a part in Everett's story.

* * *

In February, Sarge and other friends from the church crowded into the small parsonage to celebrate David's fifth birthday. He blew out his candles, and cake was passed around. His best friend gave him a wrapped gift as well as a playful punch in the arm.

While others watched, Everett lay face-up on the living-room floor and summoned his son for a leg-wrestling match.

But it's not fair, Dad. You always win.

Guess you need to get stronger, Daver. The key is to never give up.

Egged on by his friends, David lay facing the other direction, then lifted one leg and locked it with his father's. The moment Everett said go, David torqued his thigh muscles and attempted to roll his dad backward. He grunted. He twisted. Nothing he did could budge his much larger opponent.

Suddenly, Everett applied pressure of his own and flipped his son over.

See, Dad, it's no use.

One day you'll get it. You're toughening up, that's all.

When David's best friend challenged Everett, he lost just as quickly but claimed he didn't really try. Everett cautioned him about lying, even in jest. All the bigger boys laughed and began to tussle. Not to be left out, three-year-old Sharon and one-year-old Jack joined the melee.

Standing near the fireplace, Miriam rocked tiny Paul in her arms. Her baby was peaceful for the moment and that was a blessing. For one night, at least, the worries of war were forgotten.

* * *

By June 1942, the conflict that once seemed so far away beat loudly at America's backdoor. Japanese soldiers seized a number of Alaska's Aleutian Islands, and by the time US troops regained the territory, over two thousand Japanese and five hundred Americans were dead.

To meet military demands, Washington State transformed its industry in a hurry and welcomed an influx of workers. A state that hadn't produced one ounce of aluminum before Pearl Harbor would become the country's third-largest producer by war's end. Puget Sound foundries and shipyards built warships, minesweepers, and Sherman tanks. Boeing churned out B-17 and B-29 bombers. Lumber was also in great demand, as were canned salmon and halibut for the armed forces overseas.

The war machine was in high gear.

As a pastor, Everett had often performed weddings, but military funerals now became his regular duty as well. By year's end, the men's dorms in nearby colleges were nearly emptied due to the draft, and with Rosie the Riveter now a role model, thousands of women were joining the Women's Auxiliary Corps. Each time Everett prayed off departing soldiers at the train station he wondered if they would be next.

Through it all, he spoke truth and tried to love as Jesus loved. With Miriam often joining him, he led the churchgoers in song. Few things soothed a weary soul like the hope and conviction of a gospel hymn. Sunday meetings were not enough, though.

Everett later wrote: "The moment some people step through the open door of salvation . . . they sit down in a rocking chair. . . . But we need to see the needs all about, and DO something about them."

The Swansons, as a family, visited homes and farms during the week, sharing both meals and burdens. They prayed with traumatized soldiers, mourned with bereft spouses, stood graveside with hollow-eyed parents. They listened as parishioners voiced questions and doubts.

The return on this investment was an outpouring of love.

A former reverend in Mount Vernon noted that the entire community felt the impact of the Swansons' ministry and the little broken-down church was revived. Soon, the congregants built a newer, larger parsonage for their pastor and even doubled the size of the sanctuary.

* * *

Everett was thankful for this Mount Vernon community. On the weekends, when his kids weren't goofing around with Sarge, they were playing with their friends. Their stories of outdoor adventure reminded him of his own childhood escapades.

As the months ground on, Everett saw in young David the same heady mix of fear and patriotism that had gripped him as a boy during World War I. David and his best friend imagined spies and saboteurs around every corner, with the area's naval yards and army bases as obvious targets. War posters encouraged this notion with vibrant colors and cautionary slogans:

Loose Talk Can Cost Lives.

Prevent Forest Fires . . . Our Carelessness: Their Secret Weapon.

It's no joke, David said. Spies could be out in the woods this very moment, ready to burn things down. With torches, even flamethrowers!

A possibility, Everett agreed. But instead of running around on the lookout, you might better use your energy planting vegetables in the garden. "Dig for Victory," isn't that a war motto as well?

Vegetables? David pulled a face. Sure, if we feed them to the Nazis.

Just don't let me hear you griping about your mother's food.

No, sir.

In the Swanson household, gratitude was expected. Neither Everett nor Miriam accepted complaints, and if such behavior persisted, punishment was sure to follow. They might send the children to their rooms. Dessert might be canceled. More serious offenses could even lead to a spanking. Though David never saw his dad lose his temper, he did receive a couple of swats the time he was caught playing with matches in the basement.

It was hardly the first of Daver's escapades.

Everett was less than thrilled—and Miriam was horrified!—when they heard of their son's encounter with a mechanical monstrosity at a friend's nearby ranch. As David told it, the contraption, a pea viner, rose higher than either he or his friend could jump and stretched longer than a tractor. Anchored to the barn floor by giant bolts, this beast gobbled pea pods through a chute, ran them through its industrial innards, and spit them back out with the peas cleanly separated for sale.

David's friend swore he could crawl safely in one end of the machine and out the other. David told him it sounded dangerous.

Well, I'm not scared, his friend said. You're just chicken, aren't you?

David eyed the machine, his limbs tingling. What if something went wrong? What if all that metal chewed him up the way it did the pods? He feared for himself, but as a pastor's kid, he also feared reflecting poorly on his father. Wasn't shaming Dad nearly as bad as shaming God?

Can't, he said. What if I get stuck? My mom just got me these clothes.

His friend snorted, then backed up his own claims by crawling headfirst through an opening and disappearing into the belly of the beast. David's heart thudded. He heard human grunts and metallic groans. After what seemed forever, his friend wriggled out the other end in a dusty show of victory.

Victory? My foot! There's nothing victorious about it, Everett reacted when he heard the story. No, that's just plain stupidity.

He made it clear to David, Sharon, Jack, and Paul that he didn't want them ever playing on farm equipment without supervision. He loved them too much to let them do whatever they pleased. Keeping them clothed, fed, and safe was his duty.

This is the heart of a father, he explained. Nothing matters more to me.

Some evenings, Everett invited Daver to stay up with him after the other kids fell asleep. They drew the living-room shades, turned down the lights in accordance with blackout restrictions, then tuned in to war reports by the glow of the big family radio. Later, after sending David off to bed, Everett and Miriam shared their own time together while listening to songs by the classic crooners.

Hearing their soft, muffled laughter made David almost as happy as the moments he shared alone with his dad.

Chapter 10

CHICAGO CALLING

Try as he might, Everett couldn't protect his children from everything. In 1943, he found six-year-old David doubled over in pain and rushed him to Mount Vernon's municipal hospital. A doctor explained that surgery was necessary. It was appendicitis, potentially life-threatening.

David winced. What're they going to do to me?

We'll go in and remove the appendix, the doctor said, to stop you from hurting. Doesn't that sound good? I'll also need to give you stitches, which will look funny at first, but once things heal, you'll have a scar to show off to your friends.

David clung to his father. You're not going to leave, are you?

It's alright, Everett assured him. The doctor's done this many times.

Please, Dad. Please don't go.

Listen, Daver, he said, I'll be right out in the lobby. I'm not going anywhere.

True to his word, Everett waited till the surgery was over, then slept through the night beside his son in the hospital bed. He had come here to visit church members over the years, stoic and strong for them, prayerful and empathetic. Nothing, though, had prepared him for watching his own child suffer pain.

Days later, David was at home recovering on the couch when the doctor paid an old-fashioned visit. He had come to remove the stitches.

David's eyes flashed. Is it going to hurt?

Everett sat beside him and pulled a large coin from his pocket.

Might hurt a bit, he admitted, but if you sit still and don't cry, this'll be yours to keep.

A scar *and* a silver dollar? David couldn't wait to show the boys at school.

* * *

In late 1943, Rev. Swanson was presented with an opportunity both intriguing and daunting. He set the phone back in its cradle and ran a hand through his hair.

Who was that? Miriam asked.

He shook his head. I don't even know what to think, Miriam. Once again, I feel that responsibility of the opportunity.

She knew this phrase well. She'd heard her husband preach about those moments in a person's life when God presents an opportunity and a corresponding responsibility. To accept the excitement of one without embracing the hardships of the other was spiritual immaturity. To truly say yes was to commit oneself to both.

Miriam set down her tea. Was it a call to pastor somewhere else?

He nodded.

You've received many of those since we arrived here.

Somehow, he said, this seems different. Central Avenue Baptist Church wants me to come lead their congregation. He faced her, then added, They are located right in Chicago.

Everett and Miriam sat across from each other at their dining table, in this parsonage that had provided such rich memories, and discussed the possibilities and challenges big-city life would present their family. They'd spent over six years here in the Pacific Northwest, nearly half of it during this war, which still dragged on. The period had shaped them and their ministry, and they would miss these people terribly.

So many relationships. So many friends.

And Sarge, of course. Who could forget his gruff yet lovable face?

After joining hands in prayer, the Swansons believed without question this was God's hand at work. Plus, the move would put them in closer contact with both sets of their parents. Because of recent health issues, Emil and Emma Swanson had given up tenant farming to buy a small place in Sycamore. As for Miriam's father and mother, they were also in Sycamore, still in their big old house with the hen coops outside.

Everett frowned. After a decade of committed ministry, he was still questioned regularly by his recalcitrant father-in-law.

Don't worry about my old man, Miriam said. He's softening toward you. Anyway, Chicago's close but not too close. Perfect for weekends and holidays.

Have we decided, then?

Beaming, Miriam nodded. When should we tell the kids?

Everett took her hand. David will be home from school any minute. The sooner the better, don't you think?

In early 1944, with world war still raging, Emmanuel Baptist Church sent off the Swanson family with hugs and hearty back-thumps. Everett's successor watched in admiration, knowing the message of Jesus and His cleansing blood had been boldly preached in this place. He later told how his very heart was gripped by the congregation's esteem and affection for the Swansons, and he felt a solemn responsibility to carry on their legacy.

Crowding into their automobile, the Swanson family of six started the long trek east. During his own childhood, Everett had moved from Washington State back to Illinois, and he could now name every bittersweet emotion swirling in his children's eyes. Though Miriam wore a look of anticipation, she too would never forget this day of departure. They had so loved the people here, and as they headed over Snohomish Pass, Everett didn't even try to hide the tears streaming down his face.

The highways were mostly empty due to the war's gas rationing, and the grandeur of God's creation was a balm as they rolled through the Grand Tetons, the Rockies, and the farmlands of the Midwest.

On the third day, they entered DeKalb County and coasted to a stop at a rustic stone building on North Main Street, the most beautiful filling station in this section of Illinois.

They were back in the town of Sycamore.

Though the changes here were few, they were noticeable. Over there at the corner of East State Street was the National Guard armory, built by Miriam's father. Troops were gathered by the water tower to board departing trains. Flags flew at half-mast near the Soldier's Monument as reminders of suffering and loss.

Before driving the final sixty miles east, Everett and Miriam deemed it important to spend a day or two reconnecting with their extended family. What a privilege after living so far away. How Everett missed his own parents!

Let's tuck that in, he said, pointing at David's loose shirt tails. Jack, Paul, are you listening? I want you boys on your best behavior.

They nodded.

Sharon, Miriam said, you'll have fun meeting your cousin. For once, you won't be the only girl.

At Grandpa Emil and Grandma Emma's, the kids admired the flower garden, then squeezed around Grandma's old pump organ and belted out songs together. Grandpa later read them stories, peering down through his wire-rimmed glasses. They played baseball in the street and chased roosters around Miriam's old backyard. When the adults weren't looking, some of the boys even dared each other to sneak over the nearby cemetery's black wrought-iron fence.

For Everett, meeting his older brother's children was a highlight. Sally was a responsible young girl, already proficient at caring for her younger brother George, who at four years old was a rascal.

Miriam joked with them, Who is your favorite aunt?

You are, they chorused back. Aunt Miriam's the best!

And Sally meant it. She later recalled how sweet and caring Uncle Everett was and how cute his family seemed. She got along just fine with their daughter, Sharon, and laughed as her brother wrestled with Jack and Paul on the lawn.

It was a day of glorious reunion.

* * *

The next morning, Everett woke early to find his father checking the fluids of his old pickup along the curb. You headed somewhere? he asked.

Father ran a hand through thin, gray hair. You know, farming's got to be too much. This is my job now, collecting garbage for the city and making recycling runs between Cortland and Genoa. It pays the bills and at least I haven't been called up.

For the war? Could they do that?

Take a look. His father pulled a Selective Service card from his billfold. I'm still eligible. You know, we've got over two hundred German POWs barracked here in Sycamore. These fellows pick peas and shuck corn over at the old canning plant on Harvester Street. They're just boys, most of them, caught up in this awful mess.

We're all in need of a Savior, Everett agreed.

That we are, son. You must always be ready, in season and out. I still share God's Word while dealing trash about town. Being an evangelist, you know, it's a mighty powerful thing.

Right now, God's leading me to pastor in Chicago.

For the time being, sure. But you best never forget your first calling.

Everett shifted on his feet and looked across the pickup's hood at the gravestones down the block. He had packed up his evangelistic fervor along with his tent years ago, a sensitive subject for him even now, a choice made for the sake of his family. Ready to speak of something different, he faced his father.

Tell me, how's Mother doing?

Oh, she still helps at the church, sometimes plays the organ. She isn't as strong as she once was, but God is faithful. Why, the two of us still pray each and every evening for you kids and the grandkids, every evening without fail.

You've given us quite a heritage, Everett said. I'm truly thankful.

In a few days Everett would be delivering his first message from the new pulpit in Chicago. While he felt no specific pressure to perform as a minister, he certainly did feel accountable for his spiritual upbringing. He couldn't ignore the words of Luke 12:48: "For everyone to whom much is given, from him much will be required."

Yes, he had a calling to evangelize, one he knew he must return to someday. He also knew a calling involved sacrifice.

Just what would that look like?

Chapter 11

A NEST OF THEIR OWN

Everett and Miriam had been born, educated, and wed in Sycamore. As they loaded their kids back into the car for the final leg of their journey, they had a keen sense of coming full circle. They'd flown from the nest, flapped their wings, learned to fly, and soared all over the country. Soon, they would settle in Chicago and preside over a nest of their own spiritual eaglets.

They followed Route 64 toward Lake Michigan, and Everett watched the children's eyes widen as metal and glass pinnacles rose before them. It was an impressive skyline, fortresses of finance and power impervious to the everyday struggles in the city streets below.

These streets would be home to the Swansons—a sobering realization for parents from rural America, and a huge leap for their kids.

Since the nineteenth century, people from central and eastern Europe had been migrating to Chicago to take advantage of the vibrant economy. They labored in stockyards and slaughterhouses. They developed and landscaped properties, started new restaurants and businesses. From 1870 to 1900, it was the fastest-growing city in world history, adding over a million inhabitants.

And things had only sped up during World War II.

At the moment, Chicago alone produced more steel than all of Nazi Germany. Tens of thousands of African Americans came to work the mills, rail hubs, and shipping yards, and the area thrived, supplying everything for the war effort from field rations to torpedoes.

An hour after leaving DeKalb County, the Swansons rolled up at Central Avenue Baptist. Built in 1913, the building was the same age as Everett. Its wide stone edifice rose high above double doors leading inside. In the sanctuary, Everett and Miriam stepped onto the platform as their offspring wandered between the pews with the nonchalant ease of pastors' kids. Everett said a silent prayer, ran his palms over the polished wood pulpit, and gazed over the empty seats.

Here, he would spread his handwritten notes.

Here, he would read and deliver God's Word to the congregation.

Here, he would pray over weddings, infants, personal salvations, memorial services.

Climbing the stairs to the second floor, the reverend found his corner office. Through a window above the desk, he saw a drab building across the alleyway. If he tossed out a wad of paper, he could hit the structure ten times out of ten.

That three-story structure, it turned out, was their parsonage. A church janitor occupied the bottom apartment. A couple with kids rented the top. The two-bedroom middle apartment would serve as the Swanson residence.

Everett and Miriam moved into the master bedroom. The other

bedroom was shared by David, Jack, and Paul. Being the only girl, Sharon had the patio enclosure as her refuge and remained typically all smiles though she felt left out at times. To fend off the windy conditions for her, Everett provided her a space heater and hung thick quilts. Without question, this apartment was more cramped than the parsonage back in Mount Vernon.

Welcome to city life.

Miriam, nevertheless, found things for which she was grateful. For example, she appreciated the convenience of calling out the kitchen window to her husband's office just across the alley. If she needed reinforcements, he was only seconds away.

While Rev. Swanson believed this was the nest from which he and Miriam would raise and release other believers into ministry, he did not suspect it was also the perch from which he'd soon be taking flights of his own around the globe.

Chapter 12

THE NEXT STAGE

The snoring in the balcony was audible. Everett paused and glanced up from the notes on his pulpit, which he wrote and tucked into his Bible each week. Had his preaching put someone to sleep? Surely, he wasn't the only one who heard it. He cocked his head and waited.

There it was. A nasal breath, a snort—and then a long snore sounded once again through the sanctuary.

Everett allowed himself a wry smile. For two years now, he and his family had pastored here at Central Avenue Baptist. They'd discipled a congregation through the news of D-Day sacrifices in June 1944, and cheered as the troops came home after V-E Day in May 1945.

But having someone snore during one of his sermons? This was a first.

He located the responsible party, a gentleman slumped next to Mrs. Hemwall and her girls on the sanctuary's second level. Mrs. Hemwall was a quick-tempered Irish American, and she jabbed her husband with an elbow to quiet him.

The poor fellow, Everett remembered, had only just returned from medical duty in the war. He must be exhausted.

Feeling oddly endeared to the man, the reverend made a point to introduce himself after the service, and thereby encountered one of the most extraordinary people he would ever know.

Five years older than Everett, Gus "Doc" Hemwall was also of Swedish descent. He was a slim fellow, with a receding hairline and round spectacles clamped to a thin face. As a young man, Doc had hoped to be a medical missionary, but his training led him instead into the army. During World War II, he was stationed as a major in France, where his skills were tested daily.

Back in the States, Doc was already settling into work as a local physician. He was wonderfully kind, even-keeled, with a noticeable knack for dealing with his fiery wife. He never put on airs and had a place only blocks from the church, which functioned as both the Hemwall home and Doc's private practice. He was respected throughout the neighborhood as one who lived by the Christian values he professed.

Doc peered over his glasses at Everett. You heard me sawing logs, I guess.

Everett tilted his head. Seems you were resting in God's goodness.

Not a bad place to be. Do you like to fish, Reverend?

Sure, Doc. Even more than I like to sleep.

Then let me take you sometime. We have a lake house up in Wisconsin. I'll give you a run for your money.

As long as you do the gutting, Everett responded with a grin.

Why, that's the best part. My daughters, they can gut and fillet with the best of them. I use those moments to teach anatomy, right out there in nature.

Hmm. I'd rather have my hands in a Bible.

Doc and Everett soon realized they were opposite sides of the same coin. Doc Hemwall attended to physical ailments, generous with his time, still making house calls and delivering babies even after he began performing surgeries at West Suburban Hospital. No wonder he snoozed through Sunday services. Conversely, Rev. Swanson tended to spiritual ailments, making so many house calls his children complained he was hardly ever home. When he wasn't visiting the sick and the elderly, he was praying and studying in his office, counseling parishioners, or chairing committees at the pastors' general conference.

The two men's financial rewards were wildly divergent. Doc earned a good deal of money, and his stated goal was to give it all away and die destitute, whereas Everett could barely afford to eat out once a week with his family.

Joined by a mutual concern for others, they formed a close bond.

Doc, aside from being a good friend, regular church attendee, and faithful giver, also functioned as the Swansons' family physician. He treated their various ills, from ear and tummy aches to more serious matters. In three short years, he would also come alongside Everett and Miriam as they walked with their loved ones through the valley of the shadow of death.

* * *

In the summer of 1945, the future looked bright to most Americans. The war in Europe had been won and tyranny had been defeated.

Even as Chicago girded itself for a new era of prosperity, US intelligence officers sifted through the ashes of Berlin and discovered that Hitler had chosen a cowardly exit. Rather than face his own crimes, he committed suicide, swallowing a cyanide capsule before shooting himself in the head with his service pistol.

The Allies also discovered advanced enemy schematics and weaponry. They smuggled German scientists such as Werner von Braun into America, while Russia tucked away top-secret Nazi files on rocket technology.

It was a chess game for global dominance.

The Cold War was now under way.

In the South Pacific, the Japanese still put up military resistance into early August. The United States responded by dropping atomic bombs on Hiroshima and Nagasaki, killing over 100,000 civilians. The entire world was in shock. When the Japanese emperor at last announced his country's surrender, President Truman also demanded the withdrawal of troops from the Korean peninsula.

At long last, the Land of the Morning Calm was free from occupation.

This freedom was, sadly, short-lived.

Before Korea even had time to establish its own national government and agenda, the US and the USSR divided the long-unified kingdom along the 38th parallel. The Americans backed a leader in South Korea, while the Russians backed a communist-held government in North Korea.

This "temporary" arrangement signaled the next stage of the Cold War.

Back in the States, most Americans were too busy celebrating the end of World War II to pay much attention to faraway foreign diplomacy. After four years of death and destruction, they just wanted to work, feed their families, and return to normal.

Everett and Miriam were no different, awash in victory's afterglow. Time with their kids was a priority, second only to God, and they tucked away a few dollars here and there for annual vacations. One summer they camped in Yellowstone, awed by its bubbling geysers, herds of bison, and occasional black bear. Other times, they visited relatives and old friends back in Seattle and Mount Vernon.

David, always eager to please, kept a watchful eye on his younger siblings during these road trips.

Sharon laughed at almost everything. She'd accepted Jesus as her Savior at age six, and was bouncy and joyful beneath her Shirley Temple curls.

Jack was the prankster, his quick brain churning out schemes and ideas that would later make him a successful administrator.

Paul—or Paulie, as Miriam called him—rarely ventured from his mother's side, quiet and well-behaved.

When funds were tight, the Swansons found cheaper activities to enjoy. They picked blackberries, swam in lakes, played horseshoes and volleyball. The kids attended Vacation Bible Schools, spent time at summer camp, and met with their relatives for games and picnics in Sycamore.

Few things gave Everett competitive outlet like a good game of 16-inch softball. A Chicago original, this variation of America's favorite pastime was perfect for crowded neighborhoods. Putting "cloth over plate" was the pitcher's goal. No matter how hard a batter swung, the huge softball traveled only short distances—good news for nearby windows—and could be caught without a leather mitt.

On warm Saturday afternoons, Everett peeled off his jacket, loosened his tie, and rolled up his sleeves to take a turn at the plate. When he connected solidly with the ball, he pumped his fist, flashed his crooked teeth, and trotted around the bases, imagining for just a moment how Billy Sunday must've felt, the preacher who once excelled as a pro baseball player.

Even a man of God had his boyhood dreams.

Chapter 13

RESULTS

In the mornings, Everett was usually first to the dining table in their second-floor dwelling. As part of his wake-up routine, he sang without restraint, letting his warm tenor voice roll through the apartment with hymns and gospel songs. This served as a call to breakfast and devotions before the kids headed off to St. Paul Lutheran School.

Oatmeal's getting cold, Miriam barked. David, where are you?

Their oldest son was the last to arrive, dragging himself down the hall. He avoided his father's questioning look and landed in his chair. As Everett read the daily Scripture, he noticed David mechanically spooning cereal into his mouth.

You alright, son?

Head down, David didn't even look up through his blond strands of hair.

C'mon now, it's best not to let things fester.

David shrugged. I don't want to go to school, not today, not ever again.

Everett shooed the three youngest toward their mother and the stairs, then scooted his chair closer and waited.

It isn't fair, David whispered. If I goof, the other kids think they can goof too.

How exactly, Everett inquired, do you think you've goofed?

His son explained that each Wednesday they had morning chapel at the school, and yesterday the minister had called David to everyone's attention for his gum-chewing. All eyes turned his way, and he was mortified. Yes, he knew better than to chew gum during church, he told the minister. He forgot, was all.

Everett sat back in his chair. And what was the response?

He kicked me out of chapel. I had to walk back all by myself to the school building across the street. Everyone just watched me.

Were any others chewing gum? Why were you picked out?

Because, David explained, I'm Rev. Swanson's son, that's why. Everyone knows I'm the pastor's kid, and I can't make one single goof without somebody noticing. I'm only ten. I've been to church services all my life, planted smack dab in the front row, and every time, someone asks me if I'm going to be a preacher like my daddy when I grow up.

Everett mulled this over. Seems to me you've been feeling some pressure. Tell me, have I ever pressured you to be perfect?

David shook his head.

As your father, have I ever failed to show you my love?

Not once, Dad. Me, Sharon, Jack, and Paul, we've never questioned that. You don't have a mean bone in your body. I just don't want to let you or Mom down.

With a hand on his son's shoulder, Everett said, I want you to run off to school and just make sure this doesn't happen again. Jesus forgives my sins, and I see no reason your mother nor I should withhold forgiveness from you. Now go catch up with the others, alright?

David looked up and nodded.

At the door, Miriam pressed her son's coat and allowance into his hand. A little bit extra, she said. Best if you don't spend it all in one place, though, knowing that sweet tooth of yours.

He squirreled away the coins and darted down the steps.

Later that evening, Everett called David to the dining table after his siblings were tucked in. He took a seat, eyeing a radio a quarter the size of the one they'd owned in Mount Vernon.

Isn't it marvelous? These are the wonders available to us in 1947. Everett leaned closer and asked, Do you want to hear the Cubs game?

David's eyes widened. Sure, but I think it's already started.

Top of the third, Everett said, turning up the volume. Cubs have the lead. You know, one of these days I'll take you to a game at Wrigley Field. How's that sound?

Just the two of us? I'd like that.

* * *

Rev. Swanson had a farm-boy commitment to what worked. His sermons were the results of study, prayer, and preparation. When he offered God's Word to hungry souls, he trusted it was hearty fare, with no need to spice things up. "Preach the Word!" was the instruction he found in 2 Timothy 4:2: "Be ready in season and out of season. Convince, rebuke, exhort, with all longsuffering."

Over the years, he catalogued his messages in a notebook, a smorgasbord of gospel truths ready to be served at any time, at Emmanuel Baptist, Central Avenue, or wherever else he might speak.

This Sunday's message was an appetizer of sorts, and Everett was confident as the choir took their seats, the organ music faded, and he stepped to the pulpit. He prayed over the young children, released them to their classes, then scanned the sanctuary.

There were the Hemwalls in the balcony. Doc's snores, if and when they arose, were an auditory reminder of his presence. How could Everett fault him for that? And down here on the main level sat the Westerbergs, with their girls close in ages to David and Sharon. Mr. Westerberg was one of the deacons. A painter by trade, he'd done work at the church. He and his wife invited the Swansons over regularly for meals, coffee, and laughter.

In the front row, Miriam was poised and alert as always, in fashionable heels and a fitted dress. Her Bible was open in her lap. Sharon was beside her and—

Where is David?

Everett's slightly raised eyebrow got a mere shrug from his wife. Well, surely there was an explanation. Proceeding, he turned to the morning's Scripture and began his sermon. When next he looked up, he spotted a familiar blond head of hair ten rows back. As he lost his train of thought, he dropped his finger to his notes. A learned reaction, a way of finding his way back.

Was that his firstborn back there? Why wasn't he by his mother?

Seated with a group of boys, David shifted his gaze from his father's. This was a deliberate break from tradition. David knew better, all right. The Swansons worshiped as a family, not as separate, self-serving entities. Maybe, Everett reasoned, it was David resisting the pressures of being a PK. He wanted to be with friends—of course, he did—but if there was any rebellion in his heart, it would need to be addressed.

Everett returned to his sermon. He explained how important it was for believers to be people of conviction, not only speaking about the things of God but making them a lifestyle.

He asked the crowd, Have any of you ever seen me drink coffee?

People shook their heads.

No. And why not? Because years ago, while visiting a household near our church in Mount Vernon, I admonished a man for smoking a cigarette. He whipped around and said I was no better, being addicted to coffee the way I was, drinking it every chance I got. What was the difference, huh? And you know, the man was right. I vowed that day to never touch a cup of coffee again—and I haven't. Not because it was a sin for me, but because it would be wrong to point a finger at others while living by a different standard.

A few nodded from their pews. Others mulled over his words.

Which is why I drink Postum instead, he added with a chuckle.

As Everett wrapped up his sermon, he gave his call to salvation, explaining Jesus' sacrifice on the cross, His victory over sin, and His gift of eternal life. He asked to see the hands of those who wanted to repent of their sinful ways and walk in the freedom Jesus offered. Who wanted to know God as their heavenly father?

He glanced over the congregation and noticed just one hand.

To his surprise, it belonged to his son.

Everett knew from his own conversion at nine years old that such a choice was personal, stirred and sealed by God's Spirit, and he had never put expectations on his kids to do the same. Now he watched those blue eyes lift, round and full of emotion. Despite the friends on either side, David Everett Swanson was choosing publicly to follow Jesus as Lord and Savior.

In a rush, Everett understood his own father's emotion on that April Fool's Day in 1923. His thoughts turned from chastisement to jubilation. He and Miriam had prayed countless times for this moment, and he watched the room turn blurry.

Oh, wasn't God good! Praise the Lord.

He gave a brief nod to David, then acknowledged others who also lifted their hands. He thanked all of them for their boldness and encouraged them to meet in the prayer room after service. With that done, he beckoned Miriam to join him on the platform for "Hallelujah Meeting." It was their old favorite, sung today with new meaning:

> *There's a hallelujah meeting over there*
> *And a hallelujah greeting over there*
> *Angels will be there, and prophets will be there*
> *Noah will be there, and Jonah will be there*
> *And . . . my David will be there*
> *At the hallelujah meeting over there.*

After service, Everett treated his family to lunch at a nearby restaurant. It was an expensive proposition for six people, but his work was done, and his heart was full. He told his kids to get whatever they wanted. Today was a day of rejoicing.

Miriam straightened Paulie's collar and Sharon thumbed excitedly through the menu, while Jack popped the lids on coffee creamers and drank them one by one. When Everett asked what he was up to, Jack said he'd seen Grandpa Emil do this at a Sycamore coffee shop. Grandpa figured why not get everything he paid for.

Everett raised an eyebrow. Okay, but are you the one paying for this meal?

Jack wrinkled his lips and shook his head.

Across the table, ten-year-old David seemed to float above the conversation. He ordered breaded pork tenderloin, which Everett knew was his favorite. When at last their orders arrived, David took a bite and smiled as though it were the best treat available on this side of heaven.

* * *

Rev. Swanson barreled west along Route 64. Miriam was back at the apartment getting the kids ready for another school week. He was alone, en route to Sycamore as the guest speaker at a church, and as the city gave way to rolling fields, he felt like a teenager all over again, feeding his need for speed.

Best be careful, his father's old warnings rang in his ears.

There were no other cars in sight, no officers on patrol. There was nothing keeping him from pushing the limits of this Buick's V-8 engine.

It's your safety that most concerns me. Mother's words, still in his head.

Reluctantly, Everett eased just a bit off the gas. At this more reasonable pace, he spotted the DeKalb winged corn logo on a passing fence post, a variety of corn that had gained nationwide recognition during the last decade. He was proud of his county's agricultural advancements. Even in the 1800s, a locally developed grain-binding machine, the Marsh Harvester, had widely transformed farming practices.

Souls, of course, were the most important harvest.

Everett recalled his stint as an evangelist, full of long trips and gospel tents, singing and preaching, reaping and sowing. Those were the days!

After the service in Sycamore, Everett stopped by his parents' small place. Father was in his early seventies now. Mother was in her late sixties. They had been married for forty-five years. They were happy to see him, and as Mother busied herself in the kitchen, Father eased himself into his armchair.

Did you hear what happened to George, our grandson?

Picturing the little tyke, Everett shook his head.

Well, your mother and I, we were babysitting the boy when he scurried through the gate just that fast and got into a nearby field where the neighbor was plowing. George not only tore his shoes and pants under the tractor's dish, but also barely escaped with bleeding fingers. Thank God that ground was soft. You know, it could've been deadly serious.

He's an adventurous seven-year-old, Mother noted as she arrived with a tray of hot drinks and home-cooked rolls. Why, he even cut into my tablecloth, he and a friend of his, in a dare of some sort. And that's not the worst of it, is it?

Hardly, Father jumped in. When George tried chasing a ball by hopping over a spiked iron fence, he slipped and punctured his upper arm on one of the spikes. Poor kid's arm was hanging there like a chicken wing. He had to be rushed to the doctor's office to get nine stitches.

Brings to mind me and my older brothers, Everett said. And what about Sally, George's sister? I hear she's learning piano.

What a girl, Mother said. A woman, really. And such a nurturing type.

Out of necessity, Father snorted. What with that brother of hers.

Everett shared stories of his own, saving details of David's salvation for the finale. As he expected, his parents were ecstatic and cried out together with joy. Nothing made them happier than hearing of a family member won over to Christ.

Father finally muttered something about his early garbage run and headed toward the bathroom. Mother took Everett out onto the back porch and, as the sky changed from purple to star-studded black, told him Father had been suffering of late, not the usual aches and pains.

I'm worried, she confessed. Could Doc Hemwall look into it?

He'll go out of his way to help, you know that. I'll get it arranged.

As Everett drove his father into Chicago for a hospital visit a few days later, he couldn't shake the concern now lurking at the edge of his mind.

Hello, Emil, said Doc, cloaked in a white coat with a pen tucked into the pocket. I hear you're not feeling well. With your permission, we'd like to draw some blood and run some tests.

Whatever you think's best.

The results, when they came back, were even worse than expected. The gray-haired tenant farmer, family man, devout Christian, and Swedish immigrant was in the advanced stages of pancreatic cancer. Father had only months left to live.

Chapter 14

NO BOUNDARIES

The family patriarch survived well into the next year and, tough as he was, carried on his work duties until the very end. On May 4, 1948, the *True Republican* reported:

Emil Frederick Swanson, highly regarded resident of this community for many years passed away Saturday morning at 8 o'clock at the West Suburban hospital in Oak Park, following major surgery where a doctor friend of his son's attended him.

The memorial service was held in Sycamore, at the church where Emil had served for decades in various capacities. Father of five sons and a daughter, grandfather of multiple grandchildren, he was loved by all. Coworkers, church members, and relatives came from all over to celebrate the life of a humble, hardworking man—a man with dirt beneath his nails and love beating in his chest.

If there was anyone not yet on the verge of tears, surely that changed as his grown boys gathered at the front of the sanctuary.

Ray was visiting from Seattle. Les, a regular singer at revival meetings, stood next to him. Lawrence and Robert, both pastors in Michigan, stood on either side of Everett. Shoulder to shoulder in fine suits and polished shoes, the five men sang one of Father's beloved hymns. Younger sister Rose closed her eyes as her brothers' voices rolled and rose together, harmonizing into one glorious sound that glided to the heavens.

Few things were more life-affirming than the honor given in death. A life well-lived did not go unnoticed, and the sacrifices, the tough choices, did make a lasting impact. Everett believed these things to be true, and even in the years that followed Father's passing, there were no dark secrets unveiled, no scandals uncovered. There was simply the account of one man who served his God and family. In life, Father had split his boyhood between different countries and his adulthood between different centuries. Now he was in a land with no boundaries, no borders, in a place with no end of days.

At long last, Emil Swanson was home.

* * *

His body was laid to rest beneath a stone marker behind the black iron gates of the local cemetery, not far from where he and Mother dwelled. She now rented out the upstairs rooms to help cover costs. She continued her work with the Ladies' Missionary Society and at the local old folks' home. Even in her late sixties, she still reached out to those in need.

While Father had left a spiritual legacy for his descendants, he'd also left two material things: his old truck and his shotgun.

The truck went to his son-in-law, who took over the garbage route. The contraption rattled up and down the streets, wafting exhaust and stirring memories of a man well-loved.

As for the shotgun, all the Swanson boys wanted it. Lawrence had borrowed it on occasion. Everett had taken it on hunting trips with Doc. Most recently, Les used it to bring home two partridges for Thanksgiving dinner. It was special to all of them in different ways.

To settle the matter they drew lots, and when Everett won, the others grumbled.

What was he going to do with a shotgun, living on the streets of Chicago?

He kept the item tucked away, treasuring it more for who and what it represented than for any practical use it might provide. Father had raised him to be a fighter for souls, and this weapon was a symbolic reminder. Even as a family man halfway into his thirties, his task was not yet finished. There were still more battles to fight.

Chapter 15

CLOTH OVER PLATE

On May 10, 1948, only nine days after Everett's father passed, the people of Korea held their first democratic election. After protests took place in the north, voters in the south armed themselves with sharpened bamboo and, under the eye of UN troops, marched undaunted to the polls. There, they chose members of parliament who would elect for them a president and forge a constitution.

Twin nations were soon born from this land of mountains, magpies, and tigers. They were deeply connected, yet vastly different, offspring from the political womb. South Korea was recognized as its own entity, with pro-American President Syngman Rhee at the helm, while North Korea, under Russian-backed Premier Kim, became a communist enclave. Kim had been a guerrilla in the fight against the Japanese. He spun his former exploits into mythical tales, and his people revered him as a god.

By mid-1950, the two nations would be at each other's throats.

* * *

During this period, Everett did what many do in the aftermath of deep personal loss. He worked hard, focused on daily responsibilities, and tried not to let grief affect his marriage or ministry.

He also wrestled with questions of belonging and purpose.

Had he failed Father somehow? What things should he have told him before he was gone? How could he make him proud?

You best never forget your first calling.

From age fifteen to twenty-five, Everett had pursued an evangelist's calling, which his father had valued above all else. Then he'd set it all aside to serve as a traditional pastor in Mount Vernon, Washington, and in Chicago, Illinois. He was now turning thirty-seven. Under his leadership, his parishioners had grown in spiritual knowledge and application, but the majority were already saved, sanctified, and redeemed.

Had this been the most effective use of his calling?

Didn't the Good Shepherd leave the ninety-nine to find the one lost lamb?

Raised during the first half of the twentieth century, Everett couldn't ignore the bleak outlook for humanity. In 1929, the world had been brought to its knees by the Great Depression. In 1939, World War II had unleashed indescribable horrors. Then, in late 1949, it was announced the Russians had caught up with the Americans and built an atomic bomb.

As Senator Joseph McCarthy began his Red Scare, chasing down every perceived communist in Washington, DC, and Hollywood, the Cold War seemed ready to explode into nuclear war. The demand for fallout shelters skyrocketed even as schoolchildren across the country did duck-and-cover air-raid drills.

Oh, how the Lord's heart must break, Everett told Miriam. So many know nothing of God's love, but how much longer can Jesus tarry?

She rested her hand on his. You're sensing that old draw, aren't you?

I am supposed to be an evangelist, Miriam.

I've seen you up at night, she said. I've heard your prayers. For over twelve years you've pastored and provided for our family, when all along it's been in your heart to carry on with your tent ministry.

Think of Rev. Billy Graham. His crusades are front-page news and he's been leading so many souls to Christ. You know how much I love photography. Ever since high school, I've wanted to use the latest technology, and just imagine if I could film a crusade.

Well, far be it from me to stand in your way.

What about our kids, though? I must consider them. Where are they, by the way?

Paulie's in the alleyway riding his scooter, and the older boys are playing football. Sharon's at a friend's for the afternoon.

Oh, to be young again.

Stop it. You're hardly an old man.

You know, Everett said, leaning forward, when my father told me to go and do something as a boy, I felt responsible to do it. If I didn't, he had a way of making me feel responsible. Now I feel responsible to my heavenly Father. I feel a definite call to return to evangelistic work, but I'd like to know you and I are in agreement.

Listen, Everett, I know you've been struggling with this for a long time.

It will put new pressures on us as a family.

Yes. Her eyes met his. And there'll be no certainty of stable income.

No, he admitted. I'll also be gone frequently.

Are you sure this is what the Lord's telling you?

Why don't we throw out a fleece? he suggested. We want to know God's will, so let's do as Gideon did in the Bible and a : for confirmation. The Lord knows how topsy-turvy our emotions an be at times. He understands our every weakness.

Alright then, she said. What do you have in mind

Everett told her.

* * *

On a Sunday morning in mid-1950, Rev. Swanson stepped to the pulpit and spread open his notes. Before him was his most reliable sermon. If he needed to throw a perfect strike, this was the one on which he relied. This message would put "cloth over plate." Based on powerful biblical truths, it had never failed over the years to bring listeners to Christ.

To start, he led the congregation in prayer. This was God's Word, after all, and he wanted to preach it with conviction.

Never one to rely on slick presentation or emotional delivery, Everett wrapped up the message thirty-five minutes later and gave a straightforward call to salvation. Instead of the flurry of hands this sermon usually caused, he got no response. Zero movement. He gave the call again and allowed a minute of silence.

Still nothing. Not even a nervous fidget.

He invited everyone to bow their heads, then asked a third time if there was anyone who would like to receive Jesus as Lord and Savior this day.

Not one hand lifted.

Not one!

Everett's disappointment was real, as he had never come up empty like this before. How could salvation and eternal life fail to get a reaction? On the other hand, what more confirmation did he need? He'd thrown out the fleece and here was his answer.

He closed his Bible, glanced at his wife in the front row, and they exchanged knowing nods.

Their work here at Central Avenue Baptist was done.

* * *

You ready? Everett called to David from the stairs outside the apartment.

Wearing a Cubs ball cap, his thirteen-year-old son appeared on the second-floor landing. His face was aglow. We're really going?

Made you a promise, didn't I?

Together, father and son walked to the bus stop, then rode noisy city transit to the ivy-covered walls of Wrigley Field. The Chicago Cubs hadn't won a world championship since 1908, but this wouldn't keep David from becoming an avid fan and attending many more games in years to come.

As the wind gusted off Lake Michigan, Everett and David sat side by side in the bleachers, bought hot dogs from a vendor in a blue jacket—ketchup, no pickles or onions, please—and watched the Cubs pitcher deliver a pitch right over the plate.

Everett cheered, admiring the pitcher's aim.

What a feeling, he thought, *to love what you do and do it well.*

By the top of the ninth inning, the Cubs had the game in hand, a rare win on a perfect evening.

Chapter 16

THE ENVELOPE

In the coming days, Everett breathed the fresh air of excitement. Though he hadn't yet officially resigned, the unresolved burden on his heart had lifted. Revival meetings would soon fill his schedule again and he even purchased a Sterling account book in which to track his expenses. He penned in the current parsonage address, then realized his and his family's address would be changing as soon as the new minister arrived.

Where would he move his own household? They had no down payment for a home. Would they live out of their car, as in their early days of marriage?

Everett couldn't let it worry him. Not now. As never before, the needs of other nations seemed to press upon his thoughts, and he later wrote: "While God is so good to us . . . there are thousands . . . begging for a little morsel of bread. . . . America is an isle of Paradise in the midst of a world of war."

On June 25, 1950, war once again filled the headlines, as roughly 100,000 North Korean soldiers crossed the 38th parallel into South Korea. Seoul fell to the invaders, and President Truman and the UN voted quickly to provide military assistance. The US could not allow South Korea's demise, considering it was a pawn in a global struggle, a lone foothold on the Asian continent.

Too late. North Korea had already overrun the country.

When Everett pulled out pen and paper a month later, the Korean War looked to be already lost to the communists. Despite this threat, he focused his attention on the task at hand and outlined five specific promises to God. He then invited his wife to join him in the dining area. Through the window he could see his office across the alleyway, where for almost seven years he had studied and written his sermons.

Got some hot water here. Would you like tea? Miriam offered.

I'll go with Postum and a bit of sugar. Here, I want to share this list with you.

She brought the hot drinks to the table and sat beside him. What is it?

Even when it's not easy, will you agree to hold me to account?

What have you done?

It's not what I've done, but what I intend to do. Listen, we have our friends here, don't we? I have Doc. We have the Hemwalls, the Westerbergs. The kids are happy in their schools. But none of that changes my commitment to this list. He spread out the paper and stabbed his finger at each number as he read aloud.

One: To obey God's call to full-time evangelistic work wherever He may lead in this whole wide world.

Two: To resign my pastorate September 10, to take effect January 1, 1951.

Three: To trust God to provide for my every need as He has promised in Philippians 4:19.

Four: To trust God to take care of my family spiritually, physically, and materially.

Five: To redouble my efforts to win others to Christ and to pray and work for revival.

As he finished, he felt his throat catch. He took a sip of his drink. These words here held power and conviction. In the past, he had always attached responsibility to the opportunities that arose. This time, he had no specific opportunities ahead, only these vows to be responsible with whatever tasks God gave him.

He was putting to work a new level of faith.

Miriam set down her tea. What's this look like for us over the next months?

We'll need to start packing, consolidating. The parsonage will be turned over to another pastor as the new year rolls around. Where will we go? I still don't know, but I am trusting God to open a door at the right time. Numbers three and four, he said, tapping his list.

She didn't even look down. Your safety, Everett. The world is in such turmoil.

Who's to say Chicago's safer than anywhere else? We put out our fleece and we both agreed this was the next step. All I'm asking is that you pray over my list, that I might have the strength to honor it. For me, there is no turning back.

* * *

Six weeks later, Everett smoothed a sheet of paper on his desk and composed a resignation letter to the Baptist General Conference. As he folded it neatly into an envelope and affixed a postage stamp, he envisioned his father smiling down. He dropped the letter into the closest mailbox.

Soon, Everett knew, he would attend his final conference meeting as a pastor, then turn to the road as in times past, preaching wherever God led. He was already sending out notices to pastors in various states, offering to relieve them for a Sunday or two in the pulpit.

A relief pitcher, throwing strikes.

He spent the following Saturday morning packing boxes with his wife. They had agreed to look at houses for sale, including one they especially liked on North Lorel Avenue, though they didn't have the money for the three-bedroom, one-bath, with a covered back porch. On his pastor's salary, Everett could barely make ends meet.

Don't worry, I'll take freewill offerings wherever I speak, he reminded Miriam. Just like when we were younger, I'll bring every cent back to you.

You should do something for yourself every now and then.

A big wad, he pressed on. Cash for you and the kids, for food and supplies.

Miriam brushed back her auburn hair and said, I know your struggle has been far greater and longer than mine. It's our children I'm thinking of. David, if he hasn't told you, wants to join choir when he starts at Austin High. He's a good-looking boy, already catching the girls' attention. And Sharon, she's everybody's friend, turning into quite the young lady. Jack? Miriam laughed. Oh, dear Jack, he keeps me on my toes. When he's not stirring up mischief, he excels at just about anything he sets his mind to. And Paulie's almost nine already.

Paul has a soft heart, Everett noted. I love each one of them.

As though they'd been waiting to hear their names, the kids popped through the doorway, David with Paul on his back, Sharon with Jack poking at her ribs.

Aren't we going to Sycamore today? Sharon asked. You guys promised.

Why, I almost forgot, Miriam exclaimed. Your cousins Sally and George are looking forward to it. Their mom called yesterday and said it's all they've been talking about this week. Of course, Grandma Emma is always happy to see you, and my parents, well, if you're not careful, they might challenge you to a game of Monopoly.

Everett's eyebrows furrowed. No dice, though, is that understood? We don't want to give the appearance of gambling.

But, Dad, what if—

You can use a spinner, that's fine. Just no dice.

Despite being more lax on such things, Miriam encouraged the kids to honor their father's wishes and go put on their shoes. She watched them bound toward the door, then turned and looked up into her husband's eyes. Everett, don't you worry. Wherever the Lord leads us, I trust He will also provide. I've come to the place where I know beyond a doubt this is His will.

* * *

As Christmas neared, Rev. Swanson found preaching invitations flooding in from around the country, enough for nearly two years of full-time work. He had a reputation as one who spoke with spiritual authority, and his own brother, Lawrence, admitted being visibly shaken by Everett's great faith and power.

Each new day, the Swansons' mail was received with fresh expectation. What next? Where next?

Even the children joined in the fun, racing downstairs to gather envelopes from the box the moment they heard the mailman arrive.

One December day did its best to alter Everett's mood by darkening dead trees and forlorn buildings beneath a sky the same color as Father's shotgun barrel. Everett missed his father and had other family concerns as well. According to Miriam, her younger sister was butting heads with her parents and turning cold toward the things of God. Young Betty might need a place to get away, to clear her thoughts, but how could the Swansons offer any long-term solution when they themselves had no idea where they'd be living a month from now?

On his way home from praying for an ill church member, Everett spotted the mailman leaving their building. He expected one of the children to beat him to the box, but none of them appeared. They were probably cozied up in the second-floor apartment, which drew heat from below and stayed insulated above.

Boy, it was icy-cold out here.

Using his coat sleeve instead of bare skin to fumble with the metal mailbox, Everett withdrew a handful of deliveries. There were bills, advertisements, and two more responses from out-of-state churches.

There was also a sealed, unstamped envelope.

Was that Everett's name scrawled across the front? Could this be from Doc Hemwall?

At the base of the stairs, Everett split the gummed seal on the back and fished out a personal check from their dear family physician, their beloved brother in the Lord. On a handwritten note, Doc stated he had been trying to get rid of this money ever since he got it. The amount would be adequate for a down payment on a home close by, perhaps even the one Everett and Miriam had noticed over on North Lorel Avenue, only blocks away from the Hemwalls. Wouldn't it be wonderful to be so close? As for monthly mortgage payments, those would be up to Everett, of course, but this money would get the Swansons through the door into a home of their own.

This blessing was beyond Everett's wildest dreams.

Oh, Lord, You've gone beyond anything I could even ask or think!

Dashing up the steps, he cried out, Miriam, Miriam, come take a look!

She met him at the door. What's wrong? What is it?

Our best friends, he said breathlessly, we are going . . . to be . . . their new neighbors. Our own . . . a place of our very own. Isn't it incredible?

Once she could fathom what he was saying, she joined in the celebration. This provision was not only the start of God's blessings on their latest ventures, but also the safe haven Miriam and the children would need, considering the whirlwind into which Everett was headed.

Part 3

Winter 1957
Haksan, South Korea

"The only clear, deep good [of war]
is the special kind of bond welded between people
who . . . emerge knowing that those involved behaved well."
—*Marguerite Higgins, combat correspondent*

YO-HEE SHUFFLES TO THE LAKE, dragging loads of laundry. She squats by the water's edge and soaks the bedding. The water bites, then numbs her hands as she works soap into cloth. The mountains spit wind and snow at her back.

For four years, Yo-hee and her husband, Woo-yeol, have directed this orphanage at Namgang, called *Ae-Yook-Won*—meaning "to raise them in love." Her husband, formerly of North Korea, is devoted to God and popular with the children. Even now, he has gone into the small town of Haksan as he does every evening to ask for food for their charges.

The war has left devastation in its wake.

The needs here are overwhelming. Supplies are scarce.

As much as Yo-hee tries to feed and love the war orphans, she also wants to provide them with a proper education. The school lies over the mountain, a hard walk, but each day she pushes the children to go.

If they merely survive and fill their bellies, what good is that? For her fellow Koreans to rebuild their ravaged land, they must be more than survivors. They will need knowledge and determination, both of which good schooling can provide.

Yo-hee wrings out the laundry, her palms turning red and raw. She repeats the process until the bedding is done. The bags are heavier now, the sheets damp, and she groans with each step back to the dilapidated wooden orphanage. Inside, sealed clay chambers run beneath the floor, funneling heat from the kitchen's uniquely Korean *ondol* furnace into this main room. Here, the laundry will dry, and the children will keep from freezing to death during the night.

Some of these kids were found huddled under railway bridges, others sleeping in the streets on straw mats. Woo-yeol regularly takes one child with tuberculosis on long, exhausting trips to the hospital.

I will not let him die, he insists.

Yo-hee wants to believe him, but at thirty years old she has seen more death than she cares to remember. It makes her fear for the child in her womb. She wants to name this baby Ki-jong. But will she make it full-term? And if so, can she keep the baby alive?

A hand tugs at her coat. She looks down into the eyes of her six-year-old daughter. I'm busy, she snaps. Not now, Young-sook.

Her daughter won't leave. I'm hungry, she says.

The orphans are the priority, you know that. If there's enough food when your father returns, you will wait with me at the back of the line.

Yo-hee worries about going another day without food. She has been hospitalized before for severe malnutrition, completely drained of energy. This is life in postwar Korea. She knows this. Every Korean walks in the same shoes, just trying to make it through.

Two hours later, when Woo-yeol returns to Namgang Ae-Yook-Won and divvies out the meager food supplies, Yo-hee and her daughter are left without dinner to eat. Seeing the pain in her child's face causes something in Yo-hee's spirit to crack. She finds her husband and clings to him in private.

This cold, she cries. Our daughter. It's too much!

Her husband holds her, tries to comfort her. He softly pats her back—*thump, thump, thump*. God will provide, he says.

I don't want to live like this anymore. I'm so weak, I can barely stand.

The joy of the Lord is our strength, Yo-hee. I have already been at death's door with pleurisy. You remember what the doctors said. My hope of survival was slim. Then we came to this province, to the prayer retreat house, and He healed me.

Yo-hee sniffs. But the look in Young-sook's eyes, it's too much, she sobs. I can't go on.

Things always seem dark under the oil lamp, her husband responds, quoting a Korean proverb. You are too close to the situation to see the light. We must press on for the orphans, for our own child. You have a choice, my dear wife. You can think only of yourself and die, or you can think of others and live. What are you going to do?

This is a challenge she cannot ignore. Six little words. As the question takes root in her thoughts, Woo-yeol still tries to console her.

Thump, thump, thump . . .

She wonders, has their daughter heard her cries? Their family has given everything to keep this place running. They've sown the seeds of sacrifice and watered them with tears. They've done the work, and now they simply need someone to come alongside. If only they had the promise of consistent meals and of funds to repair the damaged roof.

Yo-hee realizes she could walk away. It's a very real temptation. Her husband would follow, relenting out of his love for her and their family.

I am with child, after all, she thinks. No one would blame me.

Thump, thump, thump . . .

What are you going to do?

* * *

After a fitful sleep, Yo-hee rises to an early morning calm and watches sunbeams crest the mountain peaks. A new determination wells within her, a mustard seed of faith. The Lord has healed her husband, given them a precious daughter, and trusted them with these orphans. While millions have died by bullets, bombs, disease, and starvation, the three of them have managed to survive. And a fourth member of the family will soon arrive.

God will find a way, she decides. *Yes, I must carry on.*

Yo-hee and Woo-yeol continue the tough work, make the tough choices, and a year later help comes. Funds from America. Resources to make it through.

The roof, it still needs repair, and the children's laundry gathers each day.

The money is something, though.

It's a mustard seed, sprouting up from hard soil.

Chapter 17

THIS EVENING ONLY

By January 1951, Rev. Swanson was determined to go wherever God led him.

His original plan had been to crisscross America, speaking by request at various churches, but as he set off, the Baptist General Conference presented him with an opportunity to visit foreign mission fields from Assam to Syria. Soon after, Dr. Bob Cook, cofounder of Youth for Christ, also invited him to take part in an outreach to Japan.

Are you interested? Miriam asked, already knowing the answer.

Absolutely!

Well, Everett, this checks off number one on your list, she noted. "Wherever He may lead in this whole wide world."

He frowned. It's number three on my list that concerns me. I need provision. As things stand, neither the Baptist General Conference nor

Youth for Christ is able to cover my airfare, and we certainly don't have that sort of money ourselves. I think I will have to decline.

When Doc Hemwall heard of this, his response was adamant.

Absolutely not!

You've already done more than enough, Everett countered.

There is always more to do. C'mon, Doc said, in our lines of work, you and I know that better than anyone. Anyway, if you remember, I've always wanted to do medical missions. In a roundabout way, I can fulfill that desire through you.

Who says you won't do it yourself someday?

Doc pushed up his glasses on his thin nose. Take the money, Everett, and go buy yourself an airline ticket.

The doctor and the reverend had no idea this warmhearted gift between friends was setting in motion a ministry that would one day span the globe. Like most acts of obedience, the long-term results would never be fully understood by those first stepping out.

Others might come along to take the baton.

Others might reap the rewards and bask in the glory.

Doc and Everett, they simply obeyed.

That summer, with ticket in hand and camera dangling from his neck, Everett gave hugs and kisses to his wife and children at the airport. Miriam assured Everett they would be all right during the six months he was gone. Why, fourteen-year-old David would have fun going out west to visit friends in Mount Vernon. Sharon would spend time with the Hemwall and Westerberg girls. Jack and Paul would have plenty of activities to keep them busy.

And we'll still be attending Central Avenue, Miriam added.

Even if we're not pastoring there, it remains our church home, he agreed. Oh, how I need the prayers of God's people.

You go on now, she said, giving him a kiss.

Dressed in a gray suit and tie, Everett climbed the boarding ramp of his Pan Am flight, turned once to wave, then disappeared into the plane.

He had made himself available and already God was taking him at his word. From Chicago, he would first spend a few weeks of ministry in Alaska, then visit lands throughout Asia, the Middle East, and Africa. He especially looked forward to northeastern India, staying in a compound in the jungles of Assam and preaching to the local peoples. His trip would conclude with stopovers in parts of Europe before his arrival back home for Christmas with his wife and kids.

At this point, Korea wasn't even on the agenda.

* * *

Though he had no plans of visiting, Everett kept current with developments in the Korean War and knew the country was in dire straits. The more he read about Korea, the more interested he became in the plight of her people.

In mid-September of the previous year, in the very week of Everett's official resignation, UN forces under General Douglas MacArthur had launched a bold counterattack against the North Korean offensive, landing troops at Incheon and driving a wedge through enemy lines. Possessing a legendary ego, MacArthur retook Seoul within a matter of days and decided he could also take North Korea while the enemy was in disarray.

Fighting Korea was no easy task, though.

Throughout history, she had proven her resolve. In 1592, for example, Admiral Yi refused to surrender when Japanese ships attacked and nearly overran Korean shores. He deployed the world's first ironclad warships, shaped like turtles and designed so men could fire blazing arrows out slots in the hulls. These turtle boats destroyed the enemy fleet and forced the invaders back across the sea.

General MacArthur disregarded the lessons of the past and sent infantry and tanks across the 38th parallel. UN soldiers with flame-throwers and 70-pound gas canisters torched everything in their paths. Planes dropped bombs and napalm on cities full of civilians. When it came to ousting the "dirty Reds," the general showed little restraint.

Then the freezing Korean winter set in.

Enemy resistance stiffened, making victory elusive.

When China sent hordes of communist reinforcements in from the north, 12,000 US marines found themselves trapped on the icy wastelands near Chosin Reservoir. After fighting fiercely, the American survivors of the slaughter piled their fallen comrades into trucks and escaped back to South Korea. Finally, in the spring of 1951, President Truman relieved General MacArthur of command for his insubordination and insistence on waging large-scale war.

On both sides, losses continued to mount, even as refugees trudged south in search of medical aid, food, and shelter.

* * *

In July 1951, Everett's first stop was in Alaska. Here, he filmed and photographed wildlife, preached in Spenard and Mountain View, and addressed Youth for Christ rallies in Anchorage. On his final Sunday, he spoke at a church dedication, where he recorded seventy-three decisions, some for salvation and others for consecration.

In late summer, he was at peace as he boarded his flight headed to Japan. He landed in Tokyo in early August, having lost a day as he crossed the international date line. He had never before left the North American continent, and jet lag was inevitable. He was ready for a good night's rest.

Minutes after stepping off the plane, however, he discovered he was already slated to speak. This evening? What about a meal, a shower?

Later, he was told. First, you have a street meeting.

Here it is, he thought, *the responsibility of the opportunity. What can I do but say yes?*

The reverend proved ready for the moment, delivering his message through a translator and cautioning his hearers to turn from their idols and sin. When he gave an invitation to respond, over a hundred people kneeled on the pavement and called out audibly for God to save them. The new converts were invited to local Bible classes where they could be further discipled.

Soon after, Everett also preached at the GI Gospel Hour and watched infantrymen crowd the altar as he concluded.

Wherever he went in Tokyo, God seemed to show up.

Even in a men's room.

He was surprised one early afternoon, as he stepped into the YMCA washroom, to hear a man whistling "I Shall See Him Face to Face," one of his favorite hymns. Everett was drying his hands at the sink, still chuckling at this odd coincidence, when the whistler appeared beside him, dressed in civilian clothing.

Hey, brother, Everett said. That's my song too.

The gentleman wiped his hands on a towel and introduced himself. Hello, I'm Dr. Peter van Lierop.

You're American?

The doctor nodded. I've been a missionary to Korea, while serving over twenty years as a faculty member at Yonsei University, in Seoul.

My name's Everett Swanson. I would love to go to Korea.

My family and I, we've just been evacuated due to the ongoing fighting.

I'm an evangelist. If I wanted to, I could still go there, couldn't I?

Your safety is a real concern, Everett. As beautiful as we know the land and people to be, there is widespread destruction. Things are barely recognizable.

But don't you believe there's a reason we met? For the past week I've had this burning desire to minister to Korean troops on the front lines, but I've had no connection, no way of making it happen. I'd appreciate any help you could give.

You know, Dr. van Lierop said, I'm in Tokyo this evening only, attending a field council meeting. Give me a few hours and I'll see what I can do. In fact, I'll go so far as to write you a letter of logistical support and share it with the council.

Everett beamed. Thank you, brother. Thank you!

Soon after, the field council voted in support of Everett's request to preach to the soldiers. Regardless, army chaplains in country would need to consider the council's recommendation and officially invite him into the prison camps, where thousands of Chinese and Korean POWs were held.

While awaiting such an invitation, Everett sought details on Korean customs and culture. He learned that Koreans were considered one year old at birth, that their family names were always written first—his own name, in Korean, would be Swanson Everett—and that kimchi was the national dish, with many families pickling their own recipes of cabbage and spices in large earthen jars.

He also corresponded with Miriam, noting Tokyo's strange mingling of East and West. "Unusual sights meet one's eye at every glance," he wrote. "But most of all my heart goes out to these teeming millions who, like their forefathers, go on in heathen darkness."

Any fascination on Miriam's part was overshadowed by her concern. Even as Everett sent letters from Japan telling of his desire to go into Korea, she prayed from home that he would stay out. There was a war going on there! Why couldn't he simply stick to the itinerary and proceed to the Philippines?

Everett's prayers seemed to win out, when two days later he got his invitation, signed by a Rev. Robert Rice.

He was headed to Korea's prison camps.

Chapter 18

AMBUSH

Rev. Swanson toured South Korea for three weeks in October 1951. He had no way of knowing this would be his first of many visits to the war-ravaged land.

Everett took photos of American howitzers pointed at enemy fortifications, of submarines blasted into twisted wreckage in their pens, of railroad cars blown from their tracks. Quonset huts housed hollow-eyed GIs. Refugees stumbled by in threadbare clothing. On a battlefield, poplar trees stood naked, stripped of their foliage by a hailstorm of bullets.

Everywhere he peered through his camera, he found people uprooted and towns destroyed. The numbers of sick, starving, and dead were beyond calculation.

Millions of Koreans had lost their property.

Wooden and cardboard shanties lined the riverbanks.

Impoverished families lived in straw-covered holes in the ground.

In some places, scarcely a wall or structure remained standing.

Hundreds of church buildings lay in rubble.

Boy, I ministered during the worst years of the Great Depression, Everett told Rev. Rice, *but I've never seen suffering on this scale. Where do we even start?*

Still shell-shocked myself. We help one person at a time, just one at a time.

Following Rev. Rice's lead, Everett visited the front lines where stenciled signs and sawhorses marked the 38th parallel. He went to makeshift hospitals where American and Korean soldiers faced blindness, infection, and burns. He joined chaplains who conducted daily funeral services, adding white crosses over quickly dug graves.

Lord God, were these fallen ready to meet You?

Using translators, he preached in military academies, training camps, and seminaries. He told of a God who cared about the fatherless, the destitute, and the sick. In an American medical tent filled to capacity, he addressed weary soldiers and military police over the groans of amputees. To offer biblical truths in the midst of such suffering seemed almost intrusive, but he wholly believed in humanity's need for relationship with the heavenly Father.

Jesus is here, Everett told them. He is not ignorant of the pain you have endured. He Himself went through the horrors of the cross to offer each of you eternal healing. Do you want to be forgiven today? Only God can heal your soul.

Hundreds responded to the call of salvation.

"Marines who are often thought of as being hard and tough," he wrote, "responded in large numbers."

* * *

Everett rumbled along in a military vehicle late one afternoon, his fellow chaplains bouncing beside him on hard bench seats in the back. En route to the next army base, they held on to their caps and Bibles. Billows of dust caused them to squint and shield their eyes. Dirt caked the pores on their faces. As the jeep entered a narrow pass, the grinding of the clutch reverberated off the rocky terrain. The sun had dipped below the horizon, and dim gray light cast the mountains in monochrome.

The jeep slammed to a stop, throwing bodies forward.

Stunned, Everett wondered if they'd struck a boulder.

Shouts brought them all to alert as communist guerrillas surrounded the vehicle and pointed Russian-supplied rifles. They barked commands in Korean, gestured with their weapons, and dragged the chaplains down onto the soil.

This was it. The martyrdom Everett had imagined in high school.

Spare us, Lord. Take care of my children, please. And of dear Miriam!

The other chaplains whispered similar prayers.

The guerillas poked around the vehicle and eyed this group of men, unarmed and older than expected. Sounding disappointed and upset, they argued among themselves. Then, as quickly as they had sprung their ambush, they faded away into thickening shadows.

Everett looked to the others. Are we free to go?

They had stared down death and been released. The chaplains, thanking God, climbed back onto their wooden seats, situated their caps, and drove on.

Throughout his time in Korea, Everett found himself ministering shoulder to shoulder with chaplains from multiple nations and branches of faith, and he wondered what his father would have thought. Here they were, all working together, Catholics, Baptists, and Jews, and he felt his heart expanding.

His own upbringing was based on Swedish Baptist doctrine. He'd gleaned so much—a personal commitment to holy living, an understanding that faith should be put into action, and an attitude of kindness toward unbelievers. Historically, Pietists had also shown great concern for orphans and widows, with facilities in Europe dating back hundreds of years.

Now Everett was watching people of other faith backgrounds demonstrate a similar love for God and others. Many of these were unwavering ministers who went everywhere with the soldiers and deserved much credit for their daily bravery and sacrifice.

And really, in the trenches, did sticky points of doctrine matter?

Everett focused on his initial reason for being sent here, to preach to the prisoners behind barbed-wire fences. As UN guards stood watch, he addressed throngs of POWs squatting outside rows of barracks. Many of these young Chinese and North Koreans had been forced into service, fearing for their families' lives.

Everett had lived through two world wars and, like many of his peers, was prone to viewing things as starkly good and evil.

Allies vs. Nazis. Democracy vs. communism.

From what he observed there were three types of POWs in these camps: first, a few diehard communists; second, a group of unwilling participants who would never return to communist rule; third, many who'd never been communists at all.

To men hungry for a taste of freedom, he distributed pocket-sized gospels of John. Due to limited supplies, he had to ration the books. Many times, he saw prisoners fighting over a single page of God's Word.

God, please free them from fear and lies!

He realized, of course, communism did not have the lone hold on evil.

As Everett mingled with the American troops, he saw they needed Jesus as much as the Chinese and Koreans. Many of these soldiers had enlisted enthusiastically after missing out on World War II. They had put on olive-drab fatigues and taken up M1 .30-caliber rifles, unaware of the nightmare ahead. Now they carried guilt for the things done in battle, the lives taken, the thousands who had perished. Many young faces looked shell-shocked.

On a cool October evening, Rev. Swanson addressed a packed air force chapel. The crowd included Elmer Rund, a stern, thin-lipped master sergeant, who, ten years previous, had made a vow to God at Pearl Harbor.

A vow he had failed miserably to keep.

Elmer Rund was transfixed by Everett's sermon. Though surrounded by other airmen in blue, he felt each word was aimed at him alone. He had survived World War II and the Korean War, but he'd never known peace for himself. Something was missing inside. Elmer Rund felt suddenly convicted of his broken vow and of his lifestyle of drunkenness and sin.

I want to know Christ, he told Everett. My mother is in heaven, and I want to be sure I'll see her there someday. I accept Jesus as my Savior!

Receive Him now, Everett exclaimed. Receive His joy in your heart.

Filled with excitement, Elmer Rund would go on to preach to many others in the years to come, while also becoming Everett's friend and longtime supporter.

Miriam read her husband's letters and rejoiced at what God was doing. Everett had survived thus far, experiencing provision and protection. Of course, he still had a long way to go, with stops in Manila, Bangkok, and Calcutta.

Her mounting troubles at home would have to wait.

Chapter 19

MAN ON A MISSION

Days before Christmas, Everett completed his six-month round-the-world trek. Miriam was well aware of last week's flight from Newark, New Jersey, which had crashed and left no survivors. It had been all over the news. She now watched her husband step from his flight, relieved to see him smiling, handsome as ever, and in reasonable health at thirty-eight years old.

You're alive, she greeted him at the terminal, gazing up through her glasses.

Alive and well. Coming back to you was always the plan, Miriam. He pulled her into an embrace and gave her a kiss. You've carried your own burdens here. Thank you.

The poem read at his high school graduation rang true with his recent experiences. Rev. Swanson had visited hospitals and schools in Ethiopia, where he'd laughed with schoolchildren, giving and receiving *kindness*. He'd photographed Japanese pagodas, ridden Indian oxcarts, and had *honorable dealing* with officials in Hong Kong. Using a small movie camera for *beauty in sound, form, and color*, he had recorded everything from bald eagles in Alaska to elephants in Assam. He'd visited over thirty countries and collected trinkets for his family.

Oh, Everett exclaimed, the stories I have to tell!

I have things to share as well, Miriam said.

He tilted his chin, eyes seeking hers.

Later, she said. The kids are waiting. Let's get you home and feed you.

They hefted his suitcases and camera equipment from the luggage carousel to the car, then threaded through the streets of Chicago to their new address at North Lorel Avenue, where Christmas lights twinkled along the porch and a tree stood decorated in the front window.

Home, Miriam said.

Everett nodded, but like many who travel beyond their shores and comfort zones, his vision had broadened, his horizons expanded. He was no longer a man focused on one section of the world. His ideas of ministry now had global scope. There were no longer any limits, not when airplanes could fly him in a single day to exotic places that once took months to reach.

Truly, it was a small world. And never had his heart felt so large.

Even as Everett underwent this transformation, he realized American thinking had also been reshaped over the past year. Consumerism was filling the vacuum left by Depression-era gloom and Nazi-era threats. Catalogs pitched ease and comfort to the housewives, offering shiny dishwashers and washing machines. Men were teased by images of radios, TVs, and fancy cars with tail fins. Teens were sold the wonders of fast food and drive-in movies.

As inviting as it all looked, these things seemed superficial to Everett.

Life magazine claimed that women who had once joined the workforce, empowered by wartime necessities, were again making careers out of birthing babies. Men in suits and ties carried matching briefcases to jobs where they traded crude jokes and sneaked sips of bourbon. Gangs roamed the inner cities, and kids carried knives to school.

Everett knew the spiritual struggles here in the US were real, rooted in envy, greed, and self-centeredness. In many of the other countries he'd visited, the most pressing needs were physical—food, water, and shelter.

Ready to eat? Miriam called to him and the kids.

As they convened in the dining room, Everett wrapped his children in his arms and felt his chest swell with joy. David was a young man now, getting taller by the day. Sharon, she was so full of life. Here was Jack, with his mischievous grin. And Paul, well, he seemed almost suspicious of this father who'd left him for half a year to go ride buses, airplanes, and boats.

Over dinner, Everett told of his adventures and fielded his kids' questions.

You were ambushed?

Up in the mountains, yes.

Weren't you scared of the rifles?

God was with us, but boy, did we pray.

Did you see any lions in Africa?

Everett grinned. Oh, just you wait till I show you what I brought back. Not a lion exactly, but very close. You'll have to hold tight till Christmas morning.

Dad, that's not fair!

C'mon now. After all these months, what's another day or two?

* * *

As the new year swung around, Everett traveled on weekends to speak at various churches and meeting halls. Evangelism was not only his calling but his primary source of income, and though Doc Hemwall had provided a generous down payment, Everett still had a mortgage and utilities to pay.

In mid-January 1952, the *Daily Chronicle* reported:

Rev. Everett Swanson, who recently returned from a 37,000-mile trip around the world will speak . . . during morning and evening services. . . . He spent three weeks in the front lines with the fighting forces in Korea, preaching to the servicemen while shells were flying overhead.

A later issue added:

He will appear in native costume. . . . Among his exhibits will be a nine-foot man-eating tiger and a 19-foot python.

Both exhibits had thrilled his children and his audiences. Thankfully, neither the tiger nor the python was still alive.

Everett traveled and preached in over a dozen states, wherever he was welcomed. Listeners were challenged by his faith and bravado, their religious fervor and financial backing stirred by his passionate storytelling.

It wasn't long before his perseverance was rewarded with an invitation to return to Korea. The chief chaplain at the Ministry of National Defense wanted him to come that August and September, and though Everett would need to scrimp and save, he had no doubt this was God's hand drawing him back to a country in turmoil.

How could he say no? If he did, would there be another to go in his place?

Or would the doors be shut, never to open again?

As a man on a mission, Everett later wrote: "Our responsibility does not end at the borders of our continent. Jesus said, 'unto the uttermost part of the earth.' . . . The opportunity is staggering. We must do more!"

* * *

Doing more didn't release him from the obligations close to home. Soon after Everett's return at Christmas, Miriam had shared with him her concerns about David's growing interest in the opposite sex and how it might be affecting his grades. Plus, there were several things to repair around the house. And the younger boys were truly a handful at times, especially Paulie, who clung to her even while resisting her rules.

I'll speak with them, Everett promised. A good father-to-son chat. Maybe we can get Paul into tennis or something, give him an outlet for his energy.

Thank you, Miriam said. Your being gone does present some challenges.

He mulled this over. Though his commitment was to God first and family second, the lines between the two blurred at times. He faced his wife, rested his hands on her shoulders, and said, This was my initial foray out of the country, a real chance to see the world. The next trip, I promise, will not last so long.

Far be it from me to stand in the way of your calling, Everett. I just want you to be aware. And Sharon, she's at that age when a girl can benefit from the pure affection of her father. She adores you.

Everett swallowed hard. Well, I am proud to be her dad.

Let her know it then. Me and my old man, we never had that between us.

He nodded. Is there anything else I should be aware of?

There is one thing, a situation with my youngest sister.

Betty? He frowned. Is she alright?

She's eighteen, about to graduate from Sycamore High, and—

Boy, that makes me feel old!

Miriam pressed on. Apparently, Betty and my father have been at odds, and he got violent with her a few years back. Even drew blood. You know my mother, though. She's not one to confront such issues. Some distance between Betty and Dad might do everyone good.

Betty could stay here, couldn't she? Would Sharon mind sharing a room?

Would she mind? She'd be overjoyed to have another girl in the house.

As summer rolled around, pushing hot air through the streets of Chicago, Miriam helped Betty move in and find a job along the nearest bus route.

Sixteen years apart, the two sisters barely knew each other. Betty had little interest in Miriam's faith and walked around stone-faced, avoiding conversation. Over the next months, though, their relationship blossomed. Betty was impressed by her older sister. Miriam dressed stylishly, modest jewelry and hair always in place. She was an independent woman, a fantastic baker, and a demanding mother who expected her children to kick in and help.

Betty was even more impacted by her time around Uncle Everett.

Every morning she lay in bed and heard him call out loudly from his room, Praise the Lord! Then he launched into song, filling the house with gospel tunes. Though none of it was Betty's style, she couldn't help but smile on her pillow, won over by his enthusiasm and the warm vibrato in his voice.

He was so devout, the most devout man she had ever met. He was patient, never pressuring her. When she had questions, he listened instead of pushing answers at her. Even when he gathered the rest of the family for nighttime devotionals, he gave her space. If she joined in, she joined in. If not, that was okay too.

Betty's old man was hammers and nails.

Uncle Everett was hugs and hymns.

She would one day name a child of hers after him, in honor of this uncle she both loved and respected.

Chapter 20

THE CRUCIBLE

R ev. Swanson was humbled by the history of Christian outreach to Korea.

In the early 1800s, Koreans traveling outside the country met Christians and brought back their teachings. Later, missionaries such as Horace Newton Allen, Horace Grant Underwood, and Henry Gerhard Appenzeller broached Korea's secluded shores with stories from the Bible. Despite the beheadings of thousands of believers along the Han River, Christianity grew. The next century saw Korean ministers lead waves of revival in the north, where churches again faced persecution, this time from the communists.

When Everett arrived in August 1952, he was greeted by Captain Hyung-do Kim, the tall, lanky chief chaplain, and introduced to a team of chaplains who would assist him over the next seven weeks. These men, Everett learned, were North Korean pastors, refugees of war, victims of the purges back home.

"I realize much more my debt to these heroic men and women," he noted with obvious passion. "A North Korean pastor pleaded with me to help him care for 120 children of pastors and their wives, all of whom had been martyred! In one village 600 men, women and children, members of the local Christian church, were called together by the Communists and mowed down with machine guns!"

As they traveled to hospitals and army bases, Everett found the faith of these battle-tested Christians invigorating. Though he felt insignificant by comparison, he could not turn back now. When Jesus rolled back the stone and rose from the tomb, He had opened the door for His disciples and given them power to go into all the world.

From the crucible of suffering, Everett saw many Koreans searching for meaning and truth, returning to their old religions of Buddhism and Confucianism. The troops numbed themselves with entertainment, eventually cheering on performances by comedian Bob Hope and bombshell Marilyn Monroe. Some sought escape in illicit pleasures.

Everett viewed it all as a soul-winning opportunity.

What better time than now?

He rejoiced when General Park, chief of staff of the armed forces, declared his faith in Jesus Christ. With this change of heart, Park proved sympathetic to Everett's ongoing evangelistic efforts and set up even more engagements for him.

Everett and his team of chaplains rode in black panel vans, inched over pitted roads, winched from deep ruts of mud, and ferried over engorged rivers. Bridges were unreliable. The ones not already dynamited by communist guerrillas sat in glaring states of disrepair. The team pressed on regardless, knowing there were thousands of troops expecting them at scattered military camps.

The chaplains were welcomed with paper flowers wherever they went, expressions of honor and gratitude often pinned to their lapels. Since gift giving was customary, Everett always tried to arrive with his own small tokens of appreciation—chocolates, flowers, fruit.

Few Koreans spoke fluent English, but local translators helped him communicate God's love at a rudimentary level and he did not soft-pedal the truth.

Yes, American presidents had ignored and broken treaties with Korea.

Yes, US soldiers often exhibited immorality.

Yes, millions had been forced out of the north by a bombastic leader.

Only in Jesus Christ, Everett explained, would humans find one who did not fail them.

During a meeting in a natural amphitheater, 18,000 men gathered to hear Rev. Swanson speak. Cooperating selflessly, chaplains, army chauffeurs, bodyguards, and translators made the meeting possible, and uniformed men stood for hours to hear the Word of God proclaimed. Everett was truly overwhelmed when thousands of male voices joined together and sang: "What can wash away my sin? Nothing but the blood of Jesus."

The tears flowed freely from his eyes.

Throughout his gatherings with American and Korean armed forces, Everett recorded close to 30,000 professions of faith in the Lord Jesus Christ. God alone knew how many were truly converted, but the Lord's work was evident, with chances for evangelism running in contrast with the war's atrocities.

Then a familiar face reappeared: Elmer Rund, of the US Air Force.

Elmer hadn't lost one ounce of his zeal since accepting the Lord the year before. The master sergeant was now leading others to Christ, over two hundred so far, while also giving $3,000 to gospel efforts at home and abroad.

What wondrous news, Everett cried. Thank You, God!

It was a great way to end his speaking tour, and he traveled back to Seoul with only a few days remaining before his journey home.

Then, a beggar boy stole his coat.

Then, he stumbled upon the orphans in the alleyway.

Everett's heart was broken, his world shaken, and he questioned his purpose here. He'd come and preached to the soldiers, prisoners, and civilians. He'd rejoiced at each soul saved along the way. He'd reveled in the joy of his calling.

Meanwhile, children were starving, freezing, dying.

Oh, these precious orphans of war!

Preteen girls cowered in hovels, clutching younger siblings to their sides. Malnourished kids fought over scraps in the army garbage piles. Some cowered alone, throwing stones at anyone who drew near. Empty cans were used as cooking pots over open fires, and beggar boys roamed like packs of wild dogs, scavenging, robbing, desperate to survive.

All these sad little faces just ripped Everett's heart in two.

* * *

In his window seat near the wing, Everett watched the plane's propellers spin so quickly they became almost invisible to his naked eye. How had he been so blind? How had he never before noticed all the fatherless, motherless, homeless children? Sure, he had seen them, but he hadn't really *seen* them.

He'd been focused instead on the task of winning souls.

It was what he had come here to do.

But as much as Everett had enjoyed speaking to the troops while bullets zinged by, he found even greater joy in giving soup and hugs to those children in the alleyway.

An air pocket caused the plane to drop, throwing Everett's heart into his throat and his adrenaline into overdrive. Normally, he liked this part of flying, the excitement. Not now, though. At the moment, his pulse was pounding in his ears. Or perhaps it was only the sound of the propellers applying thrust through cloud-heavy skies.

Throppp-throppp-throppp . . .

What are you going to do?

The evening sun was setting behind their flight, casting the ocean into deeper shadow. In an hour or so they would land in Seattle. An hour or two after that, he would be sleeping—or so he hoped—in a bed at his brother Ray's house. Everett was worn thin, overwhelmed by the past seven weeks, in no physical, mental, or spiritual shape to be taking on the burden of abandoned children.

What could he do anyway? He had no savings. No funding. No knowledge of the Korean language. Weren't the local people better suited for such work?

The plane lurched again, then leveled out.

He tugged a newspaper from the seat pouch and rifled through it, trying to still his swirling thoughts. He read about golfer Ben Hogan, the Chicago Bears, and Rocky Marciano, who had become the world boxing champ a few days earlier by knocking out Jersey Joe Walcott.

Hadn't another world champ, Johnny "Cyclone" Thompson, lived only two or three miles from Everett's boyhood home back in Sycamore, Illinois? Hadn't Father and Mother raised Everett to also be a fighter, a warrior in spiritual terms?

He sat up in his seat. It was time to step up. Time to pick a fight of his own.

Throppp-throppp-throppp . . .

As he gazed back out the window, that challenge, that one simple question, spun round and round like propellers in his head.

Chapter 21

A DIFFERENT FIGHT

As Everett's flight descended, fall weather lay cool and pleasant over Puget Sound. Ray picked him up from SeaTac airport, and they arrived at Ray's place by dark. They had so much to talk about, from the latest family happenings to overseas travel updates.

I shot some rolls of film, Everett mentioned. Perhaps you could help me develop them.

From Korea? Ray perked up. I'd love to.

They were interrupted by the doorbell. Ray shook hands with their visitor and invited him in. This here's Pastor Johnson, he said. From Tabernacle Baptist. Pastor, meet my brother, Rev. Everett Swanson.

A fellow minister? Everett, I'm honored. I live just across the street.

Oh, has Everett got some stories for you, Ray said. He's been evangelizing in South Korea's army bases. Can I grab you two something hot to drink?

Postum, please, said Everett. If you have it.

The three men talked deep into the night, with Pastor Johnson pressing Everett for story after story. Suitably impressed, he asked Everett to preach in his pulpit the next morning, an unexpected treat for the congregation.

Why, sure, Everett agreed. I could do that.

Sunday service at Tabernacle Baptist rolled around much too early for a man still adjusting to different time zones, but Everett came prepared. "We ought to get down on our knees and thank God," he preached from his written notes, "that our great cities do not lie in ruin. . . . We travel in great speed and comfort . . . we worship in lovely churches without fear . . . our tables are spread with good things. . . . While God is good to us, in Korea there are thousands of boys who walk the roads and the streets . . . begging for a little morsel of bread. Many Americans put more in their garbage cans every day than Koreans have to eat."

As he wrapped up and led the final hymn, Everett spotted Pastor Johnson slipping from the sanctuary. Odd as this seemed, he carried on. Before the song was over, the pastor was back.

After the service, the pastor pulled Everett aside and explained that weeks earlier a lady in this congregation had handed him a check for $50, along with specific instructions to use it for Korea. It was an unusual request since the church had not focused in any way on that particular country. The pastor, unsure of what to do, tucked the check into his desk drawer and forgot about it.

Until now, he stated. Even as you were speaking, Everett, I knew this was meant for you. I'm going to cash it for you from today's offering.

But I—

Put it to good use for the kids of Korea.

* * *

Settled into his seat for the flight from Seattle to Chicago, Everett felt his excitement about going home offset by his concerns for the Land of the Morning Calm. If he didn't step up to help the orphans, who would? There was a reason God kept giving him these little nudges to get involved, prompting instead of pushing.

A stolen coat. An alleyway. A group of tiny faces.

A $50 check.

Everett knew how highly Koreans valued their kids. Children's Day, established by a Korean writer, had been a national holiday in South Korea since 1923. Though forbidden under Japanese rule, the holiday was reinstated on May 5, 1945, highlighting the dignity of children and their need for love and respect. Already, there were Korean men and women doing their best to care for the orphans, but the need and the poverty there were so great. Most citizens could barely feed themselves.

If he turned away, Everett realized, if he ignored the orphans and widows, how could he claim to be sharing the gospel of Christ?

Holding the cash from Pastor Johnson, he gave a wry chuckle.

Fifty dollars? Why, this wouldn't even feed the orphans in the alleyway for a month.

Since childhood, he had followed his parents' lead in praying for souls, and during his youth he had heard the call to evangelism. For years, he had pursued his heavenly Father's call and honored that call for the sake of his earthly father. Now he was being drawn in a different direction, called to a different fight.

After all, if the kids died in the streets, how could they ever hear God's Word?

Jesus Himself said in Matthew 10:42, "And whoever gives one of these little ones only a cup of cold water . . . he shall by no means lose his reward." And in Matthew 19:14, Jesus told His disciples, "Let the little children come to Me . . . for of such is the kingdom of heaven."

These precious kids, Everett determined, were the ones for whom he must fight, securing safety, shelter, and sustenance. The Korean War would go down in history as the Forgotten War and many of his fellow Americans knew very little about it. To him, though, this fight for the children was even more important, a war most people had already forgotten.

How was he to convince Miriam, though?

Oh, dear Lord, help me. Have I lost my mind?

His wife's primary interest was the care of their own four children, and now here he stood, with $50 in hand, wanting to feed and clothe thousands across the sea.

* * *

Miriam realized right away something in her husband had changed. He grew animated talking about the Korean orphans. He said he could not get those images out of his mind. Many were beggar boys, he told her, using the term with affection, and he described for her their little faces, mud-caked feet, and threadbare clothes.

They are everywhere, Miriam. Roaming the streets, just trying to stay alive.

Alright, I see those wheels turning. What do you have in mind?

It's too much to even think about, he admitted. Tens, maybe hundreds of thousands. But we can help a handful, can't we? We can start with that.

Perhaps you could partner with an established agency.

He tilted his head, then nodded. Yes, good idea. A large church or missions board might want to get involved. I need someone with resources and resolve.

I'll call around, schedule you some appointments.

Fantastic. Thank you, Miriam.

Her results, though, were discouraging. At the few meetings she was able to arrange, Rev. Swanson's requests were met with veiled apathy.

The men and women he met with had goals and agendas of their own. Sincere best wishes to him, of course. And God bless.

He wondered again if this was truly his fight to fight.

Then another paper check appeared, this time in his Chicago mailbox.

Well, Miriam, what do you think of this? Everett said as he handed over the delivery and propped his hands on his hips.

Did this just come today? Who are Robert and Carrie Geary?

No idea. I've never heard those names before.

I'm not sure what to say, Miriam confessed. She proceeded to read the check aloud. To: Rev. Everett Swanson. In the amount of: $1,000. For: Relief efforts.

Everett clapped his hands together. Well, if this isn't conclusive proof that God is in this! Seems we are out of excuses.

Miriam nodded. Loony as it seems, I can't deny there is something bigger going on here. Miriam's gaze met her husband's. Her chin was set as she touched his arm, smoothed her dress, then turned back to her meal preparations. Well, she called back over her shoulder, don't just stand there. You have work to do.

Yes, I do, he said, planting a quick kiss on her cheek.

In the fall of 1952, with one solitary check in hand, the reverend sat at a desk he had squeezed into their master bedroom and opened his Sterling account book. He had no formal theological training, no business degree, no knowledge of the Korean language, but he did have a desire to serve God through practical means.

This was it. Time to climb into the ring.

Chapter 22

TWELVE-PACKS

The Korean War had reached a stalemate. What looked to be a quick victory had stretched into a third year of bloody skirmishes, and those in the West had other news now clamoring for their attention.

Meanwhile, the death toll kept rising.

Over two million civilians were dead. The Koreans had lost nearly 500,000 soldiers on both sides, and America had seen close to 40,000 killed in action.

During the presidential election of 1952, Dwight D. Eisenhower, a former five-star general, promised to end the conflict in Korea if he won. Buttons and bumper stickers proclaimed *I Like Ike*, and the popular, grassroots candidate was elected America's thirty-fourth president.

As Ike was preparing for his new post, Rev. Swanson also had new duties to consider. He must fight for the hungry and oppressed, making sure their cries did not fade away.

The bell had rung. The fight had now started.

He called his fledgling ministry the Everett Swanson Evangelistic Association. It was an unofficial entity, a humble family enterprise, using their home address as its own. He still had a heart for evangelism, but meeting the orphans' practical needs was the only way he could keep the blood pumping. They meant everything to him.

As a good steward, Everett decided to track all expenditures, keeping account of every penny in and out. He made a handwritten list.

Donations to the Korea work: $50 (Seattle), $1,000 (Gearys).

Income from preaching dates: $152 (Cadillac, Michigan), $179 (Sycamore, Illinois), and $270 (Kenosha, Wisconsin).

Expenses: $12.82 (telephone), $27 (decision cards), and $5 (projection bulb).

Everett's next priority was to fund some sort of housing for his beloved beggar boys. He wasn't interested in arranging adoptions to the United States. Turning orphans into comfortable Americans wouldn't do much to aid Korea's future. But how could he engage the hearts and minds of people in the US who were already losing interest in Korea's troubles?

Sponsors, he realized.

Instead of seeking people who wanted to adopt, Everett would sign up individuals to "parent" from afar. Each sponsor would assume financial responsibility for a child, while also praying for them. In this way, Korean orphans could grow and learn to be productive citizens of their own precious land.

It was a newer model that only a handful of other agencies had tried. Showing the needs of an entire nation often overwhelmed listeners, whereas narrowing the scope to one individual made those needs seem more manageable.

Everett also wanted Koreans, as much as possible, to oversee their own affairs instead of bowing to the demands of Westerners often ignorant of local procedures. The orphans' situation was urgent and complex. He truly believed the most effective people for ministering to them would be Korean men and women who knew their language and customs.

After prayerful consideration, Everett wrote a check for $1,000 and sent it to Rev. Robert Rice, the one who had first invited him into Korea. Rice was a wise, trustworthy man who already worked well with national pastors and chaplains. He would funnel this money to the right people for the purchase of an orphanage.

You're sure not wasting any time, Miriam told her husband.

There's none to waste. Reminds me of the sign I saw on a stake outside a Korean training camp. It said, "If you let your weapon rust, keep your coffin clean."

Help me out, Everett. I'm not much of a gun girl.

The point is, if we sit around and don't use the tools at hand, we might as well start digging graves because there are kids who will surely die.

* * *

ESEA made its initial building purchase on the mountainous fringes of Samcheok. This first orphanage was named *Shin-Ae-Won*, meaning "faith and love," and Everett shared this good report with audiences wherever he spoke. He showed color films shot by his own hand in Korea, depicting beautiful boys and girls caught in the jaws of a war they had never asked for.

Wouldn't you like to sponsor one of these little ones? he asked. We have so much, even more than we need. How can we not be moved with compassion?

To his great joy, many were eager to help.

Soon churches and Sunday school groups were signing up as sponsors. Many spoke to him in tears, hearts moved on behalf of the Korean children. They told him they had no idea how terrible things were over there, no idea at all. Though support was slow at first, it was steady. It was also followed by money from the Baptist General Conference and from Elmer Rund.

Elmer, oh boy. And to think the man could've died at Pearl Harbor!

Amid Everett's endeavors, he also had his own children to consider. David was in high school, Sharon in junior high, Paul and Jack in elementary school. They were reading their Bibles and earning good grades. Sure, they proved challenging to their mother, but that was normal, wasn't it? Hadn't he and his own brothers and sister been rambunctious at times?

Miriam was still concerned about their oldest son. David's been acting strangely, she told Everett. Especially since his latest trip out west.

He's a teenage boy, Everett noted.

That's what has me worried. Apparently, while he was with his best friend back in Mount Vernon, he—

Wait. The same friend who climbed through that pea viner years ago?

Now you see why I'm worried. They drove up to an outlook while on a double date, and David's friend tried pressuring him to get cozy with his young woman. David says he resisted, and I believe him, otherwise why would he even mention it, right? But he's struggling, I think.

I was that young man once, Everett said. Had a girl who kept me at arm's length.

And for good reason! Miriam's eyes twinkled behind her glasses.

He smiled and took her hand.

There's been other incidents, she went on. David and his brothers set off firecrackers in the cemetery out in Sycamore. They could have had a run-in with the police. And then . . . well, he doesn't want me to tell you about the Buick. He's scared you'll be disappointed in him.

Everett pulled his hand away and frowned. I know nothing about this.

Now, before you get upset, hear me out. He's already paid for the repairs—

Repairs!

From his own pocket, yes. He knows the rules. He'd taken the car out for a spin without permission when the transmission snapped. He coasted it back and crashed it into the garage.

I believe a little man-to-man chat is in order.

Please, Miriam said, go easy on him. He already feels bad enough.

After vowing to remain calm, Everett called his son into the master bedroom.

Am I in trouble? David wanted to know.

Grab ahold of the desk there, Everett said. You're a big guy now. This'll be a cinch if we both take an end.

Where're we going with it?

To the basement. As a family, we're about to get down to business, and that means we need more office space. You know, David, I've been so busy working on behalf of the orphans that I've been gone even more than usual. Please forgive me for not being around. I'd really love to go to another Cubs game together.

David shrugged. Sure, Dad. I understand.

But know this, son, from now on you will always ask permission before taking the car out. Is that clear?

Yes, sir.

Together, they hefted the desk down the stairs, its edges clunking against the railing. They positioned it on the cement floor, across from the sprawling metal ducts of the furnace—the octopus, the family called it. Everett planted a typewriter and mimeograph on the desk, then situated a rug under the chair. Miriam brought down a lamp and David tested the bulb. They opened small windows to fill the dank space with natural light and oxygen.

Pausing for a deep breath, Everett turned to face his firstborn. Listen, David, I love your mom and you kids very much. Ministry comes with its share of demands, and a calling always involves sacrifice. But you are so very important to me. You need to know that. I would not be a traveling man for anyone except Jesus Christ.

His son combed back his blond hair. Yeah, I know, Dad.

I appreciate your understanding.

So. David waved his hand around the basement. Is all this about those kids in Korea?

You know, those kids would break your heart if you could see them. As tight as things get here in our household at times, we are rich as kings compared to most others in the world. Thank you for being a part of this.

Sure thing.

Oh, I almost forgot. The boxes.

Everett led David out to the garage and revealed thousands of boxed

ESEA envelopes, earmarked *Orphanage Department.* Sponsors would receive these in twelve-packs, one for each monthly donation. Along the flaps ran the words of Matthew 25:40, "Inasmuch as ye have done it unto one of the least of these."

David's eyes widened. Do we have this many sponsors already?

We will, Everett said. I am believing for it. And our family will be sponsoring a few children of our own. Can't ask others to do what we won't do ourselves, right?

By the time father and son carted the boxes downstairs and stacked them against a basement wall, they were fanning their necks and wiping sweat from their brows. As they surveyed their work, they had no way of knowing what lay ahead.

Chapter 23

SHOVELED DIRT

By 1953, Everett appreciated the benefits of technology for the spread of the gospel, but he worried about the effects of a TV within his own home.

Dad, if we got a set, David pointed out, you could watch the news.

And I could watch *Howdy Doody*, Paul piped in.

Thing's too expensive. No, there are better uses of our time.

Everett's resistance crumbled, however, when Doc Hemwall presented him with a small black-and-white TV. Soon, he was glued to every report by broadcaster Edward R. Murrow. Murrow was a voice of reason, quoting French philosopher Bertrand de Jouvenel: "A nation of sheep will beget a government of wolves" and stating: "No one can eliminate prejudices—just recognize them."

Yes, Everett realized, he had his own prejudices. Hadn't he recently caught himself saying the only good communist was a dead communist?

This flippant remark seemed to bear bitter fruit when, on June 19, McCarthy-era anticommunism led to one American couple being put to death by electric chair on charges of espionage. The Rosenbergs claimed their innocence until the end, but their executions were fiercely debated around the world. Edward R. Murrow spoke boldly against McCarthy's bullying tactics, and Everett was saddened by the intolerance found lurking in his own heart.

God, forgive me!

Yes, a system could be evil, but individuals were created in God's image.

Then on July 27, Murrow reported that representatives of North Korea, China, and the UN had signed an armistice in a hall at Panmunjom. Though this was not an official end to the war, it would put an end to the hostilities in Korea until a peace settlement was achieved.

But South Korea refused to sign. They resented this split along the 38th parallel, dictated to them by outside forces. They wanted a unified Korea.

As thrilled as Everett was to hear of the fighting's end, he knew Korea's troubles were far from over. US planes had dropped more explosives in North Korea than in the entire Pacific during World War II. Dams had been destroyed, infrastructure crippled. Napalm had incinerated fields, huts, and humans. Though many refugees thanked UN soldiers for offering aid, the living conditions remained horrific, and war orphans numbered in the hundreds of thousands.

Everett typed in a newsletter that he wanted to "help these poor victims of war caused by the bungling of American leaders."

Despite the great need, Everett knew most of his fellow citizens were weary after years of bad news. What they wanted now were diversions of any kind.

Hey, wasn't there a new Lauren Bacall film out?

Had you heard about Sir Edmund Hillary, first man to climb Everest?

It was obvious getting and keeping sponsors would be an increasing challenge. If Everett was going to win this fight for the children, he must first get down on his knees. This was a lesson he'd learned from Father and Mother, even as a teen.

Saw you by your bed last night, his daughter told him. Bet you were praying, huh?

Since when, young lady, do we gamble or bet in this house?

But you were, weren't you? Sharon persisted. I think you fell fast asleep.

Probably so, he admitted, hoping the image would provide her a sweet memory.

Over the summer, his passion grew along with his sponsor list, and he wrote: "My hands were empty when I began this work. As we have followed God's leading, taking one step of faith at time, He has supplied the 'power that worketh in us.'"

Wherever he preached, from Chicago to Des Moines to Ogden, he shared details about Korea. He started each meeting dressed in traditional garb, flashing a beggar boy's tin pail he had purchased for display. Newspaper ads read:

Don't Miss These Meetings . . . Films Every Night!

Evangelist Everett Swanson . . . Relating the story of startling tragedies and thrilling experiences—You Must Hear This!

You'll Know Why The Throngs Are Coming This Way! Just Back From Korea! COME EARLY FOR SEATS!

* * *

As the Swansons invested what little they had in the ministry, their family bills became an even greater obstacle. Chicago bankers didn't care if Everett and Miriam were trying to save the world. They simply wanted their money.

The Lord's always been faithful, Everett assured his wife.

You know, I'm not opposed to getting a job, she commented. Then, noting his furrowed brow, she hurried on. I've given it some thought. There's a factory looking for workers, and other women in the church are already on the assembly line. This could be God's way of providing, especially since all our kids are in school now.

Would you still be here when they get home?

There'd be a gap, it's true, due to the bus route I'd have to take. David and Sharon, they can handle things. They're both responsible.

You're sure about this? What will your father think?

She waved that off. Oh, he knows I have a mind of my own. Consider it my contribution to the ministry.

Setting pride aside, Everett consented. It was one thing to make sacrifices of his own, but to have his wife do so moved him beyond words. For better or worse, they were in this together.

* * *

In the fall of 1953, ESEA furnished funds to break ground for a second orphanage. Once completed, New Life Boys' and Girls' Home would house fifty to a hundred beggar children in Daegu. This project was largely funded by Doc Hemwall and his wife. Early pillars of the ministry, they gave encouragement, financial assistance, and much-needed medical supplies.

While New Life was being built, the children dwelt in purchased army tents. A veritable black market had formed for discarded military supplies, but ESEA operated legally.

Included in Everett's introductory letter to each sponsor was a picture of an orphan, a questionnaire with the child's information, and a report on academic progress. Despite his tireless efforts, his ministry was still relatively unknown, and he got letters with questions about the $4 monthly donation and where it was sent. He spent hours each week, whether on the road or in his basement headquarters, penning responses, his cursive flowing over the pages.

In a letter he mailed from Pine Bluff, Wyoming, he replied to one lady:

Dear Mrs. W—

Thank you for your kind letter and inquiry about supporting a Korean child. . . . I am sending these funds over regularly. It actually costs a little less than $4—but there are extras time to time. So I use that as a general figure.

You may send it each month to me for transmittal. I am sending under separate care a pack of 12 envelopes for the coming year.

Thank you and God bless you. Psalm 41:1 and 2

* * *

As the leaves turned and the nights grew colder, Everett's sister, Rose, sent word from Sycamore that their mother had suffered a heart attack. At seventy-one years old, Emma Swanson spent time convalescing in Rose's home, then succumbed to a second attack the following Friday.

On October 20, 1953, the *True Republican* stated:

Her life was fully and beautifully lived. She was deeply devoted to her home and family and to her church. . . . Her many kindly traits of character won her countless friends. Left to mourn her passing are five sons and one daughter. . . . Surviving also are 23 grandchildren.

Everett and his grown siblings gathered behind the cemetery's black iron gates as Mother's casket was lowered into the earth next to Father's.

She may have faded quietly, but her impact through her kids would carry well into the next century.

An emptiness burrowed into Everett's heart. Both his parents were gone. He squared his shoulders and watched shoveled dirt go into the grave.

I'll miss you, Mother, he thought. *You've always been here for me.*

Miriam and their children circled round, mourning Grandma Emma, while Everett reflected on the life of this woman who had birthed him back in 1913. She was a quiet rock, unmoved by the floods of life. She had modeled faithful devotion at the church and also in practical service to friends and strangers. She had welcomed his wife and fawned over each grandchild. Until the end, she had never stopped working, never sought attention nor accolades.

Back in Korea, Elmer Rund had once wanted assurance he would see his own mother again someday. In this regard, Everett had blessed assurance. He imagined Mother now, adjusting the bun atop her head, cheering him on in the work God had begun.

Unlike his father, she had been alive to see ESEA's inception.

Finish what you've started, she would surely tell him. Life is all too short.

Chapter 24

ONE AT A TIME

As 1953 came to a close, the Swansons' focus turned again to Christmas. The big day was only weeks away. The tree was up in the living room, the lights strung, the tinsel hung. They sat for a family photo, to be used in their *Season's Greetings* letter to friends and relatives. While gift-giving would be sparse this year, the six of them were all together to share memories of Grandpa Emil and Grandma Emma and to celebrate the Savior's birth.

It was also, Everett understood, an important season for fundraising.

In early December, he sat at an old typewriter and composed his first sponsor newsletter for the Everett Swanson Evangelistic Association. It read, in part:

I want to take this opportunity to thank you for your faithful contributions. . . .

First of all, all the funds needed for the . . . beggar boys' orphanage are in and the building is being constructed.

Secondly, we now have 81 Christian bookshops open and carrying on a wonderful ministry throughout South Korea. . . .

Thirdly, in August our new 12-page bi-monthly revival paper, JESUS IS THE VICTOR, came off the press with 60,000 copies. These were freely distributed to all pastors, evangelists, chaplains, and Christian workers in South Korea.

Besides these main projects, substantial funds have been sent to help buy a Revival Center in Daegu, help build another orphanage up near the front lines, and care for many orphans and widows.

Last but not least, many tons of clothing from all over America have reached these very needy people and always with a Christian testimony.

Everett peeled the last page from the typewriter, read it over, then called out to his kids. They pounded down the stairs into the basement and he explained that he needed their help.

David and Sharon threw each other looks. Jack and Paul groaned.

Hold on now, it'll be fun. Consider it a gift to your Korean brothers and sisters.

I don't want more brothers, Paul griped.

And who says they would want you? Jack teased, throwing an elbow.

Enough of that, Everett said.

Let's make it a race, Sharon suggested. I bet you . . . she paused, noticing the look from her father. I'm pretty sure I can beat any of you boys.

You're on, David said.

Just out of reach of the fearsome furnace ducts, Everett cranked the mimeograph and made copies of the newsletter. As the octopus came alive, blowing warm air, he showed his brood how to stuff, seal, and stamp the sponsor envelopes. He cranked out and stacked papers in equal piles. The kids competed side by side, preparing hundreds of letters for the outgoing mail.

Not too fast. Make sure they're sealed properly, Everett chided.

I'm winning, Jack called out.

Are not, Paul reacted.

Am too.

Done, Sharon said, stamping the last envelope in her pile, with David just behind her.

The mailing of the newsletter became a quarterly routine and over the years Everett would enlist his children's assistance in other aspects of the ministry. They were learning the value of hard work and they found satisfaction in a job well done. Sure, Everett knew they dragged their feet at times, but even their cousin George noted they never seemed to show any resentment. They gave themselves to the task at hand out of love and respect for their father.

Before New Year's, ESEA took on support of a third facility, an orphanage in Suncheon, in South Jeolla, a poverty-ridden province historically shunned by the country's elite.

One orphan at a time, Everett reminded himself. One home at a time.

* * *

In 1954, Everett was not unaware of the changing world about him. Jonas Salk was beginning to vaccinate millions of children against polio, teens were singing along with Bill Haley & His Comets, and elite runners were marveling at Roger Bannister's sub-four-minute mile. As fascinating as these things were, Everett spent most of his energy seeking aid for Korea. He traveled extensively, submitting details of his meetings to local publications, then inviting audiences to support the work overseas.

Still, he couldn't turn his face from the needs in other parts of the world. Visits to far-flung lands had broadened his vision, and he wanted to prod people toward this global perspective, whether or not they contributed to his ministry. Other organizations were doing good work out there as well. Some, he noticed, were growing even faster than his.

Am I missing something? he wondered. *Is ESEA falling short somehow?*

Well, at least their numbers were growing.

This competitive streak of his was hard to ignore. It reared up while he was fishing with Doc, playing 16-inch softball with David, and leg-wrestling with his boys. As a corn-fed, farm-bred, patriotic American, Everett naturally wanted his work to grow in effectiveness and influence, but he had to check himself.

Oh, Lord, forgive me. This is not about the numbers.

Thoughts stirring, he sat at his basement desk with the evening paper. On the front page was the Supreme Court's ruling in *Brown v. Board of Education*, stating that segregation was unconstitutional. This was a good thing. He believed all were created equal by God. Even so, racism was still evident right here in Chicago.

And what about me? Do I have prejudices in my own heart?

He knew being a white-skinned, blue-eyed male of Swedish descent didn't make him any better or more capable than anyone else—a fact his Norwegian father-in-law liked to rub in his face. Certainly, ESEA did not need Westerners making all the decisions for the Korean staff. If anything, local directors should be the ones responsible for the daily operations, just as each orphan was responsible for a blanket, pillow, and shoes.

Everett set aside the paper, then opened a folder showing the directors of Shin-Ae-Won and New Life Boys' and Girls' Home. Where would he be without their faithful work? He wrote, "Directors and staff members are all Koreans, who we believe can do a much better job than any foreign missionary."

Behind him, feet padded down the stairs.

Five minutes till supper's ready, Sharon said, then moved to his side. Dad, you hardly ever stop working. You really love those Korean kids, don't you?

Oh, Sharon, I feel like a father to each one of them. And these men and women, he added, tapping the folder, these dear directors, the work they're doing over there, it's remarkable. Each day's a fight for them just to feed the kids.

From what everyone says, they all love you too, Dad. Five minutes, she repeated.

With his Sterling book open, Everett ran a finger down the page and reminded himself of the work God was already doing. Every dollar was accounted for, with money going to children in Korea, as well as to ministers in Alaska, India, Japan, and Mexico. Over $20,000.

* * *

As summer gave way to fall, Everett mailed an update to his monthly sponsors:

> By God's grace and with the help of many of you friends,
> I now have three fine houses for children. One at Daegu,
> the New Life Boys' and Girls' Home, has about 100 former

beggar boys happily situated. . . . Another is near Samcheok
on the east coast. . . . Shin-Ae-Won Orphanage has 63 boys
and girls who now look to their Heavenly Father and us for
daily bread. Our third one is located at Suncheon near the
south central coast, the New Life Children's Home. Here we
have 126 boys and girls under the finest supervision. . . . I
cannot stand to think of sending one of these children back
on to the streets again . . . we must care for them and train
them to be strong Christian leaders in that war-torn land.

One supporter responded personally to Everett:

"It was wonderful to get the pictures the other day. . . . It just
thrilled me to see all those orphans clean, well fed and with happy
beaming faces. . . . Only eternity will reveal the results of this great
work."

Another person wrote:

"I spent most of the day in prayer for you and Mrs. Swanson. . . .
Of course I am not alone for God is always with me, but sometimes
I feel so alone. Then I think of your wonderful work, and it gives me
faith and courage."

The Swansons themselves were sponsoring a handful of orphans, so
it was encouraging to have others join them in regular support. Friends
and relatives also wanted to take part. Some assisted in the mailing process, others gave generously of their finances, others donated clothing.

I even got George signed up, Miriam told Everett. Right here at
the kitchen table.

Sally's little brother? From what I hear, Sally wants to go into nursing. And George, why, he must be in his teens by now.

And still a real handful, Miriam said with a chuckle. You know
what he told me? He said, "I get more lickins than the rest of the lot
put together, but I get less lickins than I have coming." Well, the whole

thing was his idea really. "Dadburnit," he told me. "I want to sponsor my own Korean boy."

Everett pumped his fist. God is good. And He is just getting started!

Chapter 25

PUT THINGS RIGHT

Everett returned one afternoon from an out-of-town meeting and rummaged around the house for his new transistor radio. He was sure he'd left it on the dining table.

Looking for something, Dad? Jack asked.

Was hoping to listen to the Cubs game. Have you seen my radio?

Now a young teen, Jack shook his head. Maybe Paul borrowed it.

Did not, Paul shouted from down the hall.

I said maybe. Jack rolled his eyes, then turned back to Everett. Anyway, there's no asking Sharon. She's with the Westerbergs. Maybe David moved it, but these days he's got his work at the butcher shop after school and won't be home till supper.

Well, if you see it, just let me know. I'll be down in the office.

As much as he loved baseball, Everett had other things he loved even more. In the basement, he pulled out a projector and settled down to watch old film footage from his first two trips to Korea. This was his way of stirring up the gift within, the urge to help. On the screen, the boys and girls turned curiously toward him, staring into his round eyes, so hungry for love.

A cup of water.

A new coat.

A hug.

With one simple gesture, an entire life could be changed.

Everett knew there were still so many souls in jeopardy. Rev. Rice and others sent him regular updates, and Korea remained in shambles a year after the armistice. Amputees and lepers roamed muddy streets. Orphans scavenged in groups. Husbands used scraps to make ramshackle huts for their loved ones, while wives dug for vegetables and cooked fish soup for breakfast.

Anything to feed their babies, to stay alive another day.

Schools across the peninsula were starting a new session. Though many of their buildings were nothing but rubble, this didn't stop education from rolling forward. Teachers conducted classes under trees, in pastures, and on hillsides. Without knowledge, their students would be further hobbled.

And these children were the nation's future.

Despite the difficulties, Everett had great hope for Korea. Her citizens had been peaceful, home-loving, hardworking people for centuries. Even now, they rarely complained. Men and women shouldered large sacks of rice, buckets of water, and bundles of kindling, while the kids often staggered under heavy loads of their own. A bike was a luxury most could not afford.

Everett turned off the projector and recalled his recent sermon: "Although this war has cost America many lives . . . we ought to get down on our knees and thank God that our great cities do not lie in ruin; that our factories are not gutted by fire; and that our bridges have not been dynamited. . . . God's goodness and forbearance, longsuffering and kindness ought to lead every Christian to a true consecration of his whole spirit, soul, and body."

Everett believed each person had time, talents, and resources.

Each had something to give.

Since high school, he had dedicated his own time and abilities to sharing God's Word. He had traveled on a shoestring budget during the Great Depression, pastored two different congregations during World War II, and spoken to troops throughout the Korean War. No one could accuse him of not practicing what he preached.

Please, Lord, give me wisdom. Give me strength to do even more.

A noise in the dining room drew his attention. He bounded up the steps and found his flush-faced son at the dining table, transistor radio in hand.

Everett put his hands on his hips. It was you?

Sorry, David said quietly. I know I should've asked first.

David was seventeen now, nearing graduation from Austin High. He was a good kid, still fairly innocent. Everett had sat him down a few years earlier to explain the facts of life. It was an uncomfortable talk, with sex still being a dirty word that few ever mentioned out loud, but a biblical perspective was imperative now that sensuality was displayed on billboards, ads, and street corners.

Son, where'd you go with my radio? Thing's brand-new, you know?

David lowered his eyes, then confessed he'd been seated on the schoolyard steps, listening to the latest hit songs, when a pair of neighborhood bullies startled him and demanded he hand the radio over. He shook his head no. They pushed him, saying he better do it or else. David hunched over the thing and told them no way, no how.

And they left you alone? Everett was surprised. Local teens had been beaten up and even stabbed over less.

They tried getting it from me, but I just sat there, heavy as a rock.

Weren't you scared?

Losing your radio, that's what had me worried, Dad. The boys finally wandered off, laughing and saying the piece of junk wasn't worth their time.

Well, thank you for bringing it back. You know, we need a family getaway, don't we?

David's eyes lifted for the first time.

What do you say? Everett clapped a hand on his son's shoulder. We've been so busy between school, the ministry, your job, and Mom's work at the factory. We could do with a little swimming, a little fishing. It would be good for us.

Sure, but can we afford it?

* * *

Soon afterward, the Swansons headed north to Wisconsin. A family at Central Avenue Baptist had offered them free lodging at their lakeshore cabin, a place smelling of firewood and smoke. Secured to the dock was a fishing dinghy with a small outboard motor, which David, Jack, and Paul couldn't wait to test out.

Only two at a time, Everett insisted. It's all that boat can handle.

David faced the stern and let younger Jack take the throttle. Water fantailed behind them as they steered out over the lake. Sharon and Paul explored a trail through the trees, leaving Everett and Miriam on their own. She cozied up to him as they strolled toward the cabin. The sun was setting beyond the treetops, turning the lake to liquid gold.

Some hot cocoa sounds nice, Miriam suggested.

If you're cold, Everett noted, there are other ways of keeping warm.

By the time their brood regrouped on the cabin's front deck, the sky had turned deep purple, almost black, with stars quickly multiplying. One light cut across the expanse, carving a path toward the horizon.

Could be a Russian satellite, Paul pointed out.

There's American ones up there too, Everett said. He turned toward his other boys. Everything alright? You two haven't spoken a word since you docked the boat.

We, uh . . . David cleared his throat. It's the motor, Dad.

Did it run out of gas? Least you still had the oars, didn't you?

We lost it, Jack butted in. The motor. In the lake.

What? How's that even possible?

Jack explained he had just been goofing around, jerking the tiller handle this way and that to throw his older brother over the side. It was all in fun. But then the motor mounts broke loose and the outboard plummeted into the water.

We know right where it is, David insisted. We'll go back in the morning and—

You most definitely will, Everett said. That motor belongs to our friends.

The water's ten, maybe fifteen feet deep. We'll salvage it, we promise.

Sunrise found David and Jack crammed together in the boat. Everett watched them row to a spot across the lake where the piece of machinery had sunk. His sons took turns dropping the anchor, plumbing the murky depths. Once they hit the motor, Jack took a big gulp of air, followed the line down, then brought the reed-draped object to the surface. Together, he and David hefted it over the gunwale and ferried it back to the dock.

Now the real work begins, Everett said. Or you'll be buying a new motor.

Over the next few hours, the boys meticulously took apart the engine, dried out its components—no easy task—and reassembled it piece by piece. The first few pulls on the starter cord produced only hiccups and coughs, then finally the thing sputtered to life. Never had a puff of blue smoke and a steady rumble brought two boys so much joy.

I'm proud of you both, Everett told them. Remember, actions have consequences. This time the outcome was in your favor, but whenever you make a mistake, it's up to you to put things right.

Yes, sir.

In both family and ministry, Everett tried to give trust along with responsibility. Even when things went wrong, they could be rectified with a bit of honesty and hard work. It was this simple faith of his that freed ESEA's foreign workers to accomplish marvelous things.

Was he too naive, though? Too sincere and unsuspecting?

Some people described him in these terms, and some even warned it could leave him vulnerable to trouble. Maybe so. He chose, though, to err on the side of trust. Seeing the best in others and believing in their potential were keys to the way he operated. Always had been.

After all, how else could he be the man he hoped to be?

A man of true compassion.

* * *

During the winter of 1954, Rev. Swanson was thrilled to be invited once again to South Korea. His first round had given him a love for the country. His second round had made him aware of the orphans, and as a result he had taken up the fight on their behalf.

Now he was booking a third trip, to take place in the coming spring.

Time for round three.

Chapter 26

ROUND THREE

With each tour, Rev. Swanson became more comfortable in Korea. From late March through early June of 1955, he learned to bow at the waist, top off others' tea instead of his own, and leave chopsticks balanced on the rim of his bowl instead of upright in the food—which hinted at the incense sticks used after a person's death.

How do you keep it all straight? Everett asked Rev. Rice.

Believe me, I've made my share of mistakes.

Nothing was easy, from the shipping of supplies to the scheduling of trains to the ordering of bibimbap—vegetables, eggs, and bits of meat on a bed of rice. Each province, Everett realized, was proud of its unique foods and customs, and he did his best, as the apostle Paul stated in 1 Corinthians 9:22, to "become all things to all men, that I might by all means save some."

The Korean language was the biggest challenge. Translators often spoke spotty English and kept an emotional distance out of cultural respect. At age forty-one, Everett was their teacher, minister, and elder. And if he thought reading would be any easier, boy, was he mistaken. Hangul, the official written form, had been developed in the fifteenth century as a script even peasants could master, but he found it difficult to wrap his brain around.

I dearly love these people, Everett told Rev. Rice. I only wish I could communicate it better. Perhaps I'll find someone fluent in English, a translator who can share not just my words but my actual feelings.

Put it on your prayer list, I suppose. Good translators are few and far between.

Everett relied heavily on Korean Christians in their land. If he built a new orphanage or offered support to a preexisting facility, he sought their advice to make prudent decisions.

His love was evident to all, from the youngest orphan girl with weepy eyes to the proudest teenage boy. He embraced as many as he could, giving each one his attention. The orphanage workers marveled at his connection with even the most withdrawn kids. He held them on his lap and never pushed them away. To many, he was the only father they would ever know.

Papa, they cried, tugging at his legs. Papa Swanson!

Few Westerners, he was told, were so warmly received. At the orphanage near Suncheon, staff members welcomed him with gifts of traditional Korean clothing. He slipped into the colorful garb, lost in baggy long sleeves and in loose leggings cinched at his ankles. Despite the unfamiliar attire, he was a man fully at home in a country that meant the world to him.

Take picture, the workers urged. Papa Swanson, take picture with us.

Why, of course, he said, wearing a wide, easy smile.

* * *

Everett wondered, *What does a day look like in an orphan's world?*

At New Life Boys' and Girls' Home, near Daegu, he witnessed daily routines firsthand.

In the morning, workers gathered the kids for courtyard exercises and for the singing of the Korean anthem. For hygienic reasons, most orphans had helmet haircuts, even the girls. Belly-warming fish soup followed exercises, then it was time for class, where the children practiced reading and writing, studied math and science, and learned Bible stories. They especially liked singing "Jesus Loves Me, This I Know" and "Arirang," a traditional Korean song that had no direct translation but encompassed all the pain of the Korean experience—as well as the hope of a new day.

Lunchtime found kids jostling on benches at long wooden tables. Korean women in white aprons, some of them volunteers from a local church, dolloped rice into bowls and served platters of cornbread. All the kids wanted kimchi, aged in heavy earthen vessels out in the yard.

In the same yard, recess took place. The children played blindfold tag, kicked balls across the dirt, caught grasshoppers, and taunted wild goats.

Everett grinned. Oh, to be young again.

Afterward, the older kids learned vocational skills. Some practiced music on traditional instruments of wood and bamboo, while others constructed a pen for baby ducks. Girls learned to sew. Children worked side by side in the vegetable garden.

Everett then gathered all the staff and kids for a surprise. He angled his eyes toward the nearby ridgeline, over which a helicopter appeared. Thanks to US Army donations, the large-bellied beast landed in a swirl of dust to unload crates of clothing, food, dolls, and comic books. The orphans bowed in thanks, smiles flashing, as they received clean shirts and new trousers.

As night fell, staff members herded their charges into the bath house, where tubs were filled using buckets from the outside pump.

Vigorous lathering and scrubbing commenced, then the kids dried off and filed to their sleeping quarters. A worker rested at one end while the kids spread out pillows and blankets on the heated clay floor. The *ondol* system was efficient and smoke-free, warm enough to leave some hopping from foot to foot before settling down to rest.

Voices called out: Good night, Papa Swanson!

Grinning, he raised a hand. Good night.

Through these ESEA facilities, kids were given family and structure. A director saw to administrative duties and answered to a group of local overseers, while good-hearted workers served the orphans in exchange for room and board.

No one was getting rich here. This was all about the children.

It was also vital, Everett determined, to establish routines, standardize care, and observe financial transparency for the sakes of the staff, children, and sponsors.

As he laid his head down for the night, aware of soft coughs and giggles from boys and girls in their huts, he was filled with deep satisfaction. He had made the shift from tent sermons to relief work, melding his evangelistic call with a practical approach to ministry.

This was love in action.

These were miracles in motion.

* * *

Some miracles took more time, occurring in increments.

At one of the children's homes, Everett met a boy named Sung-dong Kim. Sung-dong slumped in his chair, eyes hooded and lips downturned. Many orphans lacked loving human touch, a physical deprivation that left psychological wounds. One kind gesture, in the proper time and manner, could unlock a hardened heart.

As staff members recounted Sung-dong's story through a translator, Everett listened to this precious soul beside him. What suffering the boy must've endured, what heartache. He'd been discovered on one of the region's coldest nights, nearly dead of starvation. He had no father, no mother. Both his feet were frozen solid, almost black, and the doctors had no choice but to amputate them.

Unless someone intervenes, a worker explained, he will be forced to drag himself about on a wheeled cart and continue begging. Most likely, he will die.

We are ready to step in, Everett said. Just tell me what you need.

This is good news. I will schedule a meeting at the amputee center.

Turning, Everett peered into the boy's dark, sunken eyes. Sung-dong, he said, men, women, even children in America have sent money to help you. They are praying for you, do you understand? You are loved more than you know.

A quick blink. A flicker in the darkness.

Days later, Everett visited Sung-dong again. The boy now wore a bright plaid shirt and stood on newly fitted artificial limbs. His balance was still precarious. Though he would require physical therapy as he learned to walk again, a hint of a smile tugged at his lips. With some grit and determination, he would have a new life.

As Everett rested a hand on Sung-dong's shoulder, he reflected on the words from James 1:27: "Pure and undefiled religion before God and the Father is this: to visit orphans and widows in their trouble."

This was why he was here.

Chapter 27

INTO THE TRENCHES

Ever the evangelist at heart, Rev. Swanson also spent much of his third Korean tour conducting a crusade. After years of upheaval, destitute souls were eager for something different, for a ray of hope, and they swarmed to hear him speak.

At Mount Namsan, a peak near Seoul, Everett stood in suit and tie with his hair slicked back and preached four times daily in huge revival tents. Cold winds and rain showers couldn't keep the crowds away. They grew from 17,000 on the first full day to 71,000 on the last. A cable car had not yet been installed, meaning listeners had to climb the mountain's white stone steps just to hear the presentation in person.

Sinners begged for salvation.

Many waded into a lake for baptism.

Evening prayer meetings often lasted until dawn.

There were audible cries for a move of God.

Thanks to Rev. Rice's coordination, national pastors and leaders partnered with Everett, making sure the hundreds healed and thousands converted did not stray from their new path.

Everett also traveled to schools, where uniformed students sat on cold dirt beneath leafless trees as he admonished them in steady yet urgent tones to accept Christ. Gospel trucks were part of his entourage, plastered with Scriptures in hangul and loaded with boxes of tracts and literature. In some places, he and his partners were nearly trampled in the rush for booklets.

The trucks did not stop there, but carried him to various military bases.

All of it was made possible alongside his team of local chaplains, including his lanky old friend, Captain Hyung-do Kim.

Seven weeks in, with two to go, Everett pressed on through his exhaustion. At one prison camp, he stood on a low wooden dais and gazed out over a sea of battle-hardened faces. The POWs sat cross-legged, wearing white numbered armbands. Their eyes dared him to offer some sort of meaning, peace, or absolution.

Was there any actual purpose to this existence?

Was there any way of quieting the voices of the dead?

Everett admitted he had never fought in a battle of bullets and tanks, but as "a good soldier of Jesus Christ," according to 2 Timothy 2:3, he knew well the hardships of spiritual war.

Inside each of us, he explained to the POWs, good and evil wrestle for control. God offers us love and forgiveness, while the devil offers sinful enticements. Which will it be? Jesus has not only conquered death, but He has stormed the gates of hell and set the captives free. In Him, you are free indeed. Do you want your spiritual chains to be loosed? Repent this day and receive His great love.

Many of them did, raising their hands while he prayed with them.

As he concluded, they called out: Come back soon!

* * *

Since his days as a teen evangelist, Rev. Swanson had heard the accusations:

Who are you to push your beliefs on others?

Do you think you alone hold the truth?

What right do you have to go to other countries and strip away their religious traditions?

Though Everett still had much to learn about this Land of the Morning Calm, he knew Korean spirituality had been evolving for thousands of years. The ancient shamanism that once held sway had eventually given way to Buddhism. Buddhist temples now dotted the land, but this religion of karma, rebirth, and suffering had been brought over from India and tweaked by Korean monks to fit their own land.

When Confucianism stepped in centuries later, it shifted the focus back to life's political and social realms. It also introduced hierarchies of fathers over sons, husbands over wives, elders over the young. Shintoism, which was pushed during Japanese occupation, never fully took hold, and Confucianism persisted.

Even now, Everett noticed, women were viewed as lesser than their male counterparts, though many Koreans were warming to the

Christian idea of all being equal in God's sight.

Oh, thank You, Lord! You are already softening hearts.

No, Everett did not believe he had the right to shove his beliefs down the throats of others. He had been invited here. Three separate times. And he counted each visit to this wonderful country a privilege.

Evangel meant "good news." As an evangelist, he was simply a bearer of good news.

He offered the gospel of Jesus, of everlasting life and forgiveness. Christ had brought so much meaning and joy into his own life, and it was a free gift. Available to all. You could take it or leave it. The choice was yours.

* * *

Barbed wire and forlorn wooden guard posts ran for miles along the 38th parallel, creating a demilitarized zone. This DMZ was a reminder that the war was not over officially.

Everett visited the no-man's-land before his journey's end. He stepped down into the trenches, where sandbags and stone walls provided cover, and handed free literature to Korean soldiers wearing helmets and bearing rifles. The smell of damp earth and sweat reminded him of his farm days. He posed with the men, and they all smiled for photos together.

Who was he to be here on the front lines?

He was just a kid from Sycamore, a nobody from birth.

Through Rev. Rice and his lovely family, Everett was also able to meet local pastors, medical missionaries, and gospel workers, including a blind evangelist who filled hearts with joy wherever he went. These faithful souls traversed the countryside, often on foot, preaching, praying for the sick, and constructing rudimentary church buildings.

Some, such as Pastor Choi, had survived persecution. Choi was a modern-day Job, whose mother, wife, and children had been killed by the communists before his land was confiscated.

And still the man smiled as he shared the gospel!

Truly, these men and women put Everett to shame. They were better situated than any Westerners to carry out Jesus' Great Commission in their own language and land. All they needed were the practical means to carry on.

I will find sponsors for them too, Everett decided.

He marveled at all God had done on this trip. His crusade had offered hope, and the sheer size of the crowds had overwhelmed him at times.

Back in the States, the spectacle of mass gatherings had lost its hold on the public. The pageantry of parades and Friday night games had waned. Sure, evangelists such as Billy Graham could pack stadiums, and Billy Sunday and Aimee Semple McPherson had drawn eye-popping numbers in the past, but collective experiences were giving way to individualized marketing. Everett's own children could separately under the same roof tune in to *The Mickey Mouse Club*, read a copy of *Vogue*, or listen to Chuck Berry on the latest AM/FM radio.

Oh, how the modern world was changing.

Everett kept records along the way and shot footage of cultural landmarks and religious iconography. He snapped photos of schools, orphanages, a soaring Shinto statue, and a large stone Buddha. He even posed for a picture at the base of a shrine, his large black Bible in hand. Drawing from this treasure trove of images and personal commentary, he began creating an ESEA pictorial report, a detailed account of his evangelism and relief work over three visits to the Korean peninsula.

The sixteen-page report concluded with this overview:

REASONS TO PRAISE GOD

1. In 3 evangelistic tours has preached to an estimated 850,000 people, military and civilian. Pastors and

missionaries report largest attended revival meetings in
Korean history. Thousands prayed all night long.

2. Approximately 45,000 have raised hands in a "decision to
   receive Christ."

3. Funds for millions of tracts and gospels.

4. Helped buy building headquarters for Christian Revival
   Fellowship, Daegu.

5. Full or partial support for about 30 full-time evangelistic workers (12–18 months), many of whom developed
   self-supporting churches in pioneer areas and built their
   own building in that time.

6. Funds for 1 Ford truck, 1 Austin truck, and 1 motorcycle-
   truck. Also sound equipment and sound movie projector
   for use by evangelists.

7. Provided funds to help open or plan 80 Christian book
   stalls or shops.

8. Built or bought property for 2 orphanages and a boys'
   home for former beggar boys. Total now being wholly
   or partially supported, about 400 children. The cost for
   "adopting" your own child is now $5 a month. Many are
   needed.

9. Hundreds of packages, many tons of used relief clothing
   sent for the needy.

Everett's third trip was over. His crusade was an unparalleled success. He had been obedient to his calling and used his time wisely,
making the most of every opportunity.

Oh, Miriam, now I just want to go home. To see you and the kids.
One taste of her baking sounded awfully good at the moment.

Chapter 28

DOCTOR'S ORDERS

Coming off a shift at West Suburban Hospital, Doc Hemwall was the first to bring concerns to Everett's attention. Nothing of a medical nature, not yet. There were other things on his mind.

Everett heard the knock from down in his office where he was typing up his quarterly newsletter. Miriam was still on the factory assembly line, and all four kids were still in school. Suffering jet lag from his trip, Everett was thankful for the quiet.

He cracked open the door and found Doc in scrubs and metal-rimmed glasses.

Just finished up in surgery, Doc explained.

Well, hello. You coming or going?

I was on my way home and spotted that new Packard in your driveway. Figured I'd stop.

Just a loaner from the dealer in the church. C'mon in, Doc. You must be boiling out here in this heat.

Doc pushed up his glasses, then followed Everett inside and down to the basement. Everett nudged aside a box of ESEA envelopes with his foot, moved a stack of files off an armchair, and gestured to his friend. Once Doc was settled, Everett plopped across from him in his office chair and rested his elbow on the desk, where the typewriter stood ready between trays of ingoing and outgoing mail.

You still have that TV I gave you? Doc asked. Only an hour or so until *Gunsmoke*.

We'll watch it together. I'm just finishing up a newsletter.

You're a good man, Everett, steady and faithful. It was my wife's and my privilege to have you as our pastor. Doc crossed his legs and peered over his wire rims. As your friend and as your physician, though, I'm worried about you. You look tired, run ragged. How're you sleeping these days?

Fine. When I actually get to bed. There's a lot on my plate right now.

A one-man show can only last so long.

You know, Doc, in many ways this has been one of my greatest and most fruitful years, but it's also been the most challenging. God's grace is truly sufficient.

Doc pressed his lips together, then said, I'll be honest; Miriam's been over to talk with my wife and me about the strain she's under. That woman is head over heels for you, Everett, and your absences are severely felt.

Everett tried to keep his voice steady. She said this to you?

In so many words. She's not one to complain, but the ministry's taking a toll.

Everett leaned back, eyebrows furrowed. While he might have shrugged off these admonitions from anyone else, he sensed the truth in his friend's earnest statement. He'd recently noticed worry lines at the corners of his wife's mouth.

How about David? Doc shifted the conversation. How's he faring? He graduates this weekend, doesn't he?

Comes all too quickly, Everett said, staring off.

I hear he sent off an application to Bethel College. A fine young man. He's helped Miriam while you are gone, shoveling coal for the furnace, working in the yard. You remember how he used to clean my home practice every Wednesday?

Everett chuckled. I can't begin to keep up with all the side jobs he's held.

Doc tilted his head. He's your son, Everett.

Everett swallowed hard and nodded.

He always did a fine job for me, Doc continued. Vacuuming, sanitizing, straightening chairs and magazines in my waiting room. You know, I offered to help him get into medicine, told him he could take over my practice one day since I have no son of my own. Current laws as they are, my daughters will be blocked from their desired roles as nurses and research assistants the moment they choose to marry. Ludicrous, really. Each one's as bright as any man I know.

Sharon's always admired Judith's brains, Everett agreed. He cleared his throat. So, what was my son's response to your offer?

Said he appreciated it a great deal but just couldn't find it within himself. And no, I don't blame him. Doc took off his glasses and buffed them with his sleeve. With all that our children have seen of our respective jobs—being on call, the long hours, the personal sacrifices—I won't be surprised if they pursue unrelated careers.

Everett motioned to his desk, to the boxes against the wall. All this work, it has plenty of rewards. I truly enjoy what I do.

And well you should, don't get me wrong. My wife and I are your staunchest supporters. This ministry is essential. Which is why I am speaking to you today, man to man, brother to brother. Together, we can set up some guidelines, some boundaries, not only for the sake of Miriam and the kids, but for the sake of this good work you have started.

Seems you've thought a lot about this.

I have, Everett. For legal purposes, you'd be wise to incorporate. You'd be protecting your family, while creating long-term accountability for ESEA through annual audits, reports, and disclosures. I suggest you talk it over with Miriam, run it by your brothers. Being in the ministry, they'll bring experience to the conversation.

Lawrence and I talk regularly on the phone.

Great, Doc said, then added with a wink, You sleep on it, Everett. Doctor's orders.

Everett grinned. *As iron sharpens iron*, he thought to himself. For a pastor to find an honest friend was a rarity and he would never take this man for granted.

Just don't let it sit too long, Doc added. Your son's graduating, your wife needs you, and this ministry is poised for even greater things. All I'm saying is, I don't want to lose my brother-in-arms along the way. The larger this thing grows, the greater the need for a firm foundation.

Wise words, Doc. I will not forget them.

Ah, now enough with all this serious talk. Doc Hemwall stood, clasped him on the arm, and said, You ready for some *Gunsmoke*?

* * *

The graduation ceremony had yet to begin. Seated in cap and gown with his fellow seniors, Everett's firstborn, his blond eighteen-year-old boy, his son whose name meant "beloved," would soon move into a new season of life.

David Swanson had survived encounters with a pea viner, a burst appendix, a wild friend and an attractive date, an out-of-control Buick, and a pair of local bullies. He had applied himself in class and earned good grades. He'd sung in senior choir and performed as a soloist in a major production. He had cleaned medical offices, polished rings in a jewelry store, and wrapped cutlets at a butcher shop. All the church kids looked up to David. When teachers called out random biblical references—from Habakkuk to Obadiah to Philemon—he was the fastest at fanning through his Bible to find them. He never lost. Never.

Back in 1931, Everett had received his own diploma, an idealistic farm kid champing at the bit. Had it really been twenty-four years ago? He could still see Father and Mother smiling at him from the crowd, their presence like an anchor amidst the Depression's uncertainty.

Everett squared his shoulders. May he be the father he was supposed to be. For David and Sharon, Jack and Paul. For the orphans in Korea and for kids wherever he went.

He reached for Miriam's hand. What will David do next, do you think?

Don't worry, she whispered. Our son will be alright.

Any word on his college application?

Not yet. You know, Myra from church has also applied.

Myra? He raised an eyebrow. Is there a spark between the two of them?

Time will tell, won't it?

Half an hour later, David strode across the stage and took hold of his diploma. His parents' and siblings' cheers put a sheepish grin on his face. His eyes met theirs, then shifted away, panning over the crowd, looking for someone else.

God, Everett prayed silently, *do with my son as You will.*

* * *

Per Doc's orders, Rev. Swanson had conversations with his wife, brothers, and various officials. All agreed that ESEA should apply for nonprofit status. Though the gears of the state moved at glacial speed, Everett set the process in motion.

He wasn't trying to build a kingdom here.

No, this was a safety measure.

Biblically, the precedent was established in Exodus 18:18–22, when Moses was told, "You will surely wear yourself out. . . . this thing is too much for you. . . . you shall select from all the people able men, such as fear God, men of truth, hating covetousness. . . . So it will be easier for you, for they will bear the burden with you."

Everett wanted nothing more than to come alongside the Koreans in their endeavors. They were the ones doing the real work. As much as he cared for the world, the demands on the peninsula were overwhelming. It seemed he could spend a lifetime in just this one country and there would still be needs to meet.

The orphans came first, of course. For him, this would always be true.

And now, he reminded himself, he had also committed to raising funds for Korean evangelists. These wonderful men and women, they were so full of zeal. He would make a broader appeal on their behalf.

As Chicago's summer faded, the response letters arrived in increasing numbers.

Everett's Sterling account book now proved inadequate. Daily, the ministry grew. Checks had to be cashed. Monies had to be sent to the staff in Korea. Boxes of clothing, often dropped on the Swansons' doorstep, had to be checked, resealed, marked *Orphan Gift—Not to be Sold*, then forwarded overseas through an army chaplains' orphan fund in San Francisco.

Miriam lent a hand in the basement office, and the younger kids assisted with the mailings. David helped when he wasn't carting bricks and mixing mortar for a mason, and Doc volunteered when he wasn't on rotation at the hospital.

Everett orchestrated all these activities, then on weekends threw his garment bag, film case, and notebook of sermons into his car. He traversed the Midwest, state to state, and sought new sponsors. People responded, giving joyfully, so that many more orphans were sponsored.

As winter came around, the ministry's task list seemed longer than ever. Was it time to add a staff member? Even pay an accountant? But what if the flow of donations dried up?

Everett and Miriam Swanson weighed their options and prayed for guidance, neither suspecting that this ministry, within a decade, would be the largest of its kind in South Korea.

Part 4

Summer 1959
Masan, South Korea

"All the classrooms were destroyed by war.
We studied under the trees or in whatever buildings were left."
— UN Secretary-General Ki-moon Ban

AT EIGHTEEN, EI-SUN moves through the night shadows, his eyes on a fellow Korean in a sharp suit. This businessman clearly has money. He's an easy mark.

Ei-sun does not intend to harm the man.

He simply wants to put food in his own belly.

The man strides down the street with an air of superiority. He considers a few items at the outdoor market, then moves on. Proud of his good fortune, he shows no regard for the beggar boys and thieves who still wander the alleyways.

If the man tries to resist, Ei-sun decides, *I will use my fists.*

Ei-sun already has scars from the occasional street brawl. He also has scars from his time at his first orphanage. Things there were nothing like he had heard. After being fed porridge made of corn powder, he was sent every day to work in the fields or to make bricks for a new facility. Rain or shine, ice or snow, it did not matter. There was always more work to do.

He now eases through the crowd, inching closer to the businessman. Ei-sun has already scoped out the location of the mark's money.

Jacket. Left inside pocket.

The fellow pauses, looks back over his shoulder, and Ei-sun feigns interest in a display of men's shoes. The shopping continues. Moments later a horse cart passes by, wood and iron rattling, and Ei-sun uses these sounds and smells to cover his approach, his jostling elbow and snaking hand. He is gone, swallowed by the crowd, before the robbed man has any clue.

What a fool.

* * *

Ei-sun's family name is Baek, but he has no family left. He lost both parents when he was young, and he desperately longs for a father figure. This is a ridiculous desire, of course. He has no past to speak of. No future either.

He's unwanted.

He has considered going to university someday, becoming somebody, but this is the hope of a fool, of a dreamer. He is an orphan. If he has any relatives, they're not rich. He'll be doing well just to finish his courses and complete high school.

Ei-sun now lives at his second orphanage, a facility that recently relocated to this region and took him in. The directors show genuine concern for the forty or fifty children in their care, and he is now allowed to take night classes. A small step, it still points him toward a dream.

Despite the directors' efforts to provide, food is often scarce, and Ei-sun's teenage appetite is rarely satisfied. He grapples with a desire to go steal again. When he does sneak out to the city, he often gets in fights.

Early one evening, Ei-sun slumps into a seat at a local church service. Other orphans are also here. They have nothing better to do. As uncomfortable as he feels in this revival meeting, he cannot shut his ears to the Korean evangelist. The man sounds earnest and wise. He says God is calling out to His children, offering peace and joy. Each and every person has an invitation to be part of His family.

A spiritual hunger gnaws at Ei-sun's core. What is this?

Whatever it is, it's as insistent as the hunger pangs he feels every day.

Come to Jesus now, the Korean speaker implores his audience. He knows your sins, and He wants to forgive you.

Ei-sun stiffens. He is a thief. He has taken from people, struck them down. He carries so much anger. Is this the sort of person Jesus wants?

Accept Him as your Savior, the evangelist continues.

Ei-sun closes his eyes. The hunger inside is still there.

Know God as your heavenly Father.

Yes. Ei-sun lifts his head and raises his hand. Yes, this is what he wants.

By the end of the month, the directors comment on the changes they see in him. He is no longer the scowling pickpocket. He is becoming an adult before their eyes, a good student, and mindful of other kids here at Masan's Ae-Yook-Won.

I want to be a better man, he responds.

Keep at it and stay alert, they tell him. There may be a surprise on the way.

For me? What is it?

Don't give up, they say, reminding him of the Korean proverb: One can build a mountain by moving specks of dust.

* * *

Rev. Swanson arrives at Ae-Yook-Won a few weeks later. He is here from America, and right away Ei-sun notices how he fills the orphanage with a sense of joy. Dressed in a traditional Korean hat and outfit, he looks impressive. Graying hair peeks from beneath the hat. Blue eyes sparkle behind his glasses. When the kids swarm to him in the yard, his face lights up in delight.

Papa Swanson, they cry. Papa!

Is this the surprise the directors have in mind for him? How is he involved?

Papa-papa-papa . . .

Ei-sun wants to rush in too but remains hidden on the porch. All he has are these new shoes and his school uniform. He's nobody special and certainly doesn't deserve this man's attention. Hope is a dangerous thing, coursing through his veins.

What are you going to do? he asks himself.

Papa-papa-papa . . .

Such hope could poison him once and for all with disappointment.

Don't be a fool, Ei-sun thinks. *If you step forward, the reverend might turn away. What if he's only interested in the younger, cuter children?* Even as these thoughts swirl, two of the littlest orphans tug at the man's pants and try to scale his legs. The reverend sweeps them into his arms and laughs out loud.

Papa-papa-papa . . .

What are you going to do?

Ei-sun reminds himself he is now a child of God. He too is worthy. As true as this may be, it doesn't settle into his feet and propel him forward.

What are you going to do?

He doesn't realize, not yet, that his response to these six little words could change his life. At last, with great effort, he grinds one shoe across the wooden planks. Then the other. The sun's warmth seeps into his hair, and he realizes now he is exposed. He lifts his head, stares across the yard, and hopes to catch the reverend's eye. This is the closest thing to a choice he can make—and it is enough.

In that moment, Rev. Swanson spots him. He sets down the little ones with pats on their heads, then bypasses a cluster of earthen kimchi jars. Before Ei-sun can run or resist, the man greets him and draws him into a hug.

Hello, the reverend says. You are my son, my new family.

The words chase away Ei-sun's fears. In the man's calming embrace, he feels God's love in physical form, finds a father figure he can rely on.

Papa. The word tumbles from his mouth.

Oh! the reverend says, throwing his head back. It makes me so happy to hear you call me that. You know, I've been told all about you by your directors. Lots of good things. You have an interest in the Bible and in the things of God, is that right? Well, be sure to study hard, because if you do, I would love for you to go to a seminary or university. It is something we can certainly make happen.

This is my dream, Ei-sun replies. Thank you. I will study hard.

Why the frown, then? Is something wrong?

Maybe I'm not . . . not eligible. I've stolen things. I have done many sins.

Hold on, now. Have you repented? Are you redeemed?

Ei-sun nods.

Rev. Swanson looks him in the eye. Then you are eligible.

Chapter 29

PICKING UP SPEED

In 1956, as South Korea took its first steps toward rebuilding, citizens waved their flag with pride, and businesses often featured it on their walls. Everett had seen the *Taegukgi* flying overhead during his trips to the peninsula, often at the orphanages. Soon after South Korea was established as a country in 1948, the *Taegukgi* was declared its national flag, using a basic design unveiled in the late 1800s.

The large white background spoke of peace and purity.

Black diagonal lines, trigrams, graced each corner with their own meaning.

A red and blue circle in the center, the *Taeguk*, signified the yin-yang of opposites that cannot exist without each other—light and dark, day and night. Some people viewed the red and blue *Taeguk* as a symbol of divided Korea—and they longed for the two to be made one again.

Everett knew foreign superpowers had stirred trouble and war, and he'd heard heartrending stories from both North and South Koreans who still lived on the edge of starvation. He himself prayed for a day when hearts would be one.

Here at home, he knew the more personal tug and pull between a husband and wife, the opposites who needed each other. As an idealist, he often saw the larger global picture while missing details in his own household. Miriam was a woman of style and grace, also unbending and insistent when it came to her family's needs. Through their marital squabbles over the years, they had learned to resolve their differences with more grace and less self-interest.

Now, balancing budgets and setting priorities were Everett's greatest challenges.

Boy, could things get tricky when funds dried up and time ran short.

Should he send the money to starving orphans?

Or feed four children at home?

Put gas in the tank for a weekend of travel and sermons?

Or pay the coal bill as winter drew near?

Doc Hemwall had encouraged Everett to put in place a firm foundation, to consider his family and marriage amid this booming ministry, and in the springtime these efforts paid off.

"On April 19, 1956," Everett wrote to his supporters, "the Everett Swanson Evangelistic Association (ESEA) was incorporated in the State of Illinois under the General Not For Profit Act. It was organized for the purpose of assisting Korean orphans, evangelists, and other Korean evangelist efforts. This was also implemented in order to handle the funds and attend to day-to-day business."

Per state guidelines, he went on to file articles of incorporation, and on the first day of June formed the ESEA board:

Rev. Everett F. Swanson—president
Miriam Swanson—vice president
Gus "Doc" Hemwall, MD—secretary-treasurer

An advisory board was also assembled, made up of qualified Christians: a psychiatrist; an attorney; an evangelist; a certified public accountant; two executive secretaries, including Everett's brother, Rev. Lawrence Swanson; Peter van Lierop, PhD—the whistler from the YMCA; and John Seong, a South Korean who came highly recommended as field secretary.

Without delay, they voted to give Everett a monthly salary of $200.

In the US, where the average monthly income pushed $375, this wasn't much for a household of six. Regardless, it was a significant boost for the Swanson family. Money was still tight, but now Miriam could count on buying groceries, fueling the car, and clothing her kids.

Everett was relieved as well. With an established income, he set off on another speaking tour. From Somonauk, Illinois, to Coeur d'Alene, Idaho, to Vancouver, Washington, his supplications for new sponsors continued. His meetings included orphan films, Korean highlights, and a discussion of "The End of the World."

Do you really think we're in the last days? Sharon asked while he was home one weekday.

Everett shrugged. Only our heavenly Father knows.

Sounds scary, though, the way some people talk about it. Earthquakes and wars and a moon like blood.

We're already seeing some of these things, aren't we? They're really just the birth pangs. Jesus told us simply to watch and pray. Do you trust Him? Do you believe He is with you?

She nodded.

Then again I say, rejoice!

With her own high school graduation around the corner, Sharon grimaced. Do you think He can hold off just a bit longer? I still have places I want to go and things I want to do.

Everett rested his hands on her shoulders and said, You know, I had similar thoughts at your age. We must make the most of each moment, since we have no guarantees of what our futures here may hold. But can you imagine? Oh, Sharon, to see Jesus on that final day, all of us caught up to meet Him in the air.

We've all heard, Dad, how excited you get about living in the light of eternity.

You know what I'll do when I get there?

She shook her head.

I'll spend the first hundred years just gazing at my Savior's face!

* * *

On television, Edward R. Murrow was no longer the stalwart presence of the past. Everett missed the broadcaster's even tone and direct approach. Murrow's controversial topics had caused trouble for CBS, and game shows such as *The $64,000 Question* now dominated the ratings.

Truth was truth, Everett mused. It didn't change.

These days, though, entertainment and distraction were all the rage.

More than ever, Everett was aware of life's fragile hold. Cancer had taken his father much too soon. He himself could've died in an ambush, mown down by guerrilla rifles. Sure, it was good to take time for rest and play. He liked lake-fishing with Doc, listening to songs from *Oklahoma!*, and visiting Yellowstone with his family.

But each day mattered. There were no detours around the grave.

With ESEA now an official entity, Everett was ready to give himself more fully to the work in South Korea. Just last year, he had preached in a leper colony.

What a thrilling experience!

Nearly six hundred men, women, and children crowded in to hear him, and his heart went out to them. Though fifty of the kids had leper parents, leprosy was not hereditary. These dear boys and girls were healthy as could be, yet still treated as outcasts.

Now, in May 1956, ESEA took a step of faith and decided to support Bright Star Orphanage, which would serve both orphans and leper children. In his summer prayer letter, Everett included the words of a missionary who had seen this new work firsthand:

> I want to express my appreciation to you for taking on the support of these children of leper parents in the Bright Star Orphanage. In a lot of ways they are more pitiful than regular orphans. There is not a worse stigma here in Korea than to be called the "Offspring of a Leper." There is also the haunting feeling that the disease might break out years later. . . . Ordinary orphanages here in Korea will not take such children . . .

In 1956, ESEA made other significant decisions.

First, Everett arranged for translators to assist at each orphanage. Many sponsors had asked for more than just photos and report slips about the children. They wanted back-and-forth communication. Now they could write, knowing their words would be shared directly with the kids in their own language.

Second, Everett coordinated shipping channels and urged sponsors to send individual Christmas gifts to their orphans. The directors in Korea had requested this move so that clothing and toys would no longer arrive en masse to be fought over. Now, an elderly couple in Ellison Bay, Wisconsin, could send a tablet and box of crayons to one particular boy, while a church youth group in Linton, Indiana, could send a new dress and yo-yo to their sponsored girl.

Third, by year's end, Everett created a new letterhead. He hoped its three taglines would convey his overall approach to ministry. Shivering as he smoothed the paper on his basement desk, he heard the octopus kick in and pump heat into the house. He ignored the cold and pored over each word:

Faithful in Fundamentals

"Ye should earnestly contend for the faith" (Jude 3).

Kindly in Accidentals

"If a man be overtaken in a fault . . . restore such a one" (Gal. 6:1).

Friendly in Incidentals

"He that is not against us is for us" (Luke 9:50).

Indeed, Everett set out to be *faithful* to biblical truths, *kindly* in dealing with others, and *friendly* with strangers, friends, orphans, widows, pastors, and other—even competing—relief organizations.

These taglines served as bricks in ESEA's foundation.

We shall not be shaken, he said aloud.

Though trusting by nature, Everett realized any ministry could eventually face questions or controversies. Whether these came from within or without, ESEA would need to stand firm and rest squarely on its foundation.

Fundamentals: They must trust in Scripture's reliability. Though always ready to contend for the faith, Everett aimed to be ecumenical. He wouldn't let minor doctrinal issues keep him from his task. He most often used the King James Version in his sermons, but at home he embraced more current translations. He strongly held to America's values, while also addressing its policy errors. He sent his own Baptist children to St. Paul Lutheran School—which surprised even David—before enrolling them in public schools. His Christianity was rooted in real life.

Accidentals: They must make room for human fallibility. By no means was Everett endorsing bad behavior here. In his sermons, he never depicted sin as some sad inevitability. As a seasoned pastor, however, he knew many people lived with secrets and shame. To hide sin was to let it fester. To deal with it honestly was to find healing. He believed Jesus could redeem and restore.

Incidentals: They must work with all people respectfully. Power and control were never Everett's goals. In his interactions with others, he exuded Christlike warmth. He bowed deferentially to orphanage directors, chaplains, and local officials. In photographs, he often moved to the very back, nearly hidden from view. This attitude had earned him a place of honor in Korean hearts, and he hoped it would persist throughout the organization. He and his staff would accept any person, group, or denomination that did not oppose them.

Yes. Setting down the letterhead, Everett nodded his approval.

We have here a strong biblical foundation, he decided. *And thanks to Doc, we have a solid legal foundation. Dear God, I believe we are ready. With the daily demands both here at home and in Korea, we need Your favor as never before.*

ESEA was already picking up speed, racing toward a bright future. Nothing, it seemed, could stand in the way.

Chapter 30

TO HEAL AND REBUILD

We're moving too quickly, Doc told Everett. We ought to set stipulations in place. The advisory board, they can barely respond to one request from Korea before another comes in.

Each request is an opportunity, Doc. I believe that strongly.

And how are we to fund them all?

God gives more grace when the burdens grow greater, Everett said.

I'll share the needs with our supporters. We have so many who want to do even more.

Doc looked over his glasses. You best start writing, then.

Everett was not afraid to go directly to his sponsors and state the situation. After all, he and Miriam were leading by example. At the end of 1956, they personally supported three orphans and six evangelists while still tithing at their church. Doc was correct, though. Over the course of the year, there had been a barrage of requests from Korea. Military personnel wanted help with unaided orphan groups. Politicians pled for assistance with the thousands of war widows. Local missionaries and pastors needed funding for their daily outreaches.

More earnest than ever, Everett sent out a newsletter.

Donations poured in from across America and Canada, and many sponsors expressed their deepening love for the people of Korea. Thanks to this generosity, ESEA was able to add more relief homes to its roster:

Little Lambs Orphanage, in Seoul.

Holiness and Grace Orphanage, in Yecheon.

Tender Nurture House, in Gangneung.

Good Samaritan Children's Home, in Daegu.

The next appeal came from Love and Hope Children's Home, which had opened in 1952. The Korean director now had nearly a hundred children. On the recommendation of a seminary friend, he wrote to Rev. Swanson, and Everett replied in early December, sending encouragement and a promise to support the home. In tears, the director rejoiced.

During this process, the letter translator, a Buddhist, was so moved by the words between the director and Rev. Swanson that he decided to follow Christ. Soon, his family became Christians also, and he now served as a church deacon.

Reports such as these energized Everett.

Lord, this is Your hand at work!

As the ministry dispersed funds to its growing roster, it based the amounts on the number of children in each home. The amounts increased as the home proved itself responsible with the money. The stakes were too high to expect anything less.

Just before Christmas, Everett sent out a final newsletter for the year. He described Korea's steep inflation, the staff members working so hard for the children, and the check for $6,710 recently sent for orphanages, evangelists, literature work, and building needs. There was much to be grateful for, and much more to undertake.

A few days later, Everett panted up the stairs from the basement. Miriam, where are you? He found her folding linens. Have you heard? The board's agreed to help the widows.

How about you help me with this bedspread?

Heart still pounding in his chest, he took two corners and did his best.

What'll it be called? Miriam asked, completing her task.

Great Light Widows' Home.

She touched his arm. That's great news. These dear women are very close to God's heart.

Someday you must go over with me, he said. You can meet them yourself.

And leave all the chores and our children?

You're a part of this ministry, he told her. Plus, the kids are getting older now.

Someday, she said, then stepped closer. Everett, I would truly love that.

* * *

In early 1957, the ministry's future was in the balance as it faced its first audit. Were the books in order? Were all nonprofit procedures being adhered to? The actions of Everett, Doc, Miriam, and the advisory board were all under scrutiny, until the February results revealed that the work was operating with a minimal cost, allowing a high percentage of every gift to flow directly to Korea. Through streamlined administration and marketing, ESEA provided maximum benefit to the children.

Everett pumped a fist in the air. God is good!

As a result, the board raised his pay to $400 a month, plus rent allowance, utilities, and a pension fund. Gone three weeks out of four, he would need some of it for travel. The rest would cover costs at home. David's grades were slipping as he lost interest at Bethel. Sharon was graduating soon. Though Jack and David were talking about joining the National Guard, Jack and Paul still had high school to finish.

Meanwhile, ESEA was adding more orphanages.

The story of Hillside Christian Children's Home, in Busan, caught Everett's eye. He learned about Director Lim, who had fled to the south after his father, brother, and sister were martyred in North Korea. Lim's heart was then broken a second time by the sight of all the children begging in the streets. How could Lim turn a blind eye to their needs? With the US military's help, he built a small structure for dozens of orphans, but when the military pulled out, he lost his support and turned to piano tuning and organ repairs to continue financing the work.

Such personal sacrifices sustained the orphans in his care.

ESEA required each orphanage to provide case histories of its children. These were stacked on Everett's desk for him to verify before they were filed away. He now randomly thumbed one open. Staring at him from a photo, a handsome boy stood next to a case of Korean schoolbooks and Bibles. Large buttons held shut his wool coat to his chin. His father, the brief bio stated, had died during a bombardment in the war.

Everett swallowed hard. The entire ministry was about this one orphan.

And the thousands of others just like him.

* * *

Everett's old master-sergeant friend was on the phone. Elmer Rund caught him up on his latest news, then stated the real reason for his call. He believed Everett might want to connect with Jinhae Orphanage, near Busan. Elmer had discovered the work while at a nearby air force base during the Korean War, and for over three years now he and his wife had donated to it.

What's the story there? Everett wanted to know.

The director, Yak-shin Lee, he

Wait, I know that name. I think I preached at his church once.

Yes, he says he remembers you. Yak-shin started by taking needy kids into his house. Next, he started his church in an old hotel, becoming one of Korea's best-known pastors, and moved the children over into the building with poplar trees out front. Got a photo right here. I'm standing next to some other officers behind boys in plaid shirts and girls in quilted jackets.

Jinhae, you said? All right, Everett added, let me speak to the board.

Before the board delivered a decision on Jinhae Orphanage, Yak-shin Lee died suddenly of hepatitis. It could have been the end of this vital work, but his grieving widow stepped in as the new director, aided by her grown son.

She wrote directly to Elmer Rund in early March of 1957:

I received your most welcome letter . . . which gave me and my family the most contented consolation of our Father in Heaven. . . .

We are not grieving anymore but having faith that we shall soon see our able leader who is in heaven and whom we miss. . . . things that we have to do now are to know how to keep the little boys and girls warm, how to educate them, and how to lead them in a Christian way of life. . . .

Brother Swanson is now working with the orphanage. . . . God
bless him . . .

Yak-shin Lee's death was a grim reminder of the health risks across
Korea. Disease was rampant. Open sewage was common. Most foreign armies had pulled out of the country by now, leaving it nearly
unrecognizable after millions of bullets, mortars, and bombs. Even in
these postwar years, the number of orphans grew due to malnutrition,
exposure, and tuberculosis.

If South Korea wanted to heal, she would have to rebuild.

But how?

Though the US sent over reconstruction funds, manpower and machinery were hard to come by, and there weren't many others willing to
join in. Small local crews began clearing rubble, repairing hospitals, and
reopening sanitation facilities. ESEA, World Vision, and a few other
organizations did their best to lend a hand on the peninsula, even as
apathy set in across most parts of the world.

The Cold War now made the headlines: USA, USSR, and ICBMs.

The Korean War was forgotten.

As the year reached its end, Everett was urged by Korean Christians
to make a fourth evangelistic tour in their land. While this would
require additional funds and prayer, he was committed to making it
happen. Already, ESEA had twelve homes on its roster, and he could
visit some of them along the way.

Going on faith, he booked his tickets for early the next year. He
would fly to the Philippines, then Japan, and end with a four-week
whirlwind tour through Korea.

First things first, though.

In a retrospective of 1957, the ESEA staff in both America and
Korea took time to honor Yak-shin Lee's service to the orphans. Though
Yak-shin had never learned that Jinhae Orphanage was approved for

support, his family carried on his work with others alongside.

What a legacy. Lee's memory would live on.

***

Everett's bittersweet thoughts soon gave way to a big announcement from his firstborn. David had dropped out of college and proposed. Myra, the girl from church, had said yes.

A wedding date was set for March 1958.

Chapter 31

IN THE ROUGH

E verett nodded at the third tee. You're up.

David, twenty-one now, stepped forward, took a practice swing, then drove the ball with all his might down the fairway. Thanks to his bricklaying job, his shoulders were broad and muscular, and the ball sailed two hundred yards before bouncing past the dogleg into the rough.

Put a lot behind that one, didn't you, son? Least the grass is dry.

It was a mild spring afternoon on a golf course in Sycamore. Things were quieter here and the greens fees were cheaper than in the hubbub of Chicago. This, Everett realized, might be his last time alone with his son for a while. Everett would soon be back in Korea, and David would be away on his honeymoon.

Boy, life passed all too fast.

Dad, you okay?

Sure, I was just . . .

Your turn, David said. Let's see if you can do any better.

This snapped Everett back to the moment. Though neither golfed much, he felt his old competitive edge surface. He took his stance over the ball, practiced with loose, easy movements, then drew back his club and swung through with a sharp turn of his hips. The ball lifted high, lost against the bright sky, then dropped onto the fairway and sat down quickly at the dogleg. His second shot would be a direct approach to the green.

David acknowledged all this with a tilt of his head.

Guess it's better to play it safe sometimes, Everett said, shrugging. Least mine went farther.

There's nothing wrong with sticking to the fairway.

What're you trying to tell me, Dad? Are you disappointed in me, is that it?

Everett dropped his iron into his bag. David, can you explain to me why you had to drop out of college? Couldn't you and Myra make it work while still finishing your courses? When you push too hard, drive the ball too far, you only make things tougher on yourself.

David set his chin. The golf course shimmered under a cloudless sky, silent except for the chatter of birds and the buzz of insects. He started toward his ball.

C'mon, Everett said. I'm not trying to sound critical.

Really? David shouldered his bag. You know I can't follow in your steps, Dad.

Have I ever asked you to?

As a PK, I get it from all sides, this pressure to be like my dad the pastor, my dad the evangelist. Make a difference. Change the world. I respect all the stuff you and Mom do for others. I try to help. But I have to walk my own path here. Where do I go after Bethel, huh? To seminary? That just doesn't interest me. I like working with bricks, making fireplaces, doing stuff with my hands. David stared off, his fingers tight around the strap of his bag.

Everett moved alongside him and together they walked down the fairway's fringe. He had gone about this all wrong. The questions had rolled far too quickly off his tongue.

You know, Daver, I never went past high school myself.

Yeah, well, you're smart.

So are you, son. A college education isn't the only way of getting where God wants to take you. You're earning a paycheck, aren't you? You'll need it with all the responsibilities ahead. Trust Jesus to guide you down the path that is right for you.

You think Myra and I are jumping into this too quickly, don't you?

I want the best for you, Everett said, placing a hand on his son's shoulder. You have a tender heart and a genuine faith. God alone knows the steps He has planned for you. The key is being obedient. I'm simply here if you need anything.

Everett stopped before his ball on the fairway and watched his son wander off into the rough. David searched back and forth, parting the grass with his club.

Maybe a bit to your left? Everett suggested. Yes, in that area there.

By the time they closed out the hole, he had a two-stroke lead.

You always win, David mumbled.

And you've still never beat me at leg-wrestling, have you? Everett noted the grin that played across his son's face. Listen, Everett continued, the best thing you can do is focus on your own game and not worry too much about your father's.

David stopped at the next tee and muttered, Easier said than done.

* * *

David and Myra tied the knot soon after. It was a joyous day, full of expectation. Cake was served, children darted between people's legs, and the newlyweds greeted their guests before departing on their honeymoon.

Everett and Miriam waved goodbye. He removed his glasses and dragged a hand down his face. You know, we were that age once, he said to his wife.

And I haven't aged a bit, she kidded him.

Can't argue there.

She leaned into his embrace.

Of course, at forty-four, he added with a sly grin, I can't see a thing without my glasses.

A few days later, armed with his satchel of sermons, Rev. Swanson took his window seat aboard a transcontinental flight. He'd been invited to preach for ten days each in the Philippines and Japan. The final stop would be South Korea, where beggar boys, leper children, orphans, and war widows awaited his arrival.

Doc had given him a clean bill of health, and Everett was ready.

Regardless, this trip would alter his ministry—for good and evil—over the seven years of life he had left.

Chapter 32

AT LAST

In April 1958, the river cutting through Seoul appeared below as Everett's flight neared Gimpo International Airport. He had time to read one more time through his sermon notes:

My sense of responsibility . . . has steadily grown year after year. . . .

First, I am indebted to the JEWS who gave me: 1) the oracles of God, the Holy Scriptures; 2) the concept of the true and living God in a world of idolatry; 3) the Messiah, our blessed Lord Jesus Christ; and 4) the first Christians, including the apostle Paul, who went to the Gentiles, of whom I am one.

Second, I am indebted to the MARTYRS through the ages
who laid down their lives gloriously for the "faith once
delivered." . . . I have talked with the survivors of martyred
churches. . . . In Daegu there is a home with 70 widows of
martyred pastors. . . .

Third, I am indebted to our early PIONEERS for their
faithful labors. . . . To Dr. O. L. Swanson, the Billy Sunday of
Assam, whose first convert was my maternal grandfather. . . .

The responsibility then of the open door falls upon you and
me . . . in Tokyo, I heard over and over that the only hope of
the world was in Lord Buddha. But we know only a living
Christ is the answer . . .

Wearing a light blue suit, Everett was whisked away as soon as he
landed, and at morning and evening services for the next seven days,
he shared Christ as the answer with Korean high school and university
students. He rarely raised his voice, trusting instead in the ability of
God's Word and His Spirit to transform hearts and minds.

For any public speaker, it would be an exhausting schedule.

Lord, help me, he prayed. *I am running on empty.*

His days dragged on even longer as he relied upon translators. Who
was he to complain, though? He was the guest here, the outsider, and
he knew only a few words in the local language. Still, each sentence he
delivered required a pause to let the translators do their work, and he
wondered if his meanings were communicated accurately.

Was his humor being conveyed?

Was godly conviction coming through?

While Everett's body was now accustomed to jet lag and his pal-
ate to ginseng tea and bibimbap, he felt disoriented at times. There
was always something new, some unfamiliar food or custom or bit of

history to absorb. He also felt isolated, trying to bond with his younger translators even as they kept a proper cultural distance.

Was there a bridge across this divide?

Despite the struggles, he did have moments of deep satisfaction as well.

Two, in particular, came to mind.

One morning, he had climbed into yet another army truck—this one painted in camouflage, though its layers of dirt did the job just fine—and had ridden through narrow passes and tiny villages until he reached a rundown orphanage by Haksan.

The home there was Namgang Ae-Yook-Won.

Greetings, he said with a reverential bow. I am Rev. Swanson.

The directors, a wife and husband, welcomed him. Yo-hee and Woo-yeol introduced their daughter, who stood wide-eyed, staring at this tall pale guest. They were a humble family, years of effort carved already into their faces. The file provided on this location had painted a picture of incredible poverty, steadfast commitment, and suffering.

Yo-hee, the mother, shifted her weight and cradled a half-swollen belly.

We have another child on the way, her husband said. A boy, we believe.

Great news, Everett responded. Jesus loves each little boy and girl.

If you like, Woo-yeol said, I will show you around our building. We have leaks in the roof, some repairs, but we do our best. We also have a fine *ondol* furnace, built back in—

Please. Everett held up a hand. If you don't mind, I've come to see the children.

On another daylong excursion, this one outside Daegu, Everett met a woman named Gi-sook. She explained to him how she fled from North Korea with her father in the early days of the war, how she gave her life to God at Juamsan Mountain, then married a man who also

wanted to serve Jesus. Together, with only occasional help from her father, they had directed their own ministry for the past four or five years.

Welcome to Mi-saeng Institute, she said. It means "beautiful life."

Everett clapped his hands together. I love the name.

My husband's idea.

It's good to meet you at last, Everett said. A missionary nurse at
the nearby hospital, she's the one who first told me of your work here.

Gi-sook guided him toward three small buildings. This first one,
she said, is where we live. In the other two live the prostitutes. These
women, we find them on the streets, at the train station, and we educate
them. We train them for regular jobs, and in this way, they get their
lives back. Now it's mostly orphans we look after. There are so many,
we are running out of room.

As if to confirm her words, children spilled from the structures and
rushed toward them. A smile spread across Everett's face as the kids
launched themselves forward, climbing his legs, hanging on his arms.

He patted each one on the head. They're so beautiful, he said.

At last, Gi-sook shooed them away. Time for school, no more fool-
ing around.

If you had more land, Everett asked, could you build them a bigger
home?

Gi-sook nodded. It would not be fancy, but yes, we could do this.

He lowered his chin and gazed into her eyes. Was she trembling?
He saw in her face the hopes, doubts, and years of sacrifice on the line.
If he were to follow standard procedures, he might not have an answer
for her for weeks, even months. This was a vetting process most often
left to the advisory board, which looked into and negotiated financial
relief for each home.

He was here now, though, on the ground, seeing for himself this
marvelous work.

Yes, he told her. I will help you, Gi-sook.

Dazed, she didn't even move.

Yes, he said again.

Her eyes welled with tears and then she broke down. She wiped at her cheeks and tried to speak but could not stop crying. She could barely lift her face or form a sentence.

You're doing God's work, Everett reassured her. Don't you worry. Of course, we will help you. It is a gift. You do not have to pay it back, you understand?

Still crying, she nodded.

Have you thought of a name yet for this new home?

She tried to compose herself, chest heaving. House of Hope, she replied at last.

He clapped his hands again. House of Hope! Listen, I'll make sure you and your husband get the money you need. We'll make this happen right away. God is pleased with you, Gi-sook. Very pleased.

Chapter 33

YOU MUST TAKE CARE

In mid-April, Rev. Swanson found his true compatriot, a Korean who would become his bridge to orphanages, directors, and public officials.

Everett first met the man in South Jeolla Province, a downtrodden area in which he had planned more evangelistic meetings and visits to children's homes. South Jeolla had long been a hotbed of political unrest. Its citizens faced centuries of discrimination, even hostility, from other provinces who claimed these people were hardworking yet territorial, likely to stab you in the back. No wonder many from South Jeolla hid their origins while traveling.

Suncheon, one of the province's coastal cities, dated back to the thirteenth century. Hedged in by mountains, dense reeds, and a bay, it had no beach to speak of. Its primary resources were barley, wheat, and rice.

Hordes of war refugees had been drawn to this region by the abundant agriculture, and ESEA had two outposts here: New Life Children's Home, not far outside the city, and Bright Star Orphanage, the home to orphans and leper children in Suncheon.

During Everett's first evening in Suncheon, he ordered a restaurant meal to share with staff members from these two homes. They all waited, out of respect, for him to take the first bite. When his chopsticks brought the local kimchi to his lips, its spicy bite caused his eyes to water while earning him smiles and nods of approval. After sharing bowls of rice and marinated beef bulgogi, the discussion turned to the upcoming meetings.

I'm still looking for a translator, Everett told those gathered.

This is difficult, Reverend. Not many here speak English.

This far south of Seoul, Everett knew there were even fewer proficient in another language. Please, he said, I want my Korean listeners to clearly understand the things of God.

Embarrassed looks passed around.

If I can't find anyone, he added, I may have to assign one of you to come with me.

That caused a buzz between them in their own language. One finally turned to him with an idea. There's a gentleman, a young Korean from here in Suncheon. He just moved back after courses at the Christian college in Daegu.

Great. How do I reach him?

His name is John Seong. He—

John Seong? Everett set down his teacup. He's on our advisory board, our field secretary. He came highly recommended, but I've never seen him face-to-face.

If you like, Reverend, I will take you to him tonight.

* * *

From the moment Everett and John bowed and shook hands, an intimate bond was formed. John was a lean man, a few inches shorter than Everett, with a high forehead over intelligent dark eyes that sparkled when he laughed. At twenty-five years old, he was more boisterous than his typical countrymen. Nevertheless, he had a certain stiffness in his posture, a businesslike bearing. Being from South Jeolla, perhaps he wanted to give a good impression, and as an advisory board member, he was meeting his boss, so to speak, for the very first time.

How have we never met before? Everett asked.

John shrugged. I became part of your organization in early 1956. Some local missionaries mentioned my name and offered their endorsement.

This is my first trip back since 1955. I guess you were coming as I was going. Well, we're meeting now. Thank you for all your work, John.

My pleasure, Reverend. You say you're from Chicago?

For the past fourteen years.

Does this mean you're a Cubs fan?

Everett's eyes widened. Oh, believe me, I catch every game I can.

John grinned. You know what I would like? I'd like to watch your American baseball. The younger man crouched low, thrust a hand sideways with his thumb up, and cried, Stee-rike threeee! You're outta there!

A tightness around Everett's chest broke loose. During his three previous trips to Korea, he had never felt fully free to exercise his personality. He'd worried about saying the wrong word, making an inappropriate gesture, or stepping on toes. He'd sat through bewildering formalities, often waiting until later for explanations from Dr. van Lierop or Rev. Rice. Only around the children had he felt truly comfortable.

All these concerns now vanished.

John, tell me, are you ready to help me preach Christ?

Yes, of course. I studied at a Christian college, then returned here to my province with this hope to serve Jesus in some way. My missionary friends told me of the orphan work you do here in our country, and I believed it was a good thing for Korea. This is why I decided to be part of your ministry.

Praise God! Everett exclaimed. What I need now, John, is a good translator. Assuming all goes well, you and I might even travel together more extensively.

John bowed. It would be an honor, Reverend—

Just Everett.

An honor, Everett. But I must still call you *Reverend* when we preach together. As a sign of respect, you understand?

Here, Everett realized, was an answer to his prayers, a man who would capture not only the direct translation of his words but the deeper layers of meaning, the biblical correlations, the hints at humor and shared humanity.

John Seong would be more than a translator. He'd be an interpreter.

What a joy this is! I look forward to working together, Everett said. When he saw John reach out a hand as though to seal an agreement, he extended both arms instead and wrapped the man in an embrace. He felt the stiff posture relax. We are brothers, John. Jesus has broken down every wall between us.

Gazing up, the younger man wore a radiant smile.

* * *

John Seong was a dynamic interpreter, matching Everett word for word, stride for stride, as he carried out his evangelistic meetings. Their sentences flowed in both English and Korean, communicating scriptural truths, and audiences responded. Gone were the awkward silences, the blank stares. John, a natural on stage, brought Everett's convictions to life.

He's a blessing beyond measure, Everett told Miriam over the phone. Why, that's wonderful.

We laugh together, and oh, how he loves Jesus. He's like a son to me.

So glad to hear it. I've prayed for just the right person to help.

As Everett and John crisscrossed the peninsula into May 1958, they also paid visits to ESEA orphanages and the widows' home. Everett was astounded by the great progress he witnessed. Nearly one thousand kids were being supported! Even so, John informed him, government vehicles were bringing in orphans by the truckloads who were often turned away. There simply wasn't room.

John had his own story of hardship.

Not only of hardship, he promised, but also of joy and rejuvenation.

Born in 1933, in Suncheon, John was raised under enemy occupation. As a boy, he seldom attended Sunday school due to persecution by the Japanese. At age sixteen, God directed him to preach the blessed message to people suffering for their sins.

I made up my mind then to serve the Lord, John said. And I stayed true for a time.

Everett waited, eyebrows furrowed.

A year later, John said, things fell apart. I made a great mistake and committed terrible sins, despite God's love. For some time, the Lord punished me. But even in this, I saw He was good. He never forsook me, despite my offenses against Him. As a Father, He wanted me to learn and grow.

Everett nodded in understanding. He thought of Elmer Rund, who had broken his vow to God. And of the apostle Peter, who denied the Lord three times.

Not long after, John said, my heart was filled again with joy. I didn't know what the Lord would bring in the future, but I trusted and believed He would take good care of me. I had no idea I would meet this evangelist from America, a fan of the Chicago Cubs. But here I am, going city to city with you, preaching God's Word to my countrymen.

Hallelujah! Everett exclaimed.

And then Everett's face twisted as his stomach clenched. Nothing to worry about, he told himself. Intestinal troubles were common among global travelers.

There's a clinic nearby, John suggested. We have traditional remedies.

I'll press through. I fly home tomorrow and there's too much work to do. Anyway, my good friend back in Chicago, he's a doctor. I'll see what he suggests.

For now, John said, let me make you some *yak-cha*.

Cha is tea, right?

You mustn't argue. You must take care of yourself, and herbal tea is medicinal.

Everett surrendered to his interpreter's care, convinced he would be fine.

Chapter 34

PHOTOS AND RECORDS

Back in Chicago, Doc Hemwall completed a checkup of Everett, then prescribed medication and ordered some dietary changes. He wanted to be informed of any increases in pain.

I wouldn't hide that from you, Doc. You know me.

Doc glanced over his glasses. Which is why I'll remind you every chance I get.

At home, Everett's own ailments didn't worry him as much as his wife's recent health concerns. While she wasn't one to complain, her shifts in mood and behavior served as early warning signs of discomfort. It was marvelous what physicians could do these days—and of course there was always the Good Physician—but a quiet unease settled over the household.

One day, Jack dashed in with a load of mail. Most of it's for you, Dad. As always.

Are you waiting on something?

Word back from the National Guard. Or I might join the army. You know, there's a camp up in Wisconsin.

Either way, son, you'll make us proud.

Jack thanked him, dumped the mail on the desk, and dashed back upstairs.

Everett peeled open a large envelope from Korea, containing the photos and records of a child found dying in a cave. He was skin and bones, in the last stages of tuberculosis. Symptoms included chest pain, night sweats, and coughing up blood. Given one more week, doctors claimed, he would've been a dead boy.

Dear Lord. This could've been one of my own children.

Overcome with emotion, he buried his head in his arms and sobbed. He'd seen plenty of pictures before, some even worse, and there were days when the sight did not move him as it did now. Maybe it was a side effect of his pills. Or maybe his heart was simply beating in rhythm with the heart of God.

Oh, he cried, may I never become callous!

He faced his typewriter an hour later and continued a plea to sponsors: "Then I prayed for you, my friends, that God would do the same for you . . . that we may help many more of these poor victims of war."

Even during his recent trip, Everett had noted inadequate facilities on the ministry roster. For years, Director Lim had overseen Hillside Christian Children's Home, funding it himself until ESEA intervened. On site, Everett had discovered hellish conditions for precious orphans who looked like angels.

He now pulled out his checkbook and wrote one for $4,000.

I'll run it by the board, he thought, *but it's time we do something.*

The story of the Good Samaritan came to mind, from Luke

10:25–37. May he never be like the priest who passed on by. He tore off another check for Director Park, at Love and Hope Children's Home. Everett and Rev. Rice had inspected this place outside Daegu. Its bathrooms alone posed serious health risks.

He stared once again at the photo of the boy with tuberculosis.

This is a matter of life and death, he said aloud. We cannot delay.

* * *

The Swansons drove to a weekend gathering with relatives. It was a lively event, with questions about the ministry, and excitement in the living room as kids huddled over a game of Parcheesi.

Everett was glad to see Sally and George, his niece and nephew.

You'll be going to nursing school, is that right? he said to Sally.

I will, she answered, composed as always. I'm committed to my goals.

Everett turned and handed George a photo of himself with a child in his arms. Got this taken while I was in Korea, he said. That's the little boy you are sponsoring.

Thanks, his nephew responded, staring at the picture. A lump formed in George's throat, and he fell silent for the first time all weekend.

* * *

The latter half of 1958 found Everett and Miriam taking turns in the hospital. During Everett's spring tour of the Philippines, Japan, and Korea, he had picked up an infection. What might have been easily treatable was aggravated by an attack of malaria. Neither herbal tea nor basic medicine had succeeded at fending it off. Surgery became necessary.

From his bed he smiled at his wife. I'll come through better and brighter, he assured her.

She tugged at his receding hair, where tufts of gray showed. You best let this keep growing, she said. I'm too young to have a bald husband.

But you'll love me either way, of course.

She tugged again. Let's not find out.

The surgery went smoothly.

Miriam, at forty-three years old, was then admitted for a hysterectomy. The goal was to level her hormones and prevent later infection or disease, but an attack of hepatitis complicated matters. Back home, she was still in some pain.

Nevertheless, as Thanksgiving neared, the Swansons' spirits improved.

Everett updated his supporters, informing them of a thirteenth home now covered by ESEA. Angel Orphanage, in Daegu, was a wonderful haven for fifty-five waifs, foundlings, and beggars. This was how he described the orphans, having visited there himself.

Perhaps sponsors could take on a second child, even a third, he urged.

Or make a onetime Thanksgiving offering.

The ministry was also sending monthly support to nearly one hundred Korean evangelists dedicated to preaching the gospel. Would it be smarter to send over American evangelists, funding their efforts in a foreign land? No, that wouldn't make sense, when the Koreans themselves were eager and in position to do the work.

Throughout the year, ESEA had filed quarterly reports, which tracked:

Attendance—of adults, children, and new believers.

Evangelistic work—to individuals, homes, and special meetings.

Finances—from Sunday offerings, special offerings, and rice offerings.

It was of utmost importance to Everett that all funds be handled and distributed faithfully. ESEA's standards of transparency should honor the Lord. With this in mind, their CPA sifted through records, verified every detail, and provided a 1958 year-end statement so sponsors could see where every dollar went, from postage and shipping to salaries and travel expenses, with the vast majority spent on care for the orphans.

Everett valued statements for the accountability they fostered. He also valued the feedback from individuals behind the scenes, such as John Seong, Rev. Rice, Director Lim, Director Park, and others across Korea.

What was working? What wasn't? And what could be done better? Were evangelists being fruitful in rural areas and church meetings? Most important, were the children's needs being met?

Chapter 35

PUZZLE PIECES

The news wasn't always joyful. Rev. Swanson regularly received personal letters full of despair. One director, Mrs. Kim, shared with him the worsening conditions at Blue Bird Christian Orphanage. Even their pigs and ducks were dying. The children had no food. Could the ministry step in and support her home?

ESEA responded, and also added three others:

Faithfulness and Love Orphanage, in Uiseong.
Love Valley Orphanage, in Masan.
Lazarus Home, in Daegu.

Dr. van Lierop informed him of a delegation of five Christian teachers who came begging for the sake of their own orphanage. Everett remembered the very place. He had admonished the director for mishandling funds, then withdrawn ESEA's pledge of support.

The director was now a changed man, Dr. van Lierop reported.

Was the change genuine? Was it long-term?

As a Christian, Everett felt the heaviness of these responsibilities. He wanted to believe the best, especially when partnering with other believers, but he also needed discernment since he was by nature a trusting individual.

The recently released Amplified New Testament provided guidance in 2 Corinthians 8:20–21: "[For] we are on our guard, intending that no one should find anything for which to blame us in regard to our administration. For we take thought beforehand and aim to be honest and absolutely above suspicion not only in the sight of the Lord, but also in the sight of men."

After intense prayer, he added the wayward home back to the roster.

Everett particularly looked forward to the insights of his interpreter and friend, John Seong. Like father and son, they had laughed, prayed, preached, and shared meals across Korea. They'd visited orphans and widows in their affliction.

When the phone rang one morning, he ignored it as he stirred sugar into his Postum. He heard his son pick up and tell the caller to hold on.

For you, Dad, Paul called. Sounds all garbled. I think he said Johnson. Or John Song.

Everett bolted to his feet and flew up the stairs. Across the thousands of miles, John's voice brought a thrill to Everett's heart as they caught up on health and family issues. He imagined the man's concerned expression as the conversation turned to aspects of the ministry.

Politics are complicated here, John explained. Since US troops pulled out, feelings toward foreigners have gone sour. It is hard for us to trust even good people, when we have so many times been under their shoes. For nearly fifty years, others have been telling us what to do.

That is certainly not our intent, Everett said. How can we earn trust?

Please don't take offense. This is not how everyone feels. It would help, John suggested, if we set up an ESEA office in Seoul.

Wouldn't that be expensive?

It is important to build relationships within the government. Our political leaders here could change soon, and this means new rules, shifting fees. Of course, a place on the city outskirts might be less costly. I can look around.

Don't get me wrong, John. I understand what you're saying. But all our funds are allocated to over a dozen homes and a hundred evangelists.

Even so, a representative in Seoul could save the ministry much heartache.

Let me think it over, alright?

* * *

When Everett received a good report, he was always eager to celebrate. Pacing the kitchen one evening, he read a Korean deacon's letter about the revival meetings recently conducted at his church by an ESEA evangelist.

The deacon was initially worried no one would come. This was a church full of country folks and it was the busiest season for them. To the deacon's surprise, the crowds increased night after night and the meetings were wonderful. The church filled to overflowing, and a congregation once cold and feeble became passionate for the Lord and full of grace.

The evangelist was Rev. Young-ok Pak, a blind man.

And he had given them eyes to see.

Everett clutched the letter to his heart, then raised it to the ceiling as Sharon walked through the kitchen. Hallelujah, he yelled out. Praise the Lord!

Another letter told him about Eastern Light Orphanage. Director Ki-chang Son wrote that his orphans began shouting with great joy when they heard the news that their home would be supported by ESEA.

Everett yelled out again: Hallelujah!

His daughter laughed. Good day, huh, Dad?

Even as both Everett's and Miriam's health took a downward turn, their ministry grew stronger. As a couple, their passion for evangelism and their compassion for others were moving in tandem, meeting spiritual and physical needs.

Every day, souls were saved.

Minds were educated.

Tummies were filled, faces washed, and bodies clothed.

With so much momentum behind the ministry, they didn't want anything slowing it down. Bureaucratic red tape, greedy officials, and bumbling Westerners could all impede its progress, but the right person in the right place could clear the way. Maybe John Seong was right. Maybe they needed a representative in Seoul.

And who better for the job?

Everett couldn't deny that John was a man of action, drive, and courage. He bridged the language gap. He was good at choosing leaders and delegating responsibility. He'd successfully screened a number of ESEA orphanages.

The decision was soon made to find a small office in Korea's capital, with John Seong at the helm. John would meet with officials and provide oversight.

What an answer to prayer.

It was one less thing Everett would have to worry about, alleviating his burdens and allowing him more opportunities with his wife and grown kids here at home.

With Doc at his side in Chicago, and John at his side in Seoul, Everett was now bolstered by two highly capable men, much as Aaron and Hur had been to Moses. During a battle in Exodus 17, the armies of Moses had prevailed while he held his staff aloft, but they faltered when he lowered it. His muscles grew heavy. He needed help. Aaron and Hur joined him, one on either side, supporting his weary arms as their soldiers reigned victorious.

Everett smiled and shook his head at all the what-ifs.

What if Doc Hemwall had not paid for his first plane ticket?

What if Dr. van Lierop had not run into him in the YMCA men's room?

What if Captain Hyung-do Kim had not invited him back to Korea? What if his missionary friend had not challenged him with a question? What if a woman in Seattle had not donated a $50 check? What if the Gearys, Elmer Lund, and others had not invested early on? What if there were not Korean men and women such as Gi-sook, Yo-hee, Woo-jeol, and many others who sacrificed so much for the sake of the children?

Each one had made a small choice, an act of obedience, a seemingly insignificant contribution. Each one was a puzzle piece fitted into place by God's sovereignty, providing color, contrast, and definition, becoming part of a much larger picture. Together, they formed a ministry that now served over a thousand people—and they were barely scratching the surface.

No, it wasn't just about Everett's work and vision.

This was about much, much more.

Chapter 36

TO SUFFER WITH

It was about compassion, Everett decided. Did any word describe it better?

From the Latin, *compassion* meant "to suffer with."

A search through the Bible found the word used repeatedly. In Exodus, Pharaoh's daughter had *compassion* when she laid eyes upon baby Moses hidden in a basket of reeds. In Deuteronomy, God had *compassion* on the Israelites, even in their captivity to Babylon. In the Psalms, He showed He was full of *compassion* and forgave iniquity. In Jeremiah, He promised to return and have *compassion*, giving the people back their land.

When Jesus saw the multitudes in the gospel of Matthew, He was moved with *compassion* because they were weary and scattered, and He healed them. He had *compassion*, not wanting to send them away hungry, lest they faint. In Mark, He was moved with *compassion*, teaching them many things. In Luke, He had *compassion* and told them not to weep. In John, the passion of Christ, the pain He endured on the cross, was an intentional act of suffering with sinners, becoming their sin so that the wages of sin and death would no longer have any power.

Compassion.

Jesus Himself embodied the word.

In Korea, faithful servants of the Lord had also taken up their crosses and followed His example. Daily, they gave themselves to finding the weary and scattered, to healing and feeding the children, to teaching them and drying their tears. And now, from across the US, Canada, and other lands, sponsors were giving of their own resources, often anonymously, often sacrificially.

These dear people. They were the lifeblood of this work.

This ministry wasn't simply about empathizing with others and feeling their pain. It was about striving from the core of one's being, suffering with others, and being moved to act. Compassionate people from all around the world were the beating heart of this ministry.

Inspired, Everett decided to give a new name and format to his newsletter.

The front page of the trifold read:

"I have compassion on the multitude . . . I will not send them away hungry" (Matt. 15:32).

COMPASSION
Published Bi-Monthly by the Everett Swanson Evangelistic Association
VOL. I   APRIL-MAY 1959   NO. 1

In this update he let sponsors know additional homes were being screened for approval and support. He was climbing out on a limb to even consider them, since three more had already been added to the ESEA list:

New Prosperity Christian Orphanage, in Busan.

Bethany Home, in Gimcheon.

Great Glory Orphanage, in Daegu.

Every child, every home, was another burden Everett bore. Where would he find more money and sponsors? Could he fulfill all his promises to his Korean directors?

Though he trusted God would hear the workers' and children's cries, he also believed he should do his part. Despite his recent surgery, he spent the first part of the year conducting services in New Jersey, New York, Nebraska, Minnesota, and north into Saskatchewan. He ran ads in *Christian Life* magazine and various Sunday school papers, and by the time July rolled around, ESEA was already backing twenty-eight more homes.

Chapter 37

NO INKLING

In the summer of 1959, Everett moved his own family into a new home. With whitewashed brick and tall front windows, it was only ten minutes from their old place. While this new address had less square footage, its much larger basement would soon be crammed with desks, filing cabinets, and storage boxes for the ministry.

Boy, he said, life has sure changed over twenty-five years of marriage.

Twenty-five in December, Miriam corrected.

He didn't argue. In such matters, he deferred to his wife. He slipped an arm around her waist and said, We've gone from roaming the country with our old car and revival tent to putting up World War II blackout curtains in Mount Vernon and Chicago. Now look at us, serving the Lord in ways we never dreamed of.

A delivery boy flashed by on a bicycle and tossed a newspaper their way.

Hello, Everett called out from the front steps, but the boy was gone, a blur of movement in the muggy August air.

Things have certainly grown by leaps and bounds, Miriam said.

ESEA had doubled in size over the last year and a half. A trial plan now allowed new sponsors to stop their giving after six months, no questions asked, and this had brought in many new donors. A part-time secretary had also been hired.

In the Swanson family, David and Myra were working through early marital struggles. Sharon, now a comptometer operator, had married Gorden Ronne, a crane operator. Jack and Paul were out of high school, enlisted along with David for six months' active duty in the army.

And to think we'll be grandparents soon, Miriam said.

Imagine that, Everett responded. Sharon will be a wonderful mother.

Miriam's dress swirled about her legs as she faced him. Promise me, Everett, that we'll be together as a family for Christmas. You've been on the road nonstop, it seems.

A traveling man for Jesus and no other.

Please, I want this to be a special time for all of us.

He adjusted her strand of pearls, then looked into her eyes. Our silver anniversary . . . He paused. Silver, do I have that right?

Yes. But wearing this silver, she said, tugging at his gray hairs, doesn't count. Why that silly grin? What're you hiding from me?

He held up a hand. Sorry, you'll have to wait.

Till our anniversary? That's four months away.

Time flies. Truly, who would've guessed the Lord would tarry this long? We have so much to be grateful for, Miriam. This house. Our family. The ministry. Our health after last year's scares. Do you ever regret it?

Marrying you? She pulled his face down and gave him a kiss. I do not, Mr. Swanson. Now are you going to tell me your surprise?

All he could do was laugh.

* * *

Days later, ESEA held its first board meeting in the Swansons' expansive basement at 4848 North Leonard Drive, Chicago, Illinois. They decided Rev. Swanson would receive $6,000 toward the cost of this new home, plus moving expenses. ESEA would also cover all utilities and increase his monthly salary to $500, plus a $215 housing allowance.

Once again, the provision came at just the right time.

Everett had no idea—none of them did—that this three-bedroom, one-bathroom home was the last address at which he would ever reside, or that the ESEA offices would soon outgrow even a basement this large.

Oh, Miriam, he said, squeezing her arm. God is good!

* * *

Political unrest simmered in the provinces of South Korea. With future rulership in question, the current government provided only minimal grain rations for each child. Even as American music and movies seeped into Korean culture, selling images of wealth and happiness, many Korean kids had no money for mittens, shoes, underwear, or school supplies.

Already, Everett had ten more orphanages clamoring for aid.

Since Everett's initial visit to the peninsula eight years earlier, Rev. Rice had played a foundational role in ESEA. Along with John Seong, he vetted homes for potential support, funneled resources to those already on the roster, and worked closely with the orphans.

In the September-October issue of *Compassion*, Rev. Rice shared his own recent encounters with the beggar boys:

> Last Saturday evening I returned from a 1,700-mile, nine-day tour by jeep, which completely circled South Korea. . . .

> From under railroad cars, on busy downtown streets, dry riverbeds or under bridges, we contacted boys. The last boy, contacted in Seoul, I met in a market area collecting trash paper and selling it. . . . It was only after a lot of persuasion and a friendly hand on his shoulder that he made the decision, and leaving on the sidewalk his large basket and collecting prongs, he got into the jeep with me. . . .

> These boys, living a hand-to-mouth existence, evidence little concern about their souls. We let them know that we are doing this work because we know Jesus Christ and love God who also loves them. It is always a joy to see the little battle of decision going in favor of leaving the old, futureless life for a new way of life. And it is equally disappointing to see the struggle of the will going the other way.

Everett's heart ached over these boys who so badly needed help. Many of the older ones were bigger now, streetwise, preferring to run around in "beggar clubs" while harassing neighbors and local police. They were survivors. It was all they knew.

In early September, Rev. Swanson set out again to visit North American schools and churches, sharing stories and color slides from his travels. These slide sets were available on loan, with no obligation, as a means of educating and enlisting more supporters.

Home for a brief respite, Everett went out to get the newspaper and bumped into a large box on the front step. On the side, in stenciled letters: BLANKETS.

Thank the Lord, he mumbled while massaging his shin.

Earlier, he had pleaded with sponsors to help him send five-thousand-plus blankets to Korea, where icy conditions would arrive with the first blasts of winter. Here was the first of many boxes that would soon pile at his door. ESEA had also purchased a Singer sewing machine for Love Valley Home, in Masan, where a full-time seamstress made and repaired clothes for the children. Boys wore new shorts. Girls wore dresses and bright red bows in their hair. In addition, many girls received training on the Singer.

It was important to teach each orphan a skill, a trade. With Korea facing decades of rebuilding, these orphans would grow into farmers, teachers, politicians, and engineers.

We're being proactive, Everett told his board members. These investments are worth it.

The blankets and sewing machine would be keys to survival even sooner than expected, since the weather forecasts gave no inkling of the disaster brewing off the Korean peninsula.

Chapter 38

SURPRISES

In mid-September 1959, Koreans were celebrating the harvest festival of *Chuseok*, which loosely means "Korean Thanksgiving," as a storm formed over the Pacific. Named Typhoon Sarah, the system gained strength, reached sustained winds of 190 mph, and struck the Japanese island of Miyako-jima. It then careened westward and made landfall near Busan, South Korea.

The most powerful typhoon to hit the peninsula in fifty years, Sarah's high winds and waves ravaged the port city and damaged its military bases. They decimated most of the fishing fleet, flooded coastal areas, and swept away crops and homes.

Barely a word of the catastrophe reached Chicago's newspapers. Everett heard of it from his partners in Korea. Frustrated by Western myopia and wracked with concern, he typed up an account for the November-December issue of *Compassion*:

> You have probably read in the papers of the typhoons in Japan and Mexico. But little has been published of the worst one in KOREA's weather history! One week after this indescribable tragedy hit Korea, the Ministry of Health and Social Affairs announced there were 663 dead, 2,847 injured, 259 missing and 788,249 left homeless! About 24,500 houses were completely destroyed—10,004 washed away, 50,720 half destroyed, and 44,668 flooded. . . .

> Many of our orphanages were badly damaged, but miraculously, no one was killed. Many chickens and hogs were lost, much food grain was ruined. Frantic appeals poured into our office from the directors. . . . Our funds are exhausted, but repairs must be made immediately before winter sets in. . . .

> The prospects for a happy Christmas seem very remote to many of our homes, because of the terrific typhoon. . . . But they will not go hungry, lack clothing, or fuel, because the sponsors' faithful monthly support provides all these things.

Everett was struck by the importance of these newsletters. If it weren't for his earlier plea for blankets and for a seamstress with a new sewing machine, over two thousand children in dozens of ESEA homes would currently be facing exposure, relying on nothing but the clothes hanging from their limbs.

Typhoon Sarah had delivered her worst.

Nevertheless, they had been ready.

The Lord's mercy had been shown and nature's assault mitigated by the loving efforts of ESEA, CARE, World Vision, and other relief organizations, which joined together for those in distress. Regardless, nearly every ESEA orphanage still had pressing needs. Few had the resources to handle even regular expenses, much less unforeseen damage and repairs. Many also had hopes of becoming self-sustaining, able to raise money of their own through on-site projects.

There must be more we can do, Everett implored his board members.

We don't have the resources, one member stated. There's little surplus.

What about providing loans to them?

And do we know we'll get paid back? Would it even be fair to expect?

Listening, Doc Hemwall set down his glasses and looked around the table. He said, Let's put the responsibility on the individual directors. Ah, now hear me out. We could allow each one to submit a project for their home, something with clear benefits, then extend to them an interest-free loan that they would repay over time.

I see it working, Miriam said, if each director being assisted has an amount taken out of the home's monthly allotments until the loan is settled.

It was a reasonable solution, and the board as well as the home directors were thrilled with this arrangement. Soon, projects were added to an ever-growing list:

Good Samaritan Children's Home . . . A rice cleaning mill: $3,000

Holiness and Grace Orphanage . . . Garden and pear orchard: $4,500

Great Light Widows' Home . . . New well for selling water: $750

Angel Orphanage . . . Land for rabbit ranch: $250

New Life Children's Home . . . Chicken and pigs: $300

Tender Nurture House . . . An ox to till the ground: $150

Love Valley Orphanage . . . Garden land and new toilets: $2,000

Greater Glory Orphanage . . . Bandage factory and land: $800

Despite his intense travel schedule, Everett rejoiced at these signs of progress. He also drew strength from his phone calls with Miriam and from letters in the ESEA mailbag, which he stopped to read whenever he got the chance.

From Canada:
"Enclosed is $15 which I hope will help a bit your great work. Your address was given over the radio station."

From Illinois:
"I am happy to inform you that . . . the adoption of the boy from New Prosperity Orphanage has done so much for the boys and girls of the Sunday School, and after films of the work were shown by our pastor, one of the church members approached me requesting that the Sunday School adopt a girl orphan."

From Daegu:
"Our orphanage has been changing slowly but nicely. Children have better food than we had before, also they wear good clothes. And they are happy in the Lord every day . . . through your hard work and sponsors' sacrifices."

And one he particularly loved, from a South Korean military camp:

"I am very well now. . . . I was dirty in my mind in the past, but I became a Christian and prayed to God. Now I become twenty years old and have to enter the Korean army. . . . On the way to the training place, I was thinking of Rev. Swanson who helped me to be a good soldier for the peace of the world."

Years ago, Everett had responded to a simple question by stepping into the ring, ready to fight for the needs of the children. Now this young man, this orphan whom he'd encouraged along the way, was choosing a fight of his own.

* * *

What's the surprise? Miriam wanted to know.

Hold on. Everett shook his head. Not till the family's all together. Is there any reason to rush our silver anniversary?

She folded her arms and shot him a half-hearted scowl.

Arriving from across the city on December 16, the Swansons gathered at North Leonard Drive, where they posed for their annual photo. Sets of smiling newlyweds stood in the back, Gorden and Sharon Ronne next to David and Myra Swanson. Seated in front, Everett wore a thin tie over a starched white shirt. Eighteen-year-old Paul slouched next to him. Nineteen-year-old Jack wore a smile even louder than his plaid button-up, and Miriam had coiffed auburn hair and a stylish dress, which she smoothed down over her knees.

Why, the picture's not complete, she exclaimed. Where's our grand-baby?

Jeffrey's napping, Sharon said.

Let's wake him, then.

No, Mom, her kids all groaned.

C'mon, Doc, just snap the photo, Everett urged. We're all ready to eat.

The Swansons and Hemwalls divvied out place settings and platters of food. They bowed in prayer, then dug in. Everett ate more quickly than usual.

Alright, he declared at last to the table. I have a surprise for my bride.

She tilted her head, gazing over expectantly.

Miriam, he said, touching her forearm as all eyes watched. You have stood by me for a quarter of a century. You've given so much, running the household, getting the kids off to school, seeing them through sports, choirs, graduations, even working at the factory as the ministry grew. You've rarely complained as I—

It was her turn to groan.

As I pastored and preached, he pressed on.

Sounds like a sermon right now, Jack kidded him.

Everett remained focused on Miriam. For all this time, you've let me do all the traveling. Well, there's a reason we applied for your passport. Come January, I'll be making my fifth trip to Korea, a five-month tour, and there's nothing I'd like more than to have you by my side.

Five months? My goodness. What about Jeffrey? I told Sharon I'd—

She's made other arrangements. Right, Sharon?

Their daughter nodded. What do you say, Mom? Are you going?

Miriam blinked twice, then pushed back in her seat. The excitement washed over her, adding color to her cheeks and sparkle to her eyes. She leaped up and threw her arms around Everett's neck, nearly squealing with delight.

Is that a yes? he wanted to know.

Yes, Dad, his kids all groaned again. That's a yes.

The Hemwalls and their daughters cut loose with laughter.

So, I did it? Everett asked Miriam before bed. Actually pulled off the surprise?

Oh, Everett, she gasped. I can't wait to go see those little Korean faces for myself.

Chapter 39

FIRE AND STEEL

In January 1960, Rev. Swanson and his bride boarded their flight to Seoul. Hands joined, they heard and felt the jet engines roar to life.

That sound, Everett said, it gets my heart racing every time.

Miriam gripped his hand a little tighter.

Here at the dawn of a new decade, Everett knew they weren't the only ones full of expectancy. Something was shifting. People sensed it. There was talk of robots and weather satellites. While kids were hula hooping and teens were gyrating with Elvis, adults were laughing along with Jack Lemmon and Tony Curtis in *Some Like It Hot*.

Everett got all these latest updates from his own kids.

His sights, however, were set on loftier things. He'd written to supporters that he felt a sense of urgency, believing this could be the year of the Lord's return. It was more important than ever to be renewed, consecrated, and dedicated to saving precious souls.

What an adventure this had been, starting nearly nine years ago with his first trip to war-ravaged Korea in the fall of 1951.

In 1952, he had gone back and found the orphans in the alleyway.

By 1953, he had been opening homes for the growing numbers of orphans, even as an armistice was signed to cease hostilities.

His third trip to the peninsula came in 1955, when his crusade drew in tens of thousands. And by the next year, ESEA was an official nonprofit organization, adding more homes to its roster. It grew exponentially during the following year, and by 1958, he was back for a fourth tour, during which he met his good friend and interpreter, John Seong. As for 1959, there had been many ups and downs, personally and in ministry.

I am ready for new things, Everett said, leaning toward his wife.

She sat with eyes closed as the plane accelerated down the runway. Miriam? he ventured. Are you asleep?

I'm praying, she whispered. Please, may we talk after takeoff?

* * *

ESEA now supported forty-two homes. Over the next twenty weeks, the Swansons would visit as many as possible. There was much to evaluate, not only regarding Typhoon Sarah's aftermath, but also the new interest-free loan program and the effectiveness of the blanket drive. With John Seong joining them to interpret, they would hear directly from the homes' directors.

More than anything, it was Everett's prayer that his wife would connect with the kids.

Which took only minutes at their very first stop.

Miriam strolled through the orphanage gates, heels clicking on the stone walkway, purse pressed against her hip. She peered through her sunglasses at Korean orphans with helmet-cut hair, tiny shoes, and tidy clothes.

Mama Swanson! the children greeted her.

And she fell in love.

She kneeled to hug the girls and admire the boys. She ran her hand over their heads, looked into dark, smiling eyes. They moved in, clambering to get closer to this fashionable woman in the scarf and long coat. Mama and Papa Swanson were a hit wherever they went, greeted by brightly painted banners in Korean and English, welcomed with gifts and flowers.

The kids are incredible, Miriam gushed. Each and every one of them.

* * *

The first hint of trouble came when they learned of sponsors send-ing cash directly to orphanages. This was a no-no. While the intentions were good, it put directors in an awkward position. They could cer-tainly use more money for the children, but it was illegal for them to possess US dollars. The right thing to do was send it back.

In addition, some sponsors were sending their orphans detailed de-scriptions of American homes, cars, and TVs. This accentuated the dis-parity between Western luxuries and Korean poverty. Sponsors had also shipped extravagant, personal gifts such as bikes, radios, and cameras, which quickly stirred envy and damaged morale within an orphanage. A bicycle was an item even most Korean men could not afford.

The directors, through John Seong, expressed these frustrations.

We will send out a letter immediately, Everett responded, providing strong guidelines for our supporters. We must bring this to a halt.

As the Swansons traversed mountains, rivers, and rice paddies, they discovered other disturbing scenarios. There were children wearing thin jackets, flimsy shoes, and no socks—and in the middle of winter, no less. ESEA funds were keeping orphans alive but barely meeting other needs. Things were even worse at the homes still seeking support.

Oh, Everett, we can't just leave her, Miriam cried one day.

They were at Eternal Life Orphanage, in Daegu, a home under current consideration. While Everett looked through ledgers in the director's office, his wife had gone strolling through the facility and found a sickly baby girl.

Gazing at the precious child, Everett found his own heart broken by the weepy eyes and crusty little lips. We can't take her with us, he said softly. You know this, Miriam.

But we must.

What, are you going to hide her in your purse? Take her on the plane?

Miriam glanced down at her purse as though weighing the idea. Her eyes lifted to his, full of fire and steel. I will personally sponsor her. I'll see to it she has what she needs, starting now.

Everett drew his wife into his arms, the tiny girl whimpering between them. If only we had thousands more like you, Miriam. This is why I've let so many things take a back seat these past nine years. It must break God's heart.

We have to do even better, she said. We will!

At Chunnam Children's Home, in Jeonju, the Swansons were able to make an immediate impact. A missionary had informed them of this home's dire situation and their visit confirmed it. The orphans were literally starving. Overwhelmed, the Swansons released immediate funds for food and repairs.

Director Byung-jin Yoon later wrote:

In February 1960, Rev. Swanson visited our home for the first time . . . I think that my home changed from hell to heaven. . . .

He appeared to me like a saint . . . he emphasized that to eat, clothe, and study are important, but above all to believe in Jesus Christ as one's personal savior. . . . He impressed me very much. . . . He was a real good shepherd who sacrificed himself for his sheep.

Such life-changing opportunities thrilled the Swansons. Everett saw a new resolve in Miriam, and she moved in a cloud of conviction, oblivious to observers, intent on nurturing the kids. As cameras rolled, they captured her love in action.

* * *

By March, political unrest was again rocking South Korea. In an election that many thought rigged, President Rhee retained power.

Thousands of protestors gathered, and when some concentrated themselves in the southern city of Masan, fearful police fired bullets and tear gas.

Even amidst warming air and cherry blossoms, the tensions simmered. Everett followed along in news reports, many of which were unreliable. Heeding the advice of local staff and missionaries, he kept quiet about the situation. As foreigners, it was impossible to grasp all the elements involved, and matters worsened in mid-April when the body of a missing protestor was found washed up on a beach. Though the government dismissed it as an accidental drowning, protestors forced their way into the hospital and discovered the man had actually been killed by a tear-gas canister lodged in his skull.

This revelation sparked outrage.

Riots broke out, students marched, and cars were set ablaze in the streets of Seoul.

Again, police opened fire, this time killing over a hundred people.

Instead of quashing the situation, these actions spurred even larger demonstrations. Rural and urban areas alike were angry and grieving. For twelve years, their president had suppressed opposition through violence and imprisonment, while failing to provide any viable economic future. This beautiful land needed rebuilding and was anxious for a fresh start.

Fearing for his life, President Rhee stepped down and went into exile in the US.

Still on the peninsula, Everett and Miriam could do nothing but watch and pray.

To experience these things at ground level was to have a deeper compassion for millions of South Koreans who had already endured so much. Nearly everyone had lost loved ones during the war. Many had relatives still estranged from them in North Korea. Historically, countries facing such dire circumstances struggled to ever recover.

Oh, Lord, Everett called out, how long until this land heals? Where is the new leadership who will justify this uprising?

He had no influence in these affairs. He was a bystander. Helpless. His years of investment here could be washed away in a moment, ended by a communist regime or bogged down by corrupt officials. All of ESEA's orphanages were at risk.

What do we do? he mused aloud over a meal with Miriam and John.

God's brought us here during this time, Miriam replied, reaching for his hand. Do you think our trip's been in vain? No, Everett, I don't believe that. What we do is take another step just as we've always done—through two world wars, the Depression, and the Korean War. Nothing's changed, far as I'm concerned.

She's right, John agreed. And a wise wife is a true treasure. Speaking of wives. John finished his tea and cleared his throat. I would like to tell you, I am now engaged to be married.

How wonderful, Miriam cried.

Congratulations, John. Everett pumped the man's hand. Have we met this dear lady?

She's in Daegu. A Christian nurse, very beautiful. We'll marry next spring, and she wants me to continue with this ministry. As Miriam said, we can't let this situation worry us. We just take another step.

* * *

The Swansons pressed forward with new determination. Over the next month, they met with missionaries and evangelists they supported, then dedicated a new ESEA-funded structure at Hillside Christian Children's Home. Plaques were handed out along with wreaths of flowers.

Before their return to the States, they received an unexpected blessing at the Garden of Eden Orphanage. The director there had organized some of his kids into a choir. Thirty-two voices, singing in English, performed live for Mama and Papa Swanson. They recorded twelve of the numbers, and RCA agreed to produce the album on 10-inch vinyl. *The Voices of Korean Orphans* would soon be available for sponsors free of charge—donations accepted, of course.

You know, Miriam told Everett, this is how I first came to really know you.

He frowned, not sure what she was talking about.

In choir, she said. Remember? Back at Sycamore High.

He grinned and nodded. Well, how could I ever forget?

Isn't it marvelous how the Lord thinks of everything? she went on. Here we are at the Garden of Eden, and what do we get? A sentimental gift, after twenty-five years as a couple.

But you realize, if I hadn't bought a plane ticket, we wouldn't even—

Oh, stop it. She swatted at his arm. It's not a competition to see who can give me the best gift. This is for both of us, Everett. Don't you see? Sure, we could pull back now and leave this work behind, but I truly sense God has more. So much more.

1923, Queen Anne Hill, (pictured L to R) Bob, Rose, Everett, Lawrence, Leslie, and Ray Swanson

1950, Miriam and Everett, the adoring couple in Chicago, IL

1950s, Everett, avid photographer

1950s, Everett visiting a Korean orphanage

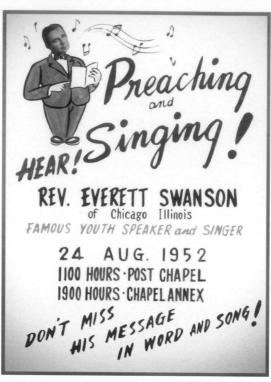

1952, Everett, the "Singing Evangelist"

1950s, Everett addressing the South Korean troops during the war

1950s, Everett filming at the YMCA in Daegu, Korea

1952, Swanson family picture, (clockwise) Everett, Miriam, David, Paul, Jack, and Sharon

1950s, Bob Morgan and Everett are greeted by children in Daegu, Korea

1950s, Everett and sons, (pictured L to R) Paul, Everett, Jack, and David Swanson

1950s, Everett at a ribbon cutting ceremony in Korea

May of 1958, Everett visits the Jinhae (Chinhae) orphanage in Korea

May of 1958, Everett approves the new renovations at Hillside Christian Orphanage

Spring of 1960, "Papa and Mama Swanson" visit an orphanage on Miriam's first trip to Korea

1960, Everett is presented with a plaque commemorating his work in Korea

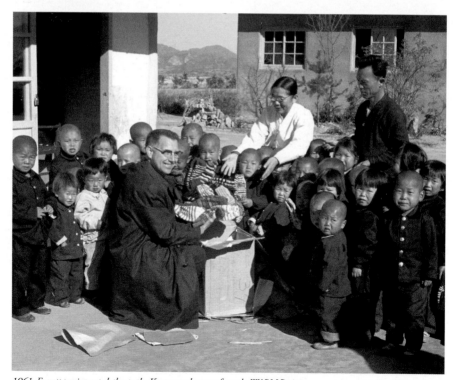

1961, Everett passing out clothes to the Korean orphanages from the WARM Project

1960s, Everett receives letter of official commendation from governor of South Gyeongsang province

1962, Everett honored by Korean superintendents at ESEA 10th Anniversary Conference

1962, 10th Anniversary of ESEA in Korea

November of 1962, a welcoming party for Everett, his brother Lawrence, and his niece Sally as she begins her duties as a nurse in Korea

November of 1963, Everett is welcomed by the Korean military

1960s, Korean orphanage welcomes Everett and Miriam, Sally Swanson, Robert Forsyth, and Bob Morgan

November of 1963, Everett is given an honorary doctorate at Konkuk University in Seoul, Korea

April of 1964, Everett inspects his trusty movie camera

April of 1965, Everett is greeted by his sponsor child in Busan, Korea

May of 1965, Everett and Miriam hold orphans during their second joint trip to Korea

Rev. Everett F. Swanson memorial photo

Part 5

Autumn 1960
Busan, South Korea

"It is only through seriousness of purpose and persistence
that we ultimately carry the day. We might liken it to riding
a bicycle. You stay upright and move forward as long as
you keep up the momentum."
— *UN Secretary-General Ki-moon Ban*

Myung-guen is not an orphan, not really. He was born in 1951, in the midst of the Korean War. Poor health and hunger pangs are part of his memories.

Now he is twelve. His stepmother, a shaman, fills his days with abuse while his father just watches him suffer. Fearing for his life, Myung-guen decides to flee. Like all who have lived through the war, he is a survivor. He's heard the Korean proverb: Even if you are caught by a tiger, you will survive if you keep your cool.

Myung-guen makes his way south to Busan, where he believes his birth mother will take him in and keep him safe. There, he will be happy again. He cannot find her, though. Busan is huge, still brimming with refugees. Many streets are unnamed, known only by their landmarks and residents. Who can help him find his mother? How can he describe their old neighborhood?

He is lost, growing desperate.

If he returns to his stepmother, he's convinced he will die.

After weeks of hopelessness and tears, Myung-guen finds himself in the care of a Busan orphanage. The place is called Seoul Ae-Lyn-Won, perhaps because it started in Seoul. He does not know. At least he has a roof over his head.

Life isn't much easier here, though.

The place is crammed with other kids. Most are tough, with hardened eyes, and some are bullies. They are all given daily tasks. His is to fetch the water in a carrier made from tin and an old tire. He must walk miles each way, the heavy carrier cutting into his skin.

Despite his weary bones, Myung-guen attends school at night and earns good grades. His teachers applaud his efforts. One evening, he even receives a grand award from the Busan superintendent of education. The orphan who is not an orphan has excelled at this one thing—and he glows with pride.

It's past midnight when he gets back to Seoul Ae-Lyn-Won.

Myung-guen, you are late! The manager is on duty, his eyes black with anger. Come with me to the office!

I won an award, sir. Please, I'm sorry, but see here, it's—

A hand slaps him hard across the face. Myung-guen is in shock. He wants to cry. On this gold-medal night when he is full of such joy, all he gets now are blows and rebukes.

Slap-slap-slap!

He wants to do something. But what? The manager's arm keeps swinging, his voice full of fury. Would the man treat his own child like this?

Slap-slap-slap!

What are you going to do? he asks himself.

Myung-guen thinks of running but has nowhere to go. Why is it that grown adults take out their anger on children half their size? He begins to cry. He feels unworthy. He tries to fend off his tormentor, to turn his head and lift his arm, but it only incites the manager to greater ferocity. Myung-guen absorbs it all, head spinning, vision blurring.

There is no plan, no escape route, no rescuer.

At twelve, all he sees is a future fading to black.

His days stretch on after that. Out of eighty kids, he's just one more mouth to feed. He doesn't complain or expect an apology. He puts his head down each morning, skulks off to fetch the water, then goes to night school and keeps silent.

Sometimes he stands too quickly. Feels a wave of dizziness.

It happens again. And again. He still feels those blows.

Slap-slap-slap!

Head spinning. Vision blurring.

Whorls of darkness.

What are you going to do? he asks himself again, but these six little words seem rhetorical, since he can only hope and pray. Perhaps there is a purpose to this life. Perhaps love even exists, somewhere beyond the walls of this wretched place.

Perhaps.

In October, as the weather begins to turn, a foreigner visits Seoul Ae-Lyn-Won Orphanage. The man strides through the building, hands on hips, taking in the situation. He might sponsor this home, but he makes it clear he is not pleased with the conditions he sees.

What is this man's name? Myung-guen wonders aloud.

Rev. Swanson, someone whispers. He's called Papa.

Myung-guen finds himself near the pale reverend and takes note of the gray sprinkles in the man's dark hair and the smile lines around his mouth.

Why, hello, Papa Swanson greets him. Here, let me look at you.

Not sure what this man wants, Myung-guen recoils and asks himself again:

What are you going to do?

He doesn't want to be made a fool of, not in front of the other boys and girls. On the other hand, what does he have to lose? If purpose and love do exist, they must require a willing heart. He steels himself and steps forward.

Hello, he says. I am Myung-guen.

Caring blue eyes peer into his and make him feel worthy. A hand touches the right side of his face. See here, this black spot by his iris? Papa Swanson motions to the director. It could be hereditary, but I suspect it's a sign of abuse. I want this checked out.

The director hesitates. But we don't have money for this. We—

I will pay for it, Papa Swanson says. He could go blind if it's not taken care of.

Doctors confirm the reverend's concerns. Myung-guen receives a painful shot, then undergoes surgery at Child Charity Hospital. His dizziness disappears and the orphan who is not an orphan can see.

Thank you, Papa, he wants to tell the man.

But Papa Swanson is gone. He has many more homes to visit.

Chapter 40

REFLECTIONS

By mid-1960, Everett and Miriam were back home on North Leonard Drive. Seated around a table in their basement, they joined the ESEA board in considering the launch of Operation Long Underwear, a campaign that would provide shoes, socks, school uniforms, and cotton long underwear for thousands of boys and girls.

I don't know, Doc Hemwall said. We may be going to the well once too often.

Everett leaned forward. And what would you do for your own daughters, Doc? If they were dying of thirst, you'd try over and over to get them even one sip of water.

You know my long-running support of this ministry, Doc countered.

I don't disagree with the idea as much as with the timing. The sponsors give each month, many contribute to projects such as last year's blanket fund, and most also sent birthday and Christmas gifts to their orphans.

Do we have a choice? Miriam said. These are orphans, Doc, beautiful little children. You really ought to see them. I mean, how can we look away?

We've already upped the monthly commitment to $8.

Are we going to start using guilt tactics next? another board member challenged.

Guilt? No, Everett said, that is never our intent. I'm well aware of sponsors who cannot give another dime. Some are living on pensions and facing hospital bills.

My point exactly, someone said, huffing.

I'll state clearly in the letter, there is no obligation. But we have many who ask what more they can do. They have the means and they've discovered the true joy of giving.

Plus, the children, Miriam reminded everyone. Isn't that what this is about?

While Chicago sweltered in a summer heat wave, the board agreed to launch Operation Long Underwear. Mailers went out, ads ran in various periodicals, and the ministry was featured in a number of magazines. As visibility spread beyond North America, the donations came pouring in, and by Christmas, over six thousand orphans directly benefited.

As of January 1, 1961, ESEA was supporting nearly seven thousand children in over ninety homes. The annual income had doubled during the previous year, reaching $455,145, with over four thousand sponsors onboard.

Didn't I say it? Miriam patted Everett's chest. God has so much more.

* * *

At dawn, Everett parked outside the Hemwall home and found Doc in his garage, moving aside his daughters' outgrown playthings, rummaging around for fishing lures. One end of a Slinky toppled from a shelf and accordioned toward the floor.

Need some help? Everett said.

Doc glanced over his wire rims. Almost ready. Go on and throw your pole and tackle box into my vehicle. It's open. Got a thermos of your favorite behind the seat. If you need sugar added, my wife will get you situated. She's already up.

Ten minutes later, the two men were headed north toward Wisconsin. A perfect day ahead, as far as Everett was concerned—some fishing, then pan-fried brookies over a fire. Beside him, Doc seemed distracted, tapping on the steering wheel.

What's on your mind? Everett ventured.

I'm what, five years older than you, Everett? Gets a man to wondering if his time here's been well spent. I've helped with the ministry, even given free physicals for various missionaries back on furlough. Truth is, though, my original desire was to be in medical missions someday.

So, what's standing in your way?

Doc checked his rearview mirror. My wife never wanted me off gallivanting around the world. Told me she didn't marry me to become a widow and raise our children alone.

Perhaps, Everett noted, it's a matter of timing. Your girls are grown now.

Doc shrugged. I've been successful in my field. Then I look at how you've walked by faith, wandering through war zones, burning the midnight oil for the orphans. I don't want to live my life selfishly, don't want that to be my legacy.

No one would call you selfish, Doc.

Day I get to heaven, Doc continued, I want to arrive empty-handed. I want there to be nothing left to give.

They crossed the state line into Wisconsin, stopped to refuel, and

Everett poured himself some Postum from the thermos. Back on the road, they passed a Sunbeam Bread billboard, then headed west through wooded valleys in the direction of Fort McCoy.

Say, Doc, weren't you based there before World War II?

How do you think I learned all the best fishing spots? Another twenty miles away is where the brookies run thickest. I used to bring my daughters fishing up here when they were still little. Judith's now finishing pre-med studies at Wheaton, and my others aren't far behind. You know, Everett, you could be right. I might soon be able to travel more.

I'm going back to Korea in the fall. Why don't you join me?

I'll keep that in mind. By the way, have you thought of Sally going over with you? She'd be a great help in the orphanages, on the medical side of things.

Sally, my niece?

She attended Wheaton with Judith, and she's now nursing at West Suburban with me. She's excellent with patients, very responsible. And pretty as she is, she still won't let a man within a foot of her. You'd have no worries in that regard.

Everett chuckled. Well, things are a lot different in Korea than in an upscale hospital. Supplies are hard to come by and she'd be dealing with the poorest of the poor.

A good nurse is a good nurse.

Hmm, wonder what my older brother would think of my stealing his daughter away on such a mission. I'll run it by Miriam since she's spent time over there. John Seong might also have some insights.

Doc aimed his vehicle off the highway onto a dirt road. Springs and metal creaked as a pothole bounced the two men in their seats.

Puts me right back on the roads in Korea, Everett joked.

Slowing a bit, Doc said, Is John still putting together an ESEA office for us?

It's been on hold with his upcoming wedding, but he'll be back at it in a few weeks.

Ah, glad to hear it. With the ministry doubling in size, you've had more on your shoulders than any one man should carry. I know I've said it to you before, but I am saying this now as your friend, Everett. Stress can severely affect your health.

I've been taking breaks when needed.

Doc shot him a look. And would Miriam corroborate that statement?

I'm going fishing with you, aren't I?

Even so, Everett, delegating tasks to John will be an important step. It'll allow you to concentrate on other matters. This isn't the little ministry you once ran from your Sterling account book, not anymore. As president, you've got to step back and take a wider view.

Speaking of views, Everett said, pointing through the trees at the river-bend, where placid green pools reflected glittering shards of sunlight.

My secret spot, Doc said. We should have the place all to ourselves.

He coasted to a stop along the bank. Both men fetched rods and tackle from the back, kidding each other about who would catch the first and the fattest fish.

Before I win this, Everett said, I ought to thank you, Doc. For sticking by me. For telling me what I need to hear. Miriam and I, we truly value the relationship between our families, and I won't forget your suggestions about John and Sally.

Doc pulled on his fishing vest. I'm telling you, Sally could be a godsend.

* * *

In Daegu, in late March, John Seong and his bride said their vows before over five hundred friends, relatives, politicians, orphanage directors, and missionaries. John's pastor from Suncheon officiated, declaring them man and wife. John wore a dark suit and tie, a boutonniere, and a self-assured smile. At his side, his bride was stunning in a white headpiece, flowing veil, and gown. Her face was a vision of fragile beauty, framed by dark wavy hair and shaped eyebrows. Her bouquet was cradled in small, white-gloved hands.

Following the reception, Mr. and Mrs. Seong honeymooned in Seoul.

Everett later placed a long-distance call and confirmed his friend's genuine happiness. Did you get the gift we sent? Miriam and I wish we could've been there.

We felt your love, Everett. Thank you.

How about we take you out for a meal, the four of us, the next time we fly over?

Some South Jeolla food, John agreed. The best in all of Korea. There's a good restaurant here in Seoul, very authentic to my province.

I appreciate all your efforts at the ESEA office, John. And I know your wife is busy working at the hospital. May God's favor shine upon the two of you. You know, we have our grandson here in the States, but we'd be proud to have a Korean grandchild as well.

We're too busy for a baby, I think. Between her nursing and my field work.

Oh, no pressure. Whenever that day comes.

With John setting up office in Seoul, Everett was now able to relinquish many duties he'd done from afar. No longer was he the first person the directors called for disaster relief, repair loans, staffing challenges, and medical emergencies. John now handled all of these and more. Whether tackling logistics, finances, or sponsor communication, the young Korean took initiative. He was comfortable with people from all walks of life—army generals, political figures, and religious leaders—and the teams he formed rarely broke into factions.

Everett, you seem happy, Miriam observed as they crawled into bed one night.

Having John over there is truly a relief. I'll be able to focus once again on traveling, speaking, and finding sponsors. The orphans are my life. And little Jeffrey, of course!

He'll be over tomorrow. He's a little live wire, Miriam said, turning off the bedside lamp. And Sharon tells me she already wants another baby. I'm exhausted just thinking about it.

In the darkness Everett thanked the Lord for new life. Even natural disasters and human free will could not stop God's goodness. Typhoons, wars, uprisings—amid tragedy, God had a way of bringing about redemption. He worked all things together for good.

Reflecting on the subjects he and Doc had discussed during their fishing trip, Everett wondered what sort of legacy he himself was creating. If his time were short, if he had only months to live, was there anything different he would be doing?

No. He'd just do it all with more gusto!

Chapter 41

AT A COST

In the fall of 1961, Korea faced another season of snow and raging winds. Encouraged by the success of recent campaigns, ESEA beseeched its donors for Winter Aid Relief Money.

WARM met a familiar yet vital need, providing jackets, pants, socks, and long underwear to thousands in the orphanages. Rev. Swanson did his part to spread the word. He made a circuit of churches, schools, and camps, presenting the ongoing needs of those across the ocean, making the realities as tangible as possible for his listeners.

He described mountains, mythical tigers, and wooden huts by icy rivers.

And the children—always the children.

Everett's own kids were grown now, making family road trips a thing of the past. One weekend, after completing his speaking circuit, he and Miriam packed bags into their used Hillman—another bargain from the car dealer in the church—and headed to DeKalb County. Father and Mother were gone, but Miriam still had her parents in Sycamore, and Everett had his brother Les nearby.

Good to see the two of you, Les greeted them. What can I carry in?

Les was lean in body, gentle in spirit. He was that rare person with a gift for both numbers and people. Ever supportive of Everett's ministry, Les had stepped up on many occasions to give monetarily and even sing at ESEA events.

As the two brothers settled into chairs on the front porch that afternoon, Everett said, So, Les, what about letting me steal your daughter away?

His older brother raised an eyebrow. Excuse me?

I'd like for Sally to work with us in Korea.

As a nurse? Les shrugged. She's certainly qualified. You know her, though, she has a mind of her own. She's in her room. If she's amenable to the idea, neither I nor her mother will stand in her way.

George arrived home as Everett rose from the couch.

Well, look at you. Everett gripped his nephew's hand. You twenty now?

Almost twenty-one.

A grown man, Miriam said, joining them.

I wanted to thank both of you, George said. That check you sent me while I was in Grand Rapids, that was a real surprise. Sorry I didn't stick with it. I'm still interested in ministry, but sitting in Bible school just wasn't my thing.

God uses each of us in different ways, Everett said.

Minutes later, he found his twenty-six-year-old niece seated by her bedroom window, her ears tuned to Moody Bible Institute on the radio. Sally's gaze was steady over wide cheekbones and a winsome smile.

She had a presence about her, attractive without drawing attention, mature beyond her years.

Sally, I hear you'd like to be a missionary nurse, Everett ventured.

She faced him from her chair. I believe it's my calling, yes.

I believe it too, which is why I'd like you to consider working for ESEA in South Korea. Yes, you have the Swanson name, but that won't automatically grant you the job. I will need to know you are prepared.

I'll jump through any hoops necessary, Uncle Everett.

It won't be easy. You'll cross the Pacific and set up in a small apartment near some of our missionary friends. You'll enroll in Korean language courses once you arrive—something I could've benefited from—and then you will start coordinating medical aid for our homes and orphanages. This means a long-term investment on your part, perhaps years before you can return here to see your parents.

She nodded. There's a personal cost. I do understand that.

A calling always comes at a cost, that's true. But oh, Sally, the rewards!

Her solemn expression cracked into a grin.

Now, I know you're smart, he went on. You've completed courses at Bethel and Wheaton, and Doc Hemwall says positive stuff about your nursing training at the hospital.

Doc's a good man, Sally noted. And a godly one.

In Korea, though, you'll face very different circumstances—supply shortages, mysterious illnesses, children with severe trauma. There's also an aspect of social work. Distant relatives show up and want to take a kid. Or even worse, drop one off.

I've had to be firm before, Sally said. It's part of the job.

Everett pushed his sleeves to his elbows. I believe it would be wise for you, Sally, to work first in an urban area to get a sense of what's ahead. There's a current opening in Chicago's Public Health Department. You'll need to apply on your own, of course. If you get the job, you'll carry a clipboard and make rounds in a nurse's uniform to help newborns in Cabrini-Green.

Sally's eyes widened but remained fixed on his.

It's a dangerous neighborhood, he went on. Much like you'd encounter in parts of Korea. Still something you're interested in?

Sally's lips pressed flat, and she gave a hard nod.

Everett pumped his fist in the air. Praise the Lord!

I will earn your trust, Uncle Everett. I will. Considering I've had George as a younger brother, I'm not one to back down easily.

They both chuckled.

Listen, Sally, if you see or hear anything that truly disturbs you, either here or in Korea, you can always come to me. Don't be afraid to speak up. I'll watch over you like my own daughter, you understand?

I know you will, she said. Thank you for this opportunity.

He smiled wider, reminded of a favorite theme of his. He believed when God gave you a shot at something, you had a responsibility to take hold and see the opportunity through. He had no doubt his niece would do just that.

As he settled into the driver's seat of the Hillman the next day, Rev. Swanson was at peace. This was one more burden off his back. Despite the growing challenges in Korea, he could trust his niece to make wise and measured decisions once she got there.

Indeed, Sally Swanson would play a pivotal role in the days ahead.

Chapter 42

THE SUMMONS

Army tanks patrolled the streets of Seoul, and soldiers bearing rifles stood guard at strategic points. The military had staged a coup in May and placed the nation under martial law. Citizens hurried past, eyes lowered, chins down.

Rev. Swanson was no stranger to such maneuvers. During the Korean War, he had witnessed his share of weapons and force. He'd visited the wounded and amputees, seen dead bodies, shallow graves, and wooden tomb markers. Nevertheless, as he made his sixth visit to the country in September 1961, he couldn't deny the oppressive mood in the air.

Just last year, hadn't he and Miriam been present during an uprising? *Lord, I'm in your hands.*

Met by John Seong at Gimpo International, Everett followed his friend onto a bus from the airport into the capital. He carried only his suitcase, garment bag, and notebook of sermons.

Doc Hemwall couldn't travel with you? John asked. I wanted to meet him.

A busy man. I'm sure he'll make it soon enough.

Since my wedding, I've put together a small office staff, John said. They're good men and women, very committed to what we're doing. But I don't have the funds to pay them.

Everett rested a hand on his shoulder. Don't worry, John. I came prepared.

In fact, he carried over $100,000 with him—$66,000 in WARM contributions so that over six thousand ESEA orphans could get two winter outfits each, and an additional $36,000 for administrative and medical concerns.

This is good news, John said, a smile brightening his face. In a quieter voice, he added, Our office is serving an important role, considering the situation with our government.

Is it safe for me to be traveling? Things turned quickly last spring.

John shrugged. You're personally safe, I think. It's the orphanages I worry about. This new leadership promises us fresh morality and a self-sustaining economy. Who doesn't want that? But they also insist all Korean children be raised in private homes instead of orphan homes.

An honorable goal, Everett said. But where do they plan to put tens of thousands of kids?

They say they're arranging domestic adoption and foster-care projects. Which could take years.

This is where our office can help, John said. Yes, ESEA will get some temporary pushback, but my staff and I will smooth over these difficulties. You've been wise, Everett, to rely on Korean directors instead of imposing your own personnel from America. Your many years here have earned you favor in the eyes of our leaders.

You don't think we'll be shut down, then?

We'll tiptoe along, John said. Eventually, these troubles will pass.

* * *

In late October, days before Everett's flight home, he toured an unsupported orphanage with its director. Would ESEA consider providing aid? Conditions here were appalling, the kids barefoot and in rags, but the tour was cut short by the arrival of a messenger bearing a summons.

Rev. Swanson was wanted back in Seoul.

Looks like I need to go, he said.

The director tried to hide his disappointment. You will come back?

Everett made no promises. He was wanted at the Blue House, the presidential residence in the capital. He had never been there before, and though he couldn't decipher everything in the letter, he knew it was serious business. His mind grew cloudy with doubts, even trepidation.

Are you alright? John asked, strolling toward him.

Everett handed over the summons. Still stunned, he wondered if this was the end. After his decade of visits to Korea, after all the time and money invested, would he be asked to leave and never return? It was a distinct possibility. This peninsula had endured centuries of invasion, deception, and betrayal at the hands of outsiders. Why should he be viewed as anything less than a threat? Korea had every right to pull back and become a hermit kingdom once more.

What about the kids, though? Would troops take over ESEA homes? *Please, God, don't let that happen.*

This is not good, John said, holding the summons to his chest. Next to him, the director frowned. You don't have much time, Everett.

What!

You'll need a dark formal suit, not this wrinkly thing you have on. My tailor is the best, able to work quickly. Hurry, we must go get your measurements.

I don't . . . what's this all about? What do they want?

President Yun has summoned you to the Blue House.

I read that part, but—

He will be awarding you the Public Welfare Medal. This is a rare honor, don't you see? Only a handful from outside our nation have ever received it. There will be a ceremony, dignitaries, photos. No, this suit of yours will not do.

Everett wanted to laugh and cry. A suit's all I have to worry about?

No offense, my friend, but you need more style.

I try to be frugal, John. You know that. I've never had a custom-made suit.

In our country this is important. We must get to work.

Still amazed at the idea of getting a medal instead of a swift kick out of the country, Everett submitted himself to professional measurements. A suit was made in record time, a perfect fit, and John slapped bills into the tailor's hand. He then combed back Everett's silver-streaked hair, propped his dark-rimmed glasses on his nose, and pronounced him ready to go.

On a Wednesday at the Blue House, Rev. Swanson stood with arms stiff at his sides as prominent figures mingled around him.

What was he doing here? This wasn't all for him, was it?

A gentleman stepped forward and introduced himself as the minister of health and social affairs. Everett warmed up, realizing this fellow could be a great contact for ESEA and for Sally once she arrived in Korea.

At last, it was time for the ceremony.

Everett's heart thumped against his ribs. Could anyone else hear it pounding? He was called forward and situated beside the podium for the presentation of a certificate. As attendees applauded, the official document was pressed into his hands. It read, in both Korean and English:

OFFICE OF THE PRESIDENT
Republic of Korea
25 October, 1961
CITATION

In recognition and appreciation of his outstanding and meritorious service, I take great pleasure, in accordance with the powers delegated to me by the Constitution of the Republic of Korea, in awarding the PUBLIC WELFARE MEDAL to REV. EVERETT F. SWANSON. Rev. Swanson, evangelist and social worker, first visited our country during the Korean conflict in 1951 to observe and promote missionary work here.

Deeply touched by the plight of thousands of children, widows and wounded veterans who were innocent victims of this terrible war, he immediately appealed for help to the people of the United States of America. He also toured the front lines to preach the gospel to both Korean and United Nations servicemen, giving them comfort and stimulating their morale.

For ten years, Rev. Swanson's devoted and unceasing activity on behalf of the Korean people has never wavered. He has not only exerted every effort in the construction of numerous welfare institutions and churches throughout the country but has provided the scholarship for needy students.

Rev. Swanson's warm-hearted humanitarianism and dedicated interest in the spiritual, social and physical welfare of our people, especially for our children, have earned our abiding appreciation, and his unselfish ministrations as a true apostle will never be forgotten.

Cameras flashed as President Yun stepped toward him and pinned the public welfare medal to the lapel of Everett's tailored suit. Everett told the president he didn't feel worthy, since a host of others had helped accomplish this. Above all, God had made it possible.

May God bless you, the president responded. I am an earnest believer, and our master of ceremonies is also a Christian.

Everett smiled. Then I will challenge him to use his influence in this high office.

President Yun gave a nod before being whisked away.

* * *

By the time Rev. Swanson arrived back in the US, the award and the ministry were already receiving attention. A reporter from Chicago's *American* insisted on doing an interview. When the fellow asked about the ministry's origins, Everett shrugged.

You know, I started out as a preacher and stumbled onto something that's now the tail wagging the dog. My only regret is I didn't begin sooner.

Why's that? The reporter's pencil hovered over his notepad.

There are still hundreds of children being rounded up off the streets, Everett replied. On this latest trip, I inspected thirty-five orphanages with no foreign support. That's over twenty-five hundred youngsters! The poor directors are pleading for help, facing bitter weather in miserable shacks. We've approved ten of the homes, which brings our total roster to a hundred and nine. We'll take more as soon as we can.

Who pays for all this relief work?

Our wonderful sponsors. We've raised over $700,000 this year for over ten thousand orphans and two hundred evangelists. Nearly 90 percent of every dollar is sent straight to Korea.

The reporter scribbled furiously.

Chapter 43

SPECIAL EDITION

Miriam Swanson was getting back her home at North Leonard Drive. It was August 1, 1962, and the office in the Swansons' basement was moving to an official location only a few miles away.

Has it really been that rough? Everett asked her.

Miriam shot him a look. For ten years, Everett, I've willingly surrendered the basements, stairways, hallways, and driveways of two separate addresses for the good of the ministry.

You've been a trouper, he agreed.

And I've been with you every step of the way. But yes, at times it's been rough. I've mopped more men's muddy shoe prints than I care to count.

Well, those days are over. Are you ready for the dedication?

The building project launched earlier in the year was now complete at 7774 West Irving Park Road, Chicago, Illinois. ESEA's humble startup had defied all odds and now filled a single-level office structure with modern machines and accounting systems. Employing staff from multiple nations and denominations, it was a truly holistic ministry that educated minds, healed bodies, and saved souls.

This would be its headquarters for years to come.

* * *

In the fall of 1962, Sally Swanson said her goodbyes and departed for South Korea. As requested by Everett the previous year, she had served in the Cabrini-Green housing project, saving her money and paying her dues. While others her age dived into political activism or married and settled down, she winnowed through her belongings and packed her luggage.

Sally's freighter embarked from Oakland, California, passed beneath the Golden Gate Bridge, and steamed into the Pacific on a monthlong voyage. She suffered terrible seasickness along the way, which she found frustrating since the food onboard was excellent. The freighter also caught the edges of a typhoon. Tossed back and forth on her bunk, she wondered how her belongings were doing. She had crates, suitcases, even a refrigerator down in the hold.

After a stop in Japan, her journey reached its end in Busan harbor, where evening lights illuminated giant cranes and container ships. Sally rode a night launch from the freighter to the dock, where she was greeted by the ministry's new field director, Mr. Robert Morgan.

He's such a kind man, Sally told Everett over the phone.

Everett was on the ground in Korea himself. Presently in Seoul, he'd already covered many miles with Mr. Morgan and John Seong, preaching, vetting orphanages, meeting with high-ranking officials, home directors, local evangelists—and the children themselves, of course.

Boy, Sally, I'm sorry you got sick. I've never made the trip by boat.

The Lord was with me all the way, she said. Did I mention the surprise Mr. Morgan brought to the dock? Sally's voice caught with emotion over the phone. He had a little orphan girl with him, the one I've been sponsoring for years.

That's wonderful!

I adore her, Uncle Everett. I just can't get enough of her.

As he listened to his niece, Everett realized she had many more adjustments ahead. Before getting her own place, she would house with some missionaries in Seoul and take language classes at prestigious Yonsei University. She would also learn how to negotiate public transport, buy food in stores and restaurants, and deal with the roaming street beggars. Poverty was still evident everywhere.

I can't wait for you to visit our orphanages, Everett said. John Seong, our man here in Seoul, he'll arrange a driver for you. Be ready for some deep-rutted roads and washed out bridges. You wouldn't even make it to many of the homes without a jeep or Land Rover.

Sounds like quite the adventure.

Afterward, I feel like I've gone ten rounds with a heavyweight champ, Everett said. These visits are important, though. You'll get to practice your language and medical skills while building rapport with directors and volunteers.

I look forward to meeting them, Sally said.

Oh, they're such dedicated, selfless people. And generous, when given a chance. They'll treat you to more rice and bulgogi than you can possibly eat.

I'm sure I'll love the diet here.

Thing is, Sally, we have nearly a hundred and fifty orphanages now. Government restrictions have tightened, so we need to standardize our health services. If there's something you're disturbed by, let Mr. Morgan know. If that doesn't work, call me. You and the local nurses can dispense medicine and vitamins, give immunizations, and treat children for their various ailments—scabies, tuberculosis, rickets, to name a few. You'll see your share of amputated limbs and severe malnutrition.

It will be a challenge, she admitted. It's the reason I came.

Then welcome to South Korea, Sally!

* * *

The world was in turmoil, with the Cold War on everyone's minds. Spies and intrigue lurked behind every headline. Earlier in the year, John

Glenn had been the first American to orbit the earth, and now Russian missiles had been discovered in Cuba, a hop and a skip from Florida.

What was next? Would the Russians invade? Was nuclear war imminent?

Amid the fearmongering and sensationalism, Rev. Swanson sensed it was time for a change within the ministry. It had relocated its offices and shed the trappings of the Swanson home. Wasn't it also time to shed the Swanson name?

Everett Swanson Evangelistic Association.

It was a mouthful.

Plus, it no longer encompassed their full mission, and it implied a ministry built around one person—the furthest thing from the truth. Everett had no ego attached to this. He'd be helpless without his family, sponsors, and the directors in Korea.

It was definitely time for a change. And Miriam agreed.

For clarity alone, he would keep his name listed as the founder, so supporters knew its direction had not changed in any way. Caring for the children and preaching the gospel were two pillars from which this ministry would never be shaken.

Needing Doc's approval to revise the name in the bylaws, Everett dictated a letter to him from the Seoul office. Best to speed up the process and make a year-end shift possible. He told Doc his idea for the name change, something more evocative, something that stirred the heart. He thanked Doc for his work back in the Chicago office and let him know he was praying for the day when Doc could see the work in Korea for himself.

Everett sealed the envelope. You mind putting this in the mail for me, John?

John Seong poked his head in from the main office next door, took the letter from Everett, and slipped it into his jacket. He was dressed sharp as always.

Everything alright? Everett asked. You like the new name?

John hesitated in the doorway, then nodded. Yes, it translates better.

You know, I want to make the big announcement in a special booklet, a tenth-anniversary tribute to everyone who's made this ministry possible. I'd love any pictures or documents you believe would fit. You have a good eye for photos.

I might need it very soon, John said cryptically. At home.

Everett gave him a blank look.

My wife will soon want lots of baby pictures. I am going to be a father.

Oh, that's marvelous! Congratulations.

I would stay to tell you more, John added with a wry grin, but the boss says I need to go mail this letter.

* * *

Doc Hemwall's signature made the name change official, and the tenth-anniversary booklet made it public weeks later. This special edition of the newsletter opened with details of ESEA's history, background, and progress, then described daily orphanage life in 157 homes, where 1,400 directors and staff members cared for nearly 17,000 children. They were doing good things. Lives were being transformed. Many national and foreign missionaries also volunteered.

Before-and-after photos showed beggar boys with threadbare clothes and matted hair now sporting clean outfits and combed heads.

A girl with a huge smile wore a hooded, fur-lined coat.

A younger girl held a ball and stuffed bear.

Among those who had received care in ESEA homes, five had become pastors, twenty-seven were evangelists, forty-seven were seminary students, 140 had graduated from college, and 750 served in the military. A snapshot provided by John showed two orphans in uniform, chaplains in the Korean armed forces.

ESEA also supported over three hundred Korean evangelists as they preached and passed out literature. One of them, a blind fellow, crossed streams and walked through bad weather, taking revival to backslidden churches. He stood next to Everett in a photo, both men smiling.

Other photos and bylines described the annual fall Bible conference, which had taken place during Rev. Swanson's visit to Daegu. Six American and Korean pastors spoke. A six-hundred-strong children's choir performed. Prayer meetings, Bible sessions, and nightly evangelistic services made it a memorable event.

Near the back of the booklet were photos of the staff in Chicago.

The staff at the Korean office was also pictured: Mr. Morgan, field director; Mrs. Morgan, his wife; John Seong, field secretary; and a number of college aides. Joining them in the front row was registered nurse Sally Swanson.

In conclusion this special edition booklet made an announcement that would change the face of the ministry:

> For ten years this challenge of caring for Korea's uncared-for children has been identified with the name of the man whose pledge God accepted literally, at face value. During these ten years, however, a vast multitude have joined Mr. Swanson and his associates in this unique ministry. It was compassion which moved the Savior when He saw the multitudes without a shepherd, and truly it is compassion which best describes the impulse to give Korean orphans a chance.

> Since compassion, in all its depth and power, most nearly speaks of the spirit and work of this association, its leaders feel that henceforth, from January 1, 1963, it should be known as COMPASSION.

It was time for Everett Swanson to decrease in stature, time for God's work to increase. His prayer was for greater compassion, for the compassion Jesus had for the multitudes.

The compassion to suffer with.

Chapter 44

PACK YOUR BAGS

By January 1, 1963, Compassion was a million-dollar ministry. In the past twelve months, its income had exceeded $1,229,000. Now, with a Christian ad agency enlisted, Rev. Swanson expected the upward trend to continue. Canada was a major contributor, second only to the United States. Early supporters Bob and Janet Forsyth had been chartered to open a Compassion office in their Ontario home. They were travel agents, sponsors, and key elements in the ministry's plans for expansion.

For Everett, none of this was about growth, dollars, and numbers. It was about orphans, widows, and beggar boys.

As he traveled across North America, he realized most supporters pictured orphan homes filled with only toddlers and elementary-school kids. In truth, many children were nearing adulthood, and their directors wished to teach them vocational skills. Going to America for adoption had never been Everett's goal for them. If they could be productive citizens in their own culture, they would have a hand in the rebirth of their fertile land.

With these things in mind, Everett contacted a Korean official.

I have an idea for you. Being a farmboy myself once, I know good soil when I see it, and your peninsula has so much potential. Thing is, typhoons and tidal waves have battered the coastal regions. What if we reclaimed some of that area?

Help me understand, Reverend, how does this involve Compassion?

You have hundreds of flooded acres, don't you? Give some of our older orphans an acre each to tend and develop, then let them reap the rewards.

And how does this benefit us?

Your national produce increases, your citizens have jobs. Instead of beggars on the streets, you have workers in the fields.

The official paused. Yes, it is good. I now understand the concept.

Wherever he went, Everett faced this challenge of helping others see what he envisioned. Couldn't an actual movie do the job for him? He spoke to an ad agency about creating a 16mm film—a story in full color, not a documentary—that captured an orphan's struggles and offered a hopeful resolution.

Love it! the agency responded.

I'm going back to Korea in October for the Bible conference. What if you send over a crew? I'll meet them, show them around, and they can film outside Seoul.

Great. It'll require funding and equipment, of course.

Not to mention a director, script, and cast.

You sound as though you've done this before, Rev. Swanson.

My oldest brother, he's done movies for years with Moody.

After a lively meeting, Compassion board members also caught Everett's zeal for the film. A Hollywood producer joined in, a screen-writer went to work, and crew travel plans were made. Everett believed a movie was the sort of tool that could hook American imaginations.

In August, however, his excitement was tempered by news that Ray Swanson, his brother, had died at age fifty-eight. This was Ray, the same brother who'd provided early guidance and inspiration for Everett's film work. Ray, who had introduced him to Pastor Johnson, the man responsible for handing over the $50 check that had launched this ministry.

Now, Ray was gone.

In his brother's honor, Everett pressed onward with the film project.

* * *

Providing a much-needed element of joy, Doc Hemwall decided to accompany Everett on his fall trip to Korea.

You're pulling my leg, Everett said.

Doc's eyes twinkled behind his glasses. Not this time. I have cut back on hours at the hospital and semi-retired. My wife's nearly as excited as I am. She knows it's been my dream all these years.

Hallelujah, Doc! This is incredible.

I'll finally meet the orphans for myself. And it'll be great to visit with Sally. She's awfully brave, that girl, pulling up stakes and moving halfway around the globe.

We might also see John's baby, Everett added. He's had a healthy little boy.

Less than a month before their departure, another name was added to the entourage:

Bob Swaney.

Bob was a Chicagoan who'd been introduced to Everett through a mutual acquaintance. A seasoned pro in the world of nonprofits, Bob had worked six years with Gideons International, traveling in Asia and Latin America. Gideons was now moving its headquarters out of Chicago, and Bob didn't like the thought of dragging his family away.

Boy, Everett told him, we could use someone with your experience.

Gotta say, I've heard nothing but good things about Compassion.

We met for a reason, don't you think? Come work with us.

Everett, I like your style, Bob said with a throaty laugh. No dragging your feet.

That's right. It seems life has been speeding up these past few years, both at home and in Compassion. Who knows how long the Lord will tarry? If the finish line's not yet in sight, it seems just around the corner.

Finish line? Bob countered. Nah, Compassion's just gaining momentum. I've been at this business a long time—and yes, Everett, as noble-minded as you are, it's a business. I'm looking at untapped potential here. And lots of it!

Within weeks, Bob Swaney was assistant executive director at Compassion. He would assist in national matters, while also directing public relations. As much as he admired Everett's humble spirit, he believed they could angle for better advertising rates and larger markets.

Gotta swing for the fences, Bob insisted. Think bigger!

Alright, Everett said. First, though, I want you to see our work on the ground.

In Korea? I'm game.

Pack your bags, then. This'll be your orientation field trip.

* * *

It was mid-October when Compassion's president, secretary-treasurer, and assistant executive director landed in Seoul, hungry and jet-lagged. To adjust to the new time zone, Everett suggested they avoid naps and stay awake till evening.

As long as we can grab a bite, Doc said.

My blood sugar's running low, Bob agreed.

I know just the man who'll lead us to a good restaurant. John Seong should still be at the Compassion office, not far away. We'll make a tour of the building, then treat him to dinner.

The hungry trio arrived unannounced at the office, where a photo of Rev. Swanson hung framed in the entryway. Men in collared shirts stopped cranking out flyers on their mimeograph machines. College-age women in dresses stopped typing sponsor communications mid-sentence. Many stood and bowed. Everett, Doc, and Bob took time shaking hands with over two dozen stunned workers.

Everett then led Doc and Bob up the stairs, leaving behind the hum of activity on the first floor. He passed Mr. Morgan's empty office. The field director handled most of his business from Daegu, where he lived.

The main office here belonged to John Seong.

Everett burst through the door, intending to surprise his old friend. There sat John, slim and handsome, with six telephones in a line on his wide wooden desk. Each phone was a different color, the red one currently held to his ear. At the sight of his visitors, John banged down the receiver and jumped up. He and Everett exchanged hugs and hearty pats on the back, sharing words about the new baby boy.

Meet John Seong, Everett said, turning. He's been our field secretary for the past seven years and now serves as Korean director. He's a leader in spiritual matters, and many say he could run for political office. There's no better man around.

You made it safely, John said. Welcome, welcome!

Six phones? Bob nodded at the desk.

This one's for my wife. This here, this is for the office in Chicago. This, for the Korean minister of health and . . . Forgive me, gentlemen. What are your names?

Doc Hemwall.

Doc! John bowed. I've heard so much about you.

And I'm Bob Swaney. The new guy on the block, just soaking it all in.

John spread his arms wide. Three American gentlemen in my office. It is my honor, truly. I plan someday to do further university studies in your country. But you're not interested in this, not after hours on a plane. Let me treat you to a meal, delicious bibimbap from my province.

Lead the way, Everett said. As the boss, I will pay. Isn't that how it works here in Korea?

Thank you, Everett. Yes. And while we eat, I'd like to suggest something that could bring in a whole new batch of sponsors and tens of thousands of dollars. A big idea.

You hear that, Bob? Everett grinned. I think you and John will get along.

Bob leaned forward. Think bigger, I like it. Tell us more.

Imagine, John said, spreading his arms. An orphan choir on tour in North America!

* * *

Before the Korea trip ended in November, it offered rich rewards.

Everett met with old friends—Dr. van Lierop, Rev. Rice, Mr. Morgan, even Sally, who was nearly conversant in Korean. He also coordinated the 16mm film, titled *Runaway*, a tale of an orphan who flees after his sponsor dies. Scenes were shot at Fragrant Forest Orphanage.

As for Doc Hemwall, he got his return on years of personal investment. He met orphans and directors. He toured temples and monuments. He and Sally also strategized on improving health conditions and procedures throughout the network of homes. It was his first but certainly not his last taste of doing the medical missions he aspired to.

Bob Swaney, new in his role, observed a ministry committed to its children. He encountered faithful directors and staff, while also noting the danger of people sneaking in with their own agendas, gearing things toward personal gain. With an experienced eye for trouble, he dedicated himself to watching Everett's back.

For all the participants, this fall tour was a success. Compassion was clearly making strides, with homes well-managed, field offices well-staffed, and nursing care better than ever.

Spreading the word's the next step, Bob said. I'm excited to get to work.

Between your ideas and John's, Doc noted, I have no doubt things will expand quickly.

Just one thing left to do here, Everett reminded them. I admit, I'm a bit nervous.

Chapter 45

ABOUT TO BREAK

The next day, dressed in their best suits, Everett, Doc, and Bob strolled along the banks of the Han River, where trees shivered in the breeze and sprinkled leaves across the path. They reached Konkuk University, one of the city's leading private institutions. Due to Japanese opposition, the university hadn't become official until 1946, but was one of the peninsula's fastest growing.

Today, Rev. Swanson had a speech to give.

May my words bring glory to You, Lord.

He was also receiving an honorary doctorate for his meritorious contributions and cultural advancements in South Korea. This degree, later reported in the Chicago newspapers, was signed by the university's president. The school's stated virtues—sincerity, fidelity, and righteousness—were ones Everett himself did his best to embody.

During his address, he highlighted Proverbs 9:10, "The fear of the LORD is the beginning of wisdom." He noted that wisdom came from God, and God alone deserved honor.

His speech was tinged with a bit of irony, considering it was delivered on the banks of the Han River where Christians were beheaded a century earlier for the faith he now proclaimed.

* * *

Back in Chicago, Bob Swaney got right to work. He streamlined operations at 7774 West Irving Park Road, Compassion headquarters, and suggested more secure ways of handling the finances. In short order, his experience fueled growth and revenue. He believed they should stop limiting Compassion's exposure to communities of faith. The time had come to go beyond displaying materials in church foyers. It wasn't only Christians who wanted to help.

Like I told you, he said to Everett. Time to . . .

Think big! Everett cried out.

Now you're getting it. I want to commit $15,000 for a spot in this month's *Reader's Digest*.

For a single ad?

It's one of the world's most popular publications, Bob said. You know, it all started with a dream back in 1922, a husband and wife in upstate New York. You were still a boy, but all this time, God's been bringing your paths together. You think I'm pulling your leg? You commit the money and just watch what God does.

A memory popped into Everett's head, of his son David cleaning Doc's medical office and straightening magazines in the waiting room. Copies of *Reader's Digest* were always front and center, the first to get picked up, the first to get read. Who didn't like all those witty anecdotes and heartwarming stories?

Alright, Bob, he said. I'll sign off on it.

Attaboy, Everett!

The ad ran immediately, in November 1963, with a mail-in sponsor form along the bottom corner. It explained how, for just thirty cents a month, a person could help lovely, yet destitute orphans receive necessities and education while being brought up in a nurturing Christian environment. The appeal was simple:

OUR GIFT TO NEW SPONSORS
A pair of lovely, colorful **Korean Baby Shoes**—
if you sponsor an orphan by December 1.

COMPASSION . . .
Cares for more than 20,000 Korean orphans.
Maintains 175 orphanages (includes 15 homes
for children of lepers; deaf, dumb, and blind children),
supervised by Bible-believing staff . . .

Provides more than 25,000,000 meals each year.

Awarded highest recognition by the Korean government.

* * *

Everett and the board at Compassion had also latched onto John Seong's idea of forming an orphan choir. If all went as planned, John and his wife would come next year with four orphans and lead them on a tour through Canada and the US, visiting schools, churches, and radio and TV stations. In Korean costumes, they would perform traditional songs and dances.

After all, who could resist the face of a child?

And what better way to educate people about the orphans overseas?

Music had long been part of Everett's ministry, since his days as the Singing Evangelist. He instructed his office staff to coordinate lodging, transportation, and an itinerary for the quartet. The office in Korea would select kids who were bright, assertive, and fit to travel.

I love it! Everett told John on an international call. This could become an annual event.

Between *Reader's Digest* and a North America tour, there were thousands, even millions, who would soon learn for the very first time of Compassion.

In terms of exposure, the dam was about to break.

Chapter 46

FLYING ARROWS

On January 1, 1964, the *Suburbanite Economist* reported the release of a 16mm film called *Runaway*. Available nationwide through film libraries, it was billed as a Korean orphan's heartrending story that would renew your faith. The movie came with a fold-out poster to display showtimes and locations.

Everett studied the child and the angled font on the cover.

He hoped his brother Ray would be proud.

Everett's own heart was heavy from news accounts of the past six weeks. Religious and political tensions were growing in Vietnam. A Pan Am flight had crashed in Maryland, killing all onboard. And the nation was still reeling from the assassination of John F. Kennedy. Everett longed for the days of Edward R. Murrow and his unbiased reporting. The news was filled instead with talk of conspiracies and coverups.

Where was the finish line? When would Jesus return?

Any day now, Everett figured. *And I'm ready!*

Meanwhile, of course, the relief work was only increasing. Responses still flooded in from *Reader's Digest*, and Everett signed off on additional ads for *Moody Monthly, Christian Life, Ladies' Home Journal, Good Housekeeping*, and *Christian Herald*. Each spot explained Compassion's work in simple terms for those who wished to participate.

Thanks to Bob Swaney, the Chicago office responsibly handled this influx of new sponsors. Honesty and transparency were top priorities, and as a result, Compassion earned high marks from the Better Business Bureau.

Pleased with this progress, Everett scheduled another trip to Korea with Doc Hemwall.

* * *

Why, look at you, Everett said, lifting his newspaper and nudging his travel companion. If it isn't Doc Hemwall, the globe-trotting physician. That's what they're calling you in this article.

Eyes closed, Doc leaned back in his window seat.

It's not every day a local doctor, and a Christian one at that, is featured in the news. Everett tilted his chin toward Doc. Young men and women will want to follow in your footsteps, serving in medical missions. Sally already thinks of you as a saint.

My wife could tell you otherwise.

Everett laughed. That goes for every husband on the planet. If it weren't for Miriam, I surely wouldn't have made it this far.

Do you always wax poetic while in flight? Doc gibed. I'd like to get some rest.

Their plane landed the next morning at Gimpo International. It was a clear spring day, a beautiful time of year, as Rev. Swanson and Doc Hemwall headed into the capital city. Magpies and red squirrels were chattering. Korean maples flashed orange and gold.

The Compassion Bible Conference was a highly anticipated event, with hundreds of evangelists, directors, and local ministers present.

Everett and others preached.

Doc shared his testimony.

John Seong interpreted and conducted the choir.

One of Compassion's sponsored evangelists was in attendance, a man named Kil-yong Choi, and he told Everett how he'd spread word of the event earlier, going door to door with gospel tracts, inviting all to come. At one home, the owner came out and cursed at Choi, threatening to pour water over his head if he didn't scram. At another, a man with badly swollen limbs asked for help, and Choi taught him how to pray to Jesus. The next day, the man said he had prayed, and look, he was healed!

Everett listened, trying to rejoice with Choi's stories.

In his gut, though, unease was stirring.

Off to the side, he noticed various directors approaching John and speaking to him in low voices. John seemed to brush them away, often brusquely. More than once the directors gestured in Everett's direction. Each time, John bristled, and his tone turned harsh. Though Everett couldn't understand the words spoken in Korean, he could read the body language just fine.

Yes, something was wrong.

I've never seen you mad before, he mentioned later to John. What were the directors saying to you? Is there something I need to address?

Rumors, John said. We don't have time for their poisonous talk. I will handle it.

Everett set a hand on the younger man's shoulder. As my Korean director, you have my full confidence, John. I love you like a son. Do you trust me?

Of course, Reverend.

What are these rumors, then? If they're so upsetting, we ought to dispel them right away.

John pulled Everett out of earshot of others. There are troubles at a children's home, a shortage in the monthly allotment received. Some directors think your office in America is cutting them short. I reacted strongly, telling them this isn't possible.

Our office operates with utmost integrity, Everett agreed.

Bob, your new assistant, could he be unfamiliar with the allotment procedures?

No, Bob is highly competent. He's been in this line of work a long time. Tell me, John, what do you think is going on?

I suspect the director has used the money for his own gain.

Director Kim? In Gimcheon? He's been with Compassion five years.

John shrugged. He bought a pear orchard for himself—this is what I've heard.

And you believe it's true?

The numbers don't lie. As I said, I'll handle it quietly.

Now, hold on, John. I like to think the best of everyone, especially my fellow Christians. I've asked directors to step down in years past, and will do so again if need be, but you and I, we ought to let this director explain himself.

After dinner, they called Director Kim to a meeting in a hotel room.

We've heard disturbing rumors, Everett told the director. I've invited John and a fellow pastor here as a witness, so tell us what's happened to the missing money at your home.

I've spent it to feed my children, the director replied.

John believes you used it to buy a pear orchard.

An orchard? If I've done such a thing, please show this to me. Where is it?

John stared over the man's shoulder, saying nothing.

I've done nothing wrong, Director Kim insisted. Go see for yourself, Rev. Swanson. My children are fed, my home is orderly. If my books show any money missing, perhaps a mistake was made, but I am innocent of this accusation.

Everett let the silence thicken. Who would crack first?

John cleared his throat. The money didn't just fade into thin air, Director Kim. The orchard theory seems the most likely.

So, you haven't seen this pear orchard? Everett asked John. It was only a guess?

John set his chin, offering no response.

We, as Christians, must do better than this, Everett said, adopting his most fatherly tone. It saddens me to find you believing ill of a brother, John, especially without going directly to him as Matthew chapter eighteen instructs us. We've now heard from Director Kim in the presence of two or three witnesses. Do you still think him guilty?

My apologies, Reverend. I shouldn't have jumped to conclusions.

Repent to Director Kim. He is the one owed an apology.

* * *

Even as the Compassion Bible Conference ended, rumors persisted about other homes. Many directors and staff members still lived at the edge of poverty. Could the ministry's unprecedented success be stirring envy and greed? Flaming arrows now seemed to be flying from all sides.

Whispers. Insinuations. Accusations.

Whereas John had misjudged the first situation, he was not wrong about others. When Everett asked the advisory board to investigate, audits revealed discrepancies at a handful of homes. Mr. Morgan expressed deep concerns. Even as the flames of accusation were growing higher, the *Reader's Digest* ad portrayed a trustworthy ministry.

Everett needed the very wisdom he'd spoken about at Konkuk University.

Oh, Lord, guide our steps. If these fires aren't put out soon, years of hard work could all burn to the ground.

Once concrete evidence was found, Everett wasted no time in dismissing two directors caught raking money from their monthly allotments. A third dismissal followed, a director who had collected for kids no longer in his care and tucked away the extra money for himself.

One of these directors turned resentful. He went to the Korean press with false claims about Compassion, and his family stirred up local animosity. Such actions poured fuel on the fire, forcing many to form opinions and take sides, including missionaries, directors, officials, and staff members at the office in Seoul.

What're you hearing? Everett asked Sally. You're in many of these homes.

Truthfully, Uncle Everett, it's hard to know what to believe. Accusations are flying. A few directors even told me that John demands kickbacks from them before releasing the funds to their homes.

Lord, help us, this is out of control. How do we stop these lies?

John's your Korean director. What does he suggest?

He's upset by it all, of course, Everett said. He insists each thief be removed before anyone else suffers. Compassion's work is too valuable to thousands of children. We have over a hundred and fifty good and faithful directors, and only five or six who have become corrupt.

Not long after, the director who had gone to the press was found guilty of embezzlement, then put in jail by Korean authorities.

As a result, the scandal flickered out.

Somewhat vindicated, Everett wrote from Seoul to sponsors of those orphanages involved and reassured them that none of the children had gone hungry or unclothed. All donations were being covered by Compassion and new directors were being put in place. God's work was moving forward.

You've handled it the best you can, Doc told him as they flew home.

Everett rubbed his temples. It's been giving me headaches of late.

Keep a water bucket handy, that's what I told my girls when we went camping.

Everett shot him a quizzical look.

Even after the campfire's put out, Doc said, the embers can still be hot. Be careful.

* * *

After the recent troubles in Korea, sponsors needed something positive to restore their faith in the ministry. As assistant executive director, Bob Swaney received a phone call that provided just the thing.

He sent out a flash announcement:

Only this morning the Korean consul general of New York
telephoned Rev. Swanson to say that the Korean government
had awarded Rev. Swanson the Korean Cultural Medal of
Honor, with a special citation! Surely this is another evidence
of God's blessing upon the ministry of Compassion in Korea.

On a warm June evening, Rev. Swanson accepted this latest honor. The Korean consul general flew in personally to present the citation at a church on Chicago's west side. This was a vote of confidence from the Korean government, a stamp of approval regarding Compassion's work, and for a blessed hour or two Everett's sole focus was on those gathered in the pews.

Then the arrows started flying again.

Chapter 47

EAGLE EYE

Miriam shrugged out of her coat and hung it by the door. She and Everett had returned from the citation ceremony. The house was quiet. Jack and Paul still occupied bedrooms here, though they were usually gone. She turned and touched Everett's arm.

What a wonderful evening, she said. All the work you've done, it's good to see Compassion receiving some recognition.

He met her eye. I've just heard of more accusations, Miriam.

In Korea? I thought things were—

It's so disheartening. Even as God gives us favor with the officials, we get news of another director's treachery. It reflects poorly on the ministry, of course, but also on all our honest, hardworking directors. Now they're under suspicion as well.

Will you need to fly back over?

Taking a deep breath, Everett weighed the idea. The latest bad news came from New Life Children's Home, in Suncheon. The director had forged letters to sponsors, begging them to send funds directly to him. This was a clear policy violation, and it was doubtful any of the money went to the children. Mr. Morgan had already confronted the man, but the damage was done.

I may need to, Everett conceded. For now, I'll write directly to the sponsors.

Oh, Miriam cried, cupping her cheek. What about the orphan quartet? John and his wife are supposed to bring them over in September. We've sent out news releases and promotional materials. Dozens of churches and schools have signed on. Why, I've even arranged our lodging in Alaska, where we'll meet them to kick off the tour. What a nightmare. Do you think we should cancel the plans?

No. Let God turn for good what the devil means for destruction.

Do you think there's any truth in the things Sally told you?

About John, you mean?

Miriam nodded, as though it pained her to even say it aloud.

I don't believe so. John's served faithfully for eight years, and I've never doubted his Christian integrity. Everett took his wife's hand and added, By defending me and the ministry, he's made enemies of those who are up to no good. Let's pray right now, Miriam, for sin to be exposed and truth to be revealed.

By month's end, Rev. Swanson had met with his advisory board and agreed upon guidelines to prevent further damage. He then sent letters to the sponsors of New Life Children's Home, assuring them their children were okay and they should continue sending support. He asked them not to be alarmed, but to have faith in God, Mr. Morgan, and Compassion to handle this correctly. No one should seek revenge. Instead, they ought to pray for the director to repent and leave quietly.

Seated at his desk one evening, he felt a dull headache, a steady, throbbing discomfort. All this stress was taking a toll. How could it not?

He'd never been a drinking man. Never chased skirts. Never been in trouble with the law. If he had any illicit pleasure, it was in the burst of boyish adrenaline brought on by the speed of a roaring car and of a jet plane taking off.

His true joys were preaching God's Word and caring for orphans and widows.

Some called that boring. He found it exciting.

And now this source of deep personal fulfillment was under attack.

A pain shot through Everett's skull. Moaning, he leaned over his desk and muttered, Dear Lord, I need Your peace.

* * *

Things took another negative turn in July, this time in regard to *Runaway*. The movie could be rented from film libraries for $15, and according to the contract, this fee was to be split 60/40: 60% to Compassion's representative and 40% to the libraries. The proceeds were then to be funneled back through the ministry to the orphanages.

For months, though, the Compassion representative hadn't remitted rental receipts in line with the agreement. Repeated letters, telegrams, and calls failed to resolve the issue.

Everett found this incomprehensible. How had a project meant for good become a point of such frustration? The *Runaway* film was an ode to his brother, the culmination of a childhood dream, the result of years of hard work. Even more important, it was an offering to God.

Now someone had pocketed these profits meant for the orphans.

The representative had become the real runaway.

Yes, some people thought Everett was too trusting. His executive assistant, Bob Swaney, suggested he was even a little naive. He wasn't blind, however, to the underbelly of human nature. Scandals were a regular part of Hollywood, Wall Street, and Main Street, USA. Marilyn Monroe's death two years back was a case as sad and sordid as any, and here in Chicago, Hugh Hefner was fast becoming an icon. Not so long ago, a movie based on Sinclair Lewis's bestselling novel *Elmer Gantry* had stirred anger with its story of a self-seeking preacher.

Yes, Everett knew scandals were rampant in this fallen world.

But to cause them in the name of God?

Oh, how he wanted to trust his fellow believers, his partners, his directors, releasing them to do the work of the ministry instead of bogging them down with regulations and suspicion. When they made mistakes, he made room for correction. Didn't one of his letterhead taglines even touch on this principle?

KINDLY IN ACCIDENTALS:
"If a man be overtaken in a fault . . . restore such a one."

But these recent thefts and deceptions were no accident.

No, this was willful sin.

In Mark 9:42, Jesus warned, "Whoever causes one of these little ones who believe in Me to stumble, it would be better for him if a millstone were hung around his neck, and he were thrown into the sea."

As the rising sun glimmered on Lake Michigan, Everett drove down West Irving Park Road to Compassion's office. He settled into his desk chair beneath a wall map of Korea and called in his assistant. Bob entered the room with purpose, shirt tucked in, tie neatly knotted.

You've dealt with this stuff before, Everett said, planting his hand on a stack of files. These are the reports from our directors, all the dates, counts, dollar amounts. You have an eagle eye. I feel like I'm missing something.

When you get that feeling, it's usually for a reason.

Can you go through all these by lunchtime?

You betcha, Bob said. I'm on it.

When noon rolled around, Bob marched back in and dropped an armload of folders on the desk. Most of the directors, he explained, were doing excellent work. The usual stragglers were a month or so behind, nothing to worry about.

Everett waited.

But, Bob said, Mr. Morgan and I talked, and he's got concerns on the ground in Korea. He's gonna airmail over copies of his findings. He's found fraudulent numbers in some of the reports, real incriminating stuff.

Everett winced as another pain stabbed through his temples.

You okay there?

He waved off Bob's concern. Let me know when those copies arrive. As much as it grieves me to fire a director, I know we need to act quickly. If we let this fester, we'll only make things harder on John Seong and his staff in Seoul.

You're a good man, Everett, a sincere man. You might be unsuspecting, but I know when called upon, you'll meet someone square on and lay them low. You'll look at the evidence, pray earnestly, and do the right thing. Of this, I have no doubt.

* * *

In early August, a month before the Seongs and the orphan quartet were set to arrive in Alaska, Everett faced the mail delivery from Korea on his desk. Mr. Morgan, his field director, was a steadfast, kindhearted man, not given to conjecture or accusation. According to Mr. Morgan, this airmailed envelope contained enough evidence to root out the real troublemaker.

Temples throbbing, Everett peeled back the seal and began reading.

The truth was even worse than expected, a betrayal by someone he loved deeply. Each page was another indictment. Each falsified document was proof. The accounts were all marked and laid open, so Everett could remove this deceit before it metastasized and killed the ministry.

No, no, no. Please, Lord. Everett gasped audibly, clutching his chest. His office seemed to spin around him, a whirlwind of numbers and names.

But not this name!

Why?

He nearly collapsed over his desk. There had to be some misunderstanding, some mistake. He had done nothing but lift up and empower this betrayer. What possible motive could there be for such wickedness? It was unfathomable. And yet, Bob's eagle eye and Mr. Morgan's thoroughness left no room for doubt.

Everett sat up in his chair and filled his lungs with oxygen.

I must hear this for myself.

He dialed long-distance on his phone, starting with the international code. He imagined electronic connections taking place, riding between phone poles, running through undersea cables, hopping back onto land, and skipping from switchboard to switchboard till reaching the peninsula he loved so much: Korea, Chosŏn, Land of the Morning Calm.

After garbled rings, a voice answered.

Sally? he said, bracing himself.

Yes, hello.

This is Uncle Everett. I have some questions, and I need you to answer honestly.

Chapter 48

NO-MAN'S-LAND

As Rev. Swanson recounted details from Mr. Morgan's report, Sally Swanson listened. She stayed calm, seeming to call upon years of nursing experience. She had been greeted nearly two years earlier by Mr. Morgan, at the dock in Busan, and she trusted the man.

I have no reason to question his findings, she told Everett. In fact, I tried to warn you.

Everett sighed. You did. How did I not recognize it?

You never even suspected?

No. John Seong and I have spent hundreds of hours together. Not once did I question his Christian witness.

Don't be too hard on yourself, Sally said. I didn't want to believe it, either. Since I first met him, I've liked John and his adorable wife. You know, I've even gone shopping with her. She's a kind person, and their baby, oh, he's so precious.

Everett pictured his adopted Korean grandbaby, as well as John's fatherly smile.

Throp, throp, throp . . .

Thoughts spinning, he planted his elbow on his desk and pressed a hand to his forehead. Sally, tell me more about John. What've you observed on your end?

He's very sharp, very dedicated to his work. His parents are quite proud of him—and for good reason. He's a natural leader. He's hired and unified a staff of over a hundred Koreans in Seoul, lots of good men and women. If anything, I suspect it's his success and sense of power that have gotten the best of him. He's well-liked by everyone, from the typist in the office to the highest-ranking province official. His smile and his enthusiasm win people over.

Do you believe he's been stealing from Compassion?

If not for my language lessons, I would've missed most of the clues. I'm sorry, Uncle Everett. It seems John has been a little dishonest.

A little? Everett would've laughed if not for the anguish involved.

More than a little, Sally conceded. I know it's tough to hear.

My personal feelings are secondary. Please, go on.

First, Sally said, I saw barrels of vitamins being delivered to the orphanages in smaller amounts than listed on the invoices. Then, I noticed there were fewer children at some of the homes than were listed on the rolls. You told me to speak to Mr. Morgan if I had any issues and that's precisely what I did. He looked over the invoices and spotted the same errors. John, it seems, has been selling off surplus supplies and collecting funds on inflated orphan counts.

You both tried to tell me something was off.

The directors, Sally noted, are the ones who helped me see it. They claim John's been demanding kickbacks from them. If they cooperate, he makes it worth their while. If they don't, he makes it hard on them. He holds all the strings. And he has also lied to them, implying you and the US office are shorting them. He's sown these seeds of distrust for a while.

I had complete faith in him. I gave him full control.

You relied on him as your interpreter, which made it easier for him to hide his actions from you. As self-confident as he is, he's used that control for not-so-good purposes. You are still loved by the directors, Everett. They are wholly devoted to the work of Papa and Mama Swanson. The few exceptions have been negatively influenced by John. As far as they're concerned, his word goes.

Everett rubbed a thumb along his eyebrows, trying to smooth out the deep furrows. So, he's turned them against me, he said, his voice catching.

I know he's been like family to you, Sally responded.

You're my niece. You're my family. I should've listened to you from the start.

You and Aunt Miriam, you've always been good to me. You both drove me to see my dad in the hospital when he had an ulcer. Do you remember that? I was a lot younger then, yet you two always treated me with respect.

It was the right thing to do. Les has been a good big brother to me.

What about now, Uncle Everett? Sally asked. Rumors are flying and things will only get worse. What are you going to do?

Throp, throp, throp . . .

There it was, the question that had kicked off this ministry amidst the drone of spinning propellers, and the question that could now end it all. Never had he needed such discernment. If he gave in to his own disappointment, he could slide into depression or—even worse—exonerate his dear friend and move on as though no real wrongs had been committed.

No, neither of these choices would suffice.

Gripping the phone to his ear, Everett said, There's only one thing I can do.

* * *

Rev. Swanson boarded the next available flight for South Korea. Already, John had turned directors against him, threatened orphans' livelihoods, and whispered rumors to the Korean press. He'd used his significant connections to further his own purposes over Compassion's.

This had to end.

By the time the Northwest Orient airplane descended into Seoul, Everett was emotionally and physically depleted. He'd replayed his many interactions with John, since meeting him in Suncheon, South Jeolla, six years ago.

Bouncing in army trucks over rutted roads.

Sampling kimchi and sipping ginger tea.

Raising their voices together in English and Korean, preaching God's Word to soldiers, prisoners, lepers, and widows.

Surely, they had been of one mind and purpose at the start. There had been genuine camaraderie and friendship between them. They'd opened their hearts to each other about past failures and moments of redemption.

Where and when had things gone wrong?

And how had Everett been so blind?

He wiped his eyes as he stared north over the plane's wing at the rugged terrain of the 38th parallel. He had visited soldiers down there in the trenches along the DMZ. After the signing of the armistice, in 1953, thousands of POWs from both sides had been exchanged at the low concrete bridge across the Sachong River. Even now, the heavily guarded strip of land separated Korean families.

For the first time, Everett truly related to their pain.

He, too, felt cut off from a man he had loved and trusted.

Though the DMZ had been off-limits to humans for over a decade, foliage and flowers now abounded there, springing to life where bullets once flew. The strip was a haven for musk deer, red-crowned cranes, and Asiatic black bears. Some even said the fabled tiger, so widely revered, prowled unseen through the no-man's-land.

Could Everett convince John of a new life ahead?

Could they bridge the divide and put hostilities to rest?

This confrontation was necessary for both biblical and business reasons. If the corruption was not dealt with, it would damage relationships with directors, orphans, and government officials. The sudden fame brought on by a *Reader's Digest* ad would backfire in a hurry.

The plane came down hard, buffeted by a crosswind. As it taxied toward the airport, Everett closed his eyes and pressed his head back against his seat.

Lord, You are the reason for this ministry. Please soften John's heart to receive what I must say to him. May he repent and receive forgiveness. May our friendship remain intact.

* * *

As John Seong stepped into the room to face Everett the next day, he wore a mask of cool detachment.

Hello, John.

The Korean director folded his arms over his business suit. His shoes were shined, pants pressed, jacket buttoned. His smile, which once seemed playful, now looked closer to a sneer.

We've shared a lot of good memories, Everett started.

None of your sweet talk, Reverend. You've come to make accusations.

You've been my right-hand man, Everett pressed on, steeling himself against the throbbing in his head. You and Doc, you've been alongside me all these years. I've relied on you both in so many ways. If I expected too much, I apologize.

Without me, John said, nothing here would get done.

You've been everything I needed and more, that's true, John. But this ministry is the Lord's. Without Him, even our best efforts would be in vain.

You know, Mr. Morgan's already asked me to step down. This is impossible. Here in our Seoul office, over one hundred people look to me for daily direction. Your orphans will not be fed if you stop the work I'm doing. Is that what you want?

Because of your theft, kids are going without food and vitamins.

Do you understand our ways, our culture? You can't even speak our language, Everett. Eating out, wearing nice clothes, these are necessary expenses when I meet with influential figures. And if I show my appreciation to a director or to one of our politicians, they show me the same in return. It is a two-way street, as you say in America.

C'mon, John. We have many honorable directors who pour their lives into the children. They don't do this for money. I've seen your doctored invoices and forged signatures. Are you telling me you're innocent?

I'm telling you Compassion needs me.

Everett's pulse struck heavier beats in his ears. Compassion, he said, needs no one. If you go or I go, the Lord will continue this work He has started.

If I go to the Korean press, John shot back, they will make life difficult for you.

The truth will win out. They've witnessed our work here for over twelve years.

John gave a bitter laugh. Maybe this humble act works in your churches back home, but here, Reverend, you'll be eaten alive. Who do you think they'll believe?

The beat grew louder in Everett's skull. Tell me, John, why did you do it? I've loved you as a son. Is it your wife and baby you are thinking of? Do you feel unappreciated? Let's talk.

John shook his head. You come to visit Korea for a month or two at a time, then think you know how tough it is here? You live in Chicago. You go to Cubs games. It is my dream to study in America and to watch baseball.

You're right, John. But when I saw the great need, I tried to help.

The Good Samaritan. Thank you. Well, we don't need you anymore.

Wincing, Everett pressed his lips together. He thought of the command in 2 Thessalonians 3:6 and 15: "Withdraw from every brother who walks disorderly. . . . Yet do not count him as an enemy, but admonish him as a brother."

Please, John, he said in an even voice. Must it come to this? As your brother in the Lord, I beg of you to repent and come clean. You once told me how you committed a terrible sin in your youth and God restored you. The same can happen now. We'll make a plan for restitution to avoid any legal action, and then—

Go to the police if you want. I don't owe you an explanation.

This must end, John. It is finished.

John scoffed. You have no proof. What is it I've done?

As Compassion's founder, I am left with no choice. You no longer work for us.

Chapter 49

PRECIOUS JEWELS

As Everett landed back in Chicago, he felt betrayed and defeated. It was late August 1964. He was fifty years old.

By mid-morning, the Swansons' garage at North Leonard Drive was sweltering. Everett lifted the garage door for some airflow as he and Miriam loaded the car for a trip to Alaska. In a week, Sally Swanson and the orphan quartet would fly from Seoul to meet them in Anchorage.

Of course, John Seong was no longer leading the tour. Since his termination, he had switched banks, tried to siphon sponsor money into his own account, then likely paid off officials to avoid prosecution. He'd gone into hiding once the ploy was discovered, and Everett would never see him again.

In the coolness of the garage, Everett drew a breath.

Why, John? Why?

As a result of this fiasco, the Compassion board had already sought legal counsel, called in a Korean advisory board, and enlisted Bob Swaney to set up new safeguards.

I gotta say, John was a real operator, Bob told Everett. Building his own little kingdom, thinking he'd never get caught. That inflated ego, it usually gets them in the end. We saw it there in his office, with that boyish charm and his six color phones.

There are others, Everett pointed out, who have sacrificed far more than we can imagine—directors who started orphanages in their own homes, who passed up meals to feed the children. They are some of the best people I've ever known, true servants of the Lord.

Agreed, said Bob. We gotta weed out the trouble so the good ones can grow.

All of it compounded Everett's headaches.

Standing in his garage, he rolled his neck and tried to ignore the hints of a migraine. He checked the fan belt on his car, topped off the oil, then dropped the hood. They were ready to go. He'd recently gifted the old Hillman to Paul, hoping to win over his youngest son, who seemed withdrawn of late.

Truth is, Everett told Miriam, Paul's lived without his father for weeks, even months, at a time. He's given to this ministry in ways others don't even know.

He's a grown man now, she replied. Don't take the blame for his acting out.

You don't think he's bitter toward me?

I think he'll come around. Paulie has a sweet spirit, much like his father.

Though Everett had pressed on since his confrontation with John Seong, the betrayal had truly devastated him. He got up each morning with praise on his lips, even as he tried to shake off the dark clouds. There was so much to be thankful for. Compassion provided homes, meals, teaching, and medical care to thousands of children. The ministry sponsored nearly four hundred Korean evangelists who spread the gospel from province to province.

Is this the last of it? Everett asked, squeezing his wife's valise into the back.

Don't forget these, she said, handing him his sermons.

He slipped the notebook between suitcases and film equipment, closed the trunk, then reached for the garage door. Old springs and hinges gave way, dropping the heavy panel more quickly than expected, and its corner caught him on the head.

He stumbled. Everything went momentarily black.

Everett! Miriam exclaimed. Are you alright?

With stars spinning before his eyes, he braced himself against the car. He groaned. Squared his shoulders. Muttered a few syllables.

What're you saying? Miriam asked. Do you want an ice pack?

He reached for her hand. I need to . . . sit down.

You're bleeding, Everett. Oh, dear. Here, let's get you inside.

Once he was settled on the sofa, she found some antiseptic and bandages, then kept the conversation light, listing stops on their North American tour, from Canada down to California, over to South Dakota, Iowa, Missouri, Illinois, and Ohio.

I just can't wait to see the children, she said. What a trip it will be!

God is good, he responded in a whisper.

Black spots still wavered before his eyes, and he felt sick to his stomach. It would pass, of course. He'd be fine. He simply needed to rest.

* * *

Everett and Miriam arrived in Anchorage the following week. Everett's head seemed much better, with only brief jolts of pain, and he found abundant distraction in the natural beauty along their route.

They embraced Sally the moment she got off the plane. In tow, she had two boys and two girls, handpicked from Compassion orphanages to form a quartet.

Papa! Mama! they cried.

Everett and Miriam swept them up in their arms.

It wasn't long before Sally, as a registered nurse, noted something off in Everett's behavior. When he mentioned the incident with the garage door, she suggested he get the wound checked out. There could be internal damage.

I'm sure it'll heal, he told her. I'm already feeling better.

After stops in Alaska, their tour headed south to Vancouver, British Columbia. They visited churches and troops of Boy Scouts and Girl Scouts. They started each performance with a greeting in English: "How do you do, everybody? How do you do? We are Korean children small, and we love you one and all."

The quartet's evening performances brought smiles and applause as they danced, sang Korean folk songs, and recited Bible verses. One song, "Precious Jewels," seemed to describe the orphans perfectly. The boys were adorned in bright blue vests and the girls in traditional red dresses. They left their audiences full of good cheer.

What an adventure this must be for them, Everett told Sally. Did you notice how their eyes popped open when they saw running water in the motel, not to mention the TV? And I've never seen children so excited about fresh bananas.

Why, these kids will be spoiled before the tour's over, Miriam noted.

Sally pursed her lips. It's a dream come true for them, like nothing they have back home. I wonder how they'll adjust when they go back to communal living.

Should we be concerned? Everett asked. They say you speak better Korean than the Koreans. Have they made any comments to you?

The girls wish they didn't have to wear short-cropped hair. They're jealous of all the women they've seen, with braids and long flowing hair.

What about the boys? Have they said anything?

Sally grinned. They think all Americans have big noses.

Everett and Miriam laughed.

* * *

The tour, Everett wrote to Doc Hemwall, was already a fine success. Sally was such an asset and clearly the children adored her. Their music broke down barriers at each performance, and the offerings were more than adequate to cover expenses. Best of all, there was increasing interest in the work of Compassion.

It was now their last morning in Vancouver. Everett strolled from the motel to the car, luggage in hand. His head was hurting again, a dull reminder of his run-in with the heavy garage door. Still, he remained upbeat. With over sixty scheduled venues, the tour was only getting started and he looked forward to the next performance.

He would show slides and a film.

Sally would play a bit of piano and lead the little ones in song.

Miriam would sign up sponsors at the table, handing them Korean wood carvings as gifts.

Everett reached for the car door, then stared through the window and noticed something was missing. He clearly remembered setting his notebook in here the night before.

Oh, no! he cried. Where is it?

As if recent scandals at the orphanages weren't enough, someone had broken into his car and stolen his most valuable possession. It represented years of study, prayer, and hard-won wisdom. It was his life's work!

The incident even made it into a section of the *Chicago Tribune*:

THIEF ROBS CHICAGO CLERIC—OF SERMONS
VANCOUVER, B.C., Sept. 5 (AP)—This thief apparently
was seeking solace. He left untouched a camera and a film
projector, taking only the notebook of sermons belonging to
the Rev. Everett Swanson.

For Everett, it was final insult to injury. His son David had always
claimed that to hear his father's preaching and his passion for the gospel was priceless. If so, this collection of sermons was an irreplaceable
treasure. Why would someone nab his notebook, of all things? Why
would they leave objects of more cash value untouched?

If there was any consolation, perhaps the sermon notes would lead
the culprit to salvation.

By this point, Everett's headaches had returned with a vengeance. At
each performance, he saw John Seong's name on the pre-printed tour
programs, and he was besieged again with questions, guilt, and grief.
He grimaced through the physical pain and tried not to dwell on the
ministry's teetering reputation in Korea.

Are you alright, Uncle Everett? Sally asked.

It'll pass, he said. Now what do you say we go treat the kids to their
first ice cream cones? We don't want them to be deprived, do we?

At tour's end, Everett and Miriam waved goodbye to their niece
and the dear orphans. They promised to visit Korea in the spring for
the annual conference.

I'll have my eye out, Miriam said, for kids who can form next year's
quartet.

You think we'll do this again? Sally asked.

I can't imagine why not. What a joy it's been! Don't you agree,
Everett?

As much as he wanted to confirm every word, his lips wouldn't
move. Couldn't move. He felt stuck, as though his brain signals weren't

reaching his vocal cords. He blinked, swallowed hard, then simply nodded and looked away.

Chapter 50

THE DRIVE HOME

On many fronts, 1965 was a pivotal year. Folk singer Bob Dylan released "Like a Rolling Stone" and the Beatles played at Shea Stadium. Selma, Alabama, saw Martin Luther King Jr. march across a bridge, even as protests intensified against the war in Vietnam. In a highly anticipated boxing match, Muhammad Ali retained his championship belt during a bout with Sonny Liston.

Father and Mother raised you to be a fighter, Everett reminded himself. He wished they were here now to advise him.

Though John Seong was nowhere to be found, his dirty dealings had left rot and debris in their wake. Everett spent hours making phone calls and typing letters to board members. Soon after, Compassion published an ad in *Moody Monthly* for a stewardship director, someone to work with the office in Seoul and oversee all operations.

Everett was fighting to repair the breach. He must never again let the ministry suffer from the actions of one individual. He must protect the sponsors, directors, and children.

You're taking the right steps, Miriam assured him.

I should've never allowed it to happen.

Well, it did, and you're doing your best to put things right. There's no need to be so despondent. You're not eating or sleeping. Perhaps you should go in for an exam.

We have the conference coming up in Korea.

When we get back then, she said. Please, do it for me.

April in Seoul was glorious as ever, with cherry blossoms drifting on the breeze. Doc Hemwall and Mr. Morgan spoke at the conference, as did Rev. Swanson. Despite the recent scandal, the Swansons were greeted with great love and fanfare in all the orphanages. In Busan, Everett and Miriam met with two of the girls they personally sponsored. What a treat to spend time with their Korean "daughters." Both had grown into courteous young women.

Everett saw the joy written across Miriam's face. She was always happiest with the children. She had gone from being a bride, traveling evangelist, and young mother to being a sponsor, supporter, and full-fledged board member of Compassion. She was as committed and capable as anyone in this ministry.

And everywhere Miriam went, she was on the lookout for her next quartet.

In Seoul, she met Jung-won Lee. Jung-won was a darling girl, having been brought to Mercy Life Christian Orphanage after being abandoned by her father at a police station. Her name meant "peaceful garden," which matched her disposition. Though small in stature, she led the younger kids to school over muddy fields and roads full of buses and trucks. She took care of her assigned quilt. She bowed and thanked the US soldiers who brought candy and Christmas gifts.

Jung-won is very obedient, the director told Miriam. And she sings beautifully.

She's going on next year's tour, Miriam told Everett.

Who was he to disagree?

* * *

Miriam's focus shifted once they arrived back in America. Over Everett's objections, she set up an appointment for him at West Suburban Hospital, and Doc Hemwall confirmed her concerns. Everett's mental and emotional states were exacting a physical toll.

It's time you take a leave of rest, Doc ordered. You're not well.

Can I still go for a drive if I like?

Doc tilted his head. If you manage to keep a reasonable speed.

A few days later, Everett turned up the radio and rested his elbow out the window as he cruised past fields of corn. He frowned when he heard the announcement that Edward R. Murrow, former radio and TV broadcaster, had died of lung cancer. This speaker of truth, this man Everett had long respected, was now gone.

He pulled in his elbow, rolled up the window, and turned off the radio. He moved to hit the brake, but his foot failed to respond. He sat up straight. Tried again.

Still, no response.

What was wrong? A cramped muscle, a spasm?

Fidgeting in his seat, he coaxed the car to the side of the road and rolled to a stop. Minutes passed before his foot would obey any messages from his brain.

Still not convinced of his dire situation, Everett popped in one morning at the offices on West Irving Park Road. He had survived the Great Depression. He'd been on the front lines of a war zone. Even with his increasing migraines, he could surely visit with his staff for an hour or two. He cared for each one of them, after all.

Stepping from his vehicle, he looked around.

Across the street, the gates of Irving Park Cemetery guarded emerald lawns dotted with tombstones and mausoleums. It was a peaceful spot, a wide swath of land in the middle of this concrete jungle, a reminder that everyone's days were numbered.

Everett sauntered into the Compassion building and greeted men and women with a warm smile. Some time later—minutes or hours, he wasn't sure—Bob Swaney found him at his desk. Everett responded to a question or two, then his attention wandered off. He leaned back, fixing his eyes on his map of Korea.

Bob's voice. Growing louder.

Everett? You okay, there? Say something, will you?

He tried, he really did. He felt as though he were underwater. His chest was tight, his breathing labored. His words came out garbled.

Several hospital visits occurred during the spring, and more significant tests were conducted in June, including an electroencephalogram (EEG). The intention was to track Everett's brain waves and detect any abnormalities. When the results came back clear, Doc Hemwall and the other doctors were stumped. They met with the Swanson family and suggested Everett wait, rest, and see if things got any worse.

It's this whole deal with John Seong, Miriam confided to Doc. You know, Everett hasn't been the same since. I truly believe it's contributed to his poor health.

David agreed. Dad's been really disappointed. It's just broken his heart.

Rev. Swanson couldn't argue. Back in 1952, he had made a total shift and determined for the sake of orphans and refugees that ministry must encompass spirit, mind, and body. Now his own body needed help, suffering from the afflictions of his heart and mind.

Slipping speech. Loss of muscle control.

Oh, Lord, I need Your strength.

Sensing it might be his last opportunity, Everett agreed to a morning round of golf with his oldest son. David drove him to a course in DeKalb County, where cicadas buzzed in the sycamores and sunlight sparkled on the water traps.

You ready? David said. Guess we could call this a rematch.

Everett nodded, then followed his son to the first tee. They took a few practice swings. This wasn't a day for winners or losers or bragging rights. Everett was just glad to be on his feet.

You're looking rusty, David kidded him.

It was true, Everett hadn't hit a ball in a while and the signals between head and limbs seemed muddled. By the time they reached the second hole, one of his legs had locked. It was like that moment in the car all over again. No response. Nothing.

He dragged it behind him through the grass.

David's gaze softened. Do you want to keep playing? We can stop anytime.

Everett waved them onward, still stutter-stepping.

Seriously, Dad, we don't have to do this. I just wanted to spend time with you. You're not only my father, you're my best friend.

One step. Drag leg.

Another step.

Drag.

As they drove their shots and approached the green, Everett had so much he wanted to say. Here they were, two grown men away from work, wives, and responsibilities. A chance to catch up. He knew David and Myra had faced some marital difficulties. He wanted to encourage his son, offer him words of wisdom.

But his jaw was locked, his lips numb.

This life, it's not easy, he wanted to say. I love you, son. You've been your mother's and my beloved since the day you were born. Don't lean on your own understanding. Live your own life and make your own mistakes, but never stop growing. Be the man God created you to be.

Your shot, Dad.

Everett tried to get out a few words. Then lost the thought. He imagined an operator at a telephone switchboard, tugging at cables to end a connection.

David tried to fill in the space. Hey, Dad, you remember that time—man, it was years ago—when you were roaring down some rural road not far from here? Jack and Paul, they kept begging you to slow down. I'm not sure why, but I started fiddling with my door behind you.

Scrunching his eyebrows, Everett grunted. Yes, he tried to say.

Suddenly, my door swung open, and I just about got sucked out. You remember?

Everett leaned on his putter and nodded.

Just like that, David said, you snapped around, grabbed hold of my arm, and yanked me back inside. How you did it, I still don't know. That always amazed me.

It was a . . . God is . . .

David waited for his dad to finish.

Frustrated as he lost the words again, Everett gazed across the green. He believed God was a good father, ready to turn and rescue His children even when their ignorance got them into trouble.

God is . . .

It's okay, Dad. It's getting hot out here anyway. David tapped in his ball, then assisted his father back to the car. From the driver's seat, David made another attempt to communicate, but to no avail. Together, in silence, they made the drive home.

* * *

With symptoms worsening, Rev. Swanson was admitted to the Mayo Clinic in Rochester, Minnesota. Through exploratory tests and X-rays, doctors discovered a malignant brain tumor, and on July 6, 1965, he underwent brain surgery.

Everett returned home under the watchful eye of his wife and visiting nurses. Miriam fawned over him like never before, and he wanted nothing more than to respond to her. Here he was, a lead foot on the road now relegated to a wheelchair. A man who had talked about God all his life, now unable to speak.

Alright, Lord, looks like I'm stuck here. I'm all ears.

A sweet mercy, like anointing oil, eased over him during these days. Where his burdens had increased over the past year, grace was now given, providing a peace which surpassed all understanding. It was so tempting to be angry and morose, and at times he felt these emotions. Lord, he felt them deeply!

Yet, there was joy in the morning.

Though he couldn't shout out as he had in times past, his heart sang of the Lord's mercies. It was a deep river running through him, cool and refreshing.

After all you've done for others, David confided to him, it's just so disappointing. I don't understand, Dad. I mean, they had to open a flap in the side of your head just to operate and keep you alive. How can this be right?

Right. Wrong. Fairness. Injustice.

These were concepts too weighty for a man in his last months on earth.

Instead, he focused on showing kindness and love, and he rejoiced as his brothers, Les and Lawrence, paid him regular visits.

Everett, Lawrence told him, you've spent the last eleven months in frustration, physical difficulty, and suffering. Yet at no time has your testimony been brighter. You realize, don't you, the nurses often walk out of here in tears, saying they've never cared for such a kindly man.

At a family picnic that summer, Everett struggled anew with his situation. He watched relatives play pranks, compete in games, eat lots of food, and laugh. Boy, what a wonderful sound! Unable to join in the activities, though, he found himself getting depressed.

I know it's tough, Miriam said, settling on his lap in the wheelchair. She played with his hair, then wrapped her arms around him. But you still have me, Everett Swanson.

He swiveled his head and looked up.

You've been betrayed by a friend you loved. Your body's not acting right. But please, she said, I want to see that old spark in your eyes. I'm not going anywhere.

The smile came naturally, without restriction.

There it is! she exclaimed. I knew it was still in there.

While Miriam remained hopeful, she was also honest with herself and sponsors. In letters, she told them of her gratitude for Doc Hemwall, who was a real brother and a Christian doctor seeking divine help. Few men had his ability to deal with any situation. She also thanked sponsors for their letters, cards, and prayers regarding Everett. She wrote: "We have been told that medically there is no hope at all for his recovery, so he is in God's hands."

As Everett's role at Compassion faded, Miriam became heavily involved in the operations. He watched her rise to the occasion, proud of this godly woman who had been his partner for thirty years. It was the Lord's work, and it would go on. That was a fact.

Thank God, though, for Miriam, who had picked up the torch.

In no time at all, a large group of Compassion sponsors would be traveling to Korea to tour the orphanages and meet their sponsored children. While Everett still hoped to fly over with them, he knew it was unlikely. He could only imagine the memories they would bring home—the joy and unforgettable experiences.

To think it had all started thirteen years ago.

In the Swansons' basement.

With a $50 check.

Compassion had grown beyond anything he had ever imagined. It was truly compassion to suffer with—and he would suffer with it until he crossed the finish line.

By mid-October, it was clear he wouldn't be joining the tour. As things stood, he couldn't even make it to the office for the board meetings. Regardless, the tour would proceed—yes, he insisted on it—and Doc Hemwall, as interim director, would lead the way, along with Canada's Bob Forsyth.

Everett had to wonder if Father and Mother could see how much this ministry had grown. Surely, they could. How he longed to see the two of them again.

And oh, to gaze upon my Savior's face!

* * *

In early November, Everett was helped into the car by Miriam and their son Jack, then they headed to O'Hare International for the tour's big send-off.

This was a milestone. Today, one hundred and thirteen men and women were flying over the Pacific to the Korean peninsula, where they would be exposed to the foreign mission field. This would solidify Compassion's commitment to the children, while also producing sponsors and missionaries for years to come.

At the curb, Everett was maneuvered into the wheelchair. Miriam snugged his coat, kissed him on the forehead, then rolled him through the terminal. This was in violation of his medical orders, but he was not going to miss this.

Almost there, Miriam assured him.

Through the tall concourse windows, he spotted the Northwest Orient airliner being fueled out on the tarmac. Milling around the gate, Doc and the throng of sponsors awaited departure.

Despite the wheelchair, despite the loss of speech and movement, Everett was filled with excitement for these wonderful people who would get to experience Korea for themselves.

Why, I've been nine or ten times, he realized. Cumulatively, I've spent over a year on the peninsula. I've been blessed beyond measure. I have done my part.

Now, it was their turn.

A sponsor pivoted and caught sight of him. Rev. Swanson, the woman called out.

Miriam locked the wheels on his chair as people swarmed round.

She met her husband's eye and grinned. She knew him all too well, knew the joy he felt in this moment. These were the ones who had given monthly to support the ministry, who had lived and breathed the pure religion of God's Word, devoting themselves, their time, and their money to the welfare of the orphans and widows.

Everett expects a good report from all of you, she told them. We'll see you when you return at the end of the month.

With handshakes, hugs, and a final prayer, the group was off. Everett managed to fan his fingers in a wave as the plane accelerated down the runway and its bright red tail blurred. He'd come here against his surgeon's wishes. Now his job was done. Alone, only he and his wife, he felt the adrenaline begin to fade. He was just one man. He'd given it the best he could.

You ready to go? Miriam ventured, curling her fingers around his.

He stared up at the bright blue sky, eyes watering in the sunlight. Was he ready? Yes, he was. He squeezed her hand twice as travelers rushed on by. They barely noticed him there, just a sickly old man in a chair. They had places to go and schedules to keep.

Well, so did he. He grinned.

Yes, so did he.

Chapter 51

AND NOW THIS

At 6:00 a.m., Monday, November 15, 1965, Everett Francis Swanson breathed his last after lying six days in a coma. He was one month from his fifty-second birthday and two months from his thirty-first anniversary. He left his wife with four grown children and more grandbabies on the way.

Hours later, halfway around the world, Doc Hemwall returned to his hotel in Seoul and found a cablegram from Bob Swaney. Doc was exhausted. Since the tour's arrival, they had been hounded by newspaper, television, and radio outlets. Police escorts had even followed their buses in from the airport. Compassion's work in the orphanages was big news across the peninsula, and when a flowered wreath was placed around Doc's neck, he had felt honored—if not a little embarrassed.

Each morning, Doc had led the team in devotions before they set out for the orphan homes, widow homes, and the home for leper children.

Each day had been exhilarating.

And now this.

Doc didn't need to read the cablegram. He already knew.

He had known it when he boarded the flight back in Chicago. And when he peered over his glasses at the shapes of Everett and Miriam still watching from the airport concourse. Being in the medical profession, he understood fluid was building around Everett's brain, and even the best attempts to drain it had done nothing but reveal more solid mass. Doc thought fondly of his revered pastor and fishing buddy. He pictured Everett standing behind the pulpit on a sleepy Sunday morning, or casting his line into the river, or rolling up his sleeves for some 16-inch softball.

Everett had inspired him for fifteen years through genuine love, tireless work, and earnest faith. In fact, Doc was already forming his own ministry, which he would call the Christian Medical Society. Lord willing, he would soon travel to Africa, Haiti, India, and beyond.

Doc set the cablegram on the table, then stared out the hotel window at the lights of Seoul. Removing his glasses, he wiped his eyes.

Godspeed, my dear friend, he whispered. Godspeed.

Days later, Doc Hemwall, the tour group, home directors, evangelists, pastors, and various officials gathered from across South Korea to celebrate the life of Papa Swanson. The news of his death came as a shock to many, causing directors and children to cry out passionately with loud voices.

Director Lim, of Hillside Christian Children's Home, wrote: "He was . . . humble before anyone . . . frugal . . . a man of great love for the Korean children and people. This will long be remembered by many Koreans."

As the ceremony ended, dozens donated funds to build a lasting memorial.

* * *

Rev. Swanson was laid out at Peterson's Funeral Home in Chicago, Illinois. Cards, flowers, and condolences poured in from churches, pastors, politicians, sponsors, and other ministries in the United States, Canada, and countries around the world. Ted Engstrom, of World Vision, sent a personal letter offering to help in any way possible.

The memorial took place on November 18, 1965, at Central Avenue Baptist, Everett's last pastorate and home church. Compassion closed its offices so all staff members could attend. It was a quiet yet joyous service, with favorite memories and songs shared by those closest to Everett. His brother Lawrence led everyone in a round of "Hallelujah Meeting" and invited them to imagine Everett rejoicing in heaven alongside his parents, the rest of the saints, and Christ Jesus in all His glory.

"Everett's not here," Lawrence explained. "In fact, a few short weeks ago, he told me, 'When you see me in the casket, it won't be me. I will be with the Lord.'"

After the service, a hearse delivered the casket to Irving Park Cemetery, directly across from the offices at 7774 West Irving Park Road. On this gray winter day in the southwest corner of the graveyard, the casket was prepared for burial beside a flat granite marker hardly visible from ten yards away.

Miriam, David, Sharon, Jack, and Paul comforted each other.

Onlookers huddled round and offered a prayer.

Standing at attention next to the casket was one of the Swansons' longtime acquaintances from their church back in Mount Vernon, Washington. Sarge was older now, still gruff but in full regalia, here to honor the man he once called pastor and friend.

* * *

The Compassion board gathered for a special meeting to officially report their founder's homegoing. Even in mourning, they realized tough decisions must be made to keep the ministry alive and well. They needed a new leader, as well as men and women of integrity to grapple with the complexities in Korea.

Six weeks later, Rev. Henry Harvey accepted the role of president. He was a good friend of Doc Hemwall, with a degree in business administration and years of experience as a missionary in India. Right away, Rev. Harvey outlined a plan to visit Seoul during the next spring conference, hire field representatives to inspect the orphanages, and rebuild trust with Korea's minister of health and welfare.

Answering to Rev. Harvey was his board of directors:

Gus "Doc" Hemwall, MD—chairman of the board
Miriam Swanson—vice president
Elmer Olson—treasurer
David Swanson—secretary
Bob Swaney—general manager, domestic operations
James Johnson—field representative for the US
Mr. Robert Morgan—director, Korean operations

Miriam, the brave yet grieving widow, was vital to the continuation of this ministry and she was proud to have her firstborn son join her on the board. She was a spokesperson loved and respected by all, the

North American sponsors and the Korean staff and directors. She was needed now more than ever.

And she rose to the task.

No one, she determined, was going to mess up her husband's work.

To honor his legacy, she sat at his old desk and typed a letter for all those impacted by his recent passing:

> My husband was so much a part of my life that to try to put into words what I feel now that he is gone is most difficult. The love we shared, the togetherness, the loneliness without him—all these things are impossible to describe. Still, the comfort that I have found in the promises of God's Holy Word has sustained me. . . .
>
> I think that I can best describe my husband as a man who lived each day as if it might be his last. He awakened each morning with a prayer on his lips . . . he would bounce out of bed and start singing songs of praise. . . . He was one of the happiest men I have ever known, full of joy, of living, and happy in the service of the King . . .
>
> We have many wonderful memories as a family. . . . We miss him more than words can say, but we all rejoice for his sake that his suffering and helplessness are past. . . . What joy and wonder must be his as he gazes upon the face of Him whom he loved and served with such devotion all these years.

Miriam had been there thirty-four years ago as Everett stood in cap and gown at Sycamore High School. His class motto had been *Not the Sunset but the Dawn*. She pulled the letter from the typewriter, then clutched it to her heart.

This was not the sunset, not if she could help it.

No, this was not the end.

Today

AN EXCLAMATION POINT

Today, Compassion International is a Christian child development organization that partners with more than 8,500 local churches in twenty-seven countries. Consistently ranked in the top ten on Forbes' America's Top Charities List, Compassion is a founding member of the Evangelical Council for Financial Accountability and an accredited member of the Better Business Bureau's Wise Giving Alliance.

Compassion International does holistic relief work on multiple levels. It delivers spiritual, economic, social, and physical care to over two million babies, children, and young adults in poverty. Program children receive medical care, supplemental meals, clothing, and biblical instruction, while also attending local schools.

Everett knew children were valuable to God, and Compassion still sees the protection of young ones as central to God's heart. No violence against a child is justifiable. Compassion believes children should be known, loved, and protected. This is especially important for those in poverty who are at higher risk of abuse and trafficking.

Compassion is serious about keeping children safe.

Over three quarters of a century, Compassion has had only five presidents at the helm, creating a pattern of steady leadership.

In 1952, Everett Swanson had the initial vision, starting with a few dozen children in one Korean orphanage. Preaching the gospel and meeting practical needs were the foundations of his ministry, and he personally exemplified the deep care in which the ministry's name was rooted. Though he was gentle, trusting, and sensitive to God's leading, he was also driven.

When he passed, Compassion served close to 15,000 children.

In 1966, Henry Harvey took over and implemented processes for integrity and greater accountability, while also expanding the ministry's program options into seventeen other countries. The orphans would always be a focus, but there were impoverished families whose children were also in great need of help.

When he left, Compassion served 25,000 children.

In 1975, Wally Erickson became a hands-on leader. He established systems for securing sponsor and donor information, and stressed the importance of hiring qualified staff whose work matched the marketing message. He believed the educational component was paramount in providing services for children. Under his guidance, headquarters moved from Chicago to Colorado Springs, Colorado.

When he resigned, the ministry served 180,000 children.

In 1993, Wess Stafford stepped into the lead role with open arms and a servant's heart. He not only bonded with domestic and field workers but shared his vision for child advocacy. As an effective writer and communicator, he helped local churches awaken to the needs of the children and the poor.

When he stepped down, Compassion served 1,350,000 children.

In 2013, Santiago "Jimmy" Mellado came in with lofty goals and the zeal to match. As current president, he wants the ministry to be the benchmark in child sponsorship, globally partnering with Christians and local churches to disciple, equip, and free children from the cycles of poverty. With a billion children still in impoverished conditions worldwide, he intends to reach as many as possible.

By the time of its seventieth anniversary in 2022, Compassion was serving well over 2,000,000 children.

International leaders have long recognized the vital work of Compassion. Using the pseudonym George Walker, one US president sponsored a child after hearing about Compassion through a Michael W. Smith concert. He wrote letters to his sponsored child for years.

His actual name? George H. W. Bush.

Compassion's tagline, *Releasing children from poverty in Jesus' name,* is much more than a catchy phrase. It is the mission statement, included in the very name of the organization. It's a strategy they have followed since the days of Rev. Swanson.

* * *

After her husband's passing in 1965, Miriam Swanson stepped up and served on the board until 1982. She traveled all over the world, loving children and encouraging sponsors. She passed in 1994, laid to rest next to Everett in Irving Park Cemetery.

David Swanson sat on the board until 1968, and visited orphanages in Korea with his wife, where they were treated like celebrities, though he knew his dad would want nothing to do with such behavior.

Sharon helped at Compassion headquarters and sponsored children of her own. She followed the ministry's growth over the years, glad to see her father's vision did not fade.

Jack worked in administration in Chicago's public school system, also serving children, though in a different arena.

Paul, falling ill, received a kidney from Jack and lived into his forties—though his early passing was another heartbreak for his mother.

Les Swanson, after his brother Everett's demise, served for a brief period as Compassion's general manager.

Sally Swanson continued as a registered nurse with Compassion in Korea, then worked with Holt International, an adoption agency. In 1973, she married a director from one of the Korean orphanages.

George Swanson, to this day, still treasures the photo of his "adopted" boy, given to him by Uncle Everett.

Doc Hemwall served as Compassion chairman till 1983. He fulfilled his lifelong wish, circling the globe to places in need of medical attention. He passed in November 1998, ninety years old, a full thirty-three years after his dear friend and Compassion founder had left the bonds of this earth.

On the Korean side, Gi-sook, who fled North Korea and then founded Mi-saeng Institute and House of Hope with her husband, served the orphans for decades. She is retired now, yet House of Hope still serves abused and neglected children, carrying on the work started decades ago with a donation from Everett Swanson.

Yo-hee and Woo-yeol, who directed Namgang Ae-Yook-Won, raised their own kids amidst the hardships of the orphan home. For many years Young-sook and Ki-jong resented this, but today they praise their mother and father's sacrifices. Because of their parents' prayerful tears, three generations of the family now do full-time social work.

Ei-sun, who became Pastor Ei-sun Baek, graduated from Seoul Theological University in 1966, thanks to Compassion's financial backing. He founded the Swanson Memorial Foundation in 1969, and for twenty-five years worked at Compassion Korea. In 1981, he met with Miriam in Chicago and visited Rev. Swanson's grave. Pastor Ei-sun Baek couldn't hold back tears as he considered this loving man who had forever changed his life.

Myung-guen, the boy who would have gone blind without an operation paid for by Compassion, has now pastored for fifty years, the first pastor to graduate from his orphanage. He spent thirty years ministering to those with disabilities, helping vulnerable children receive the loving care and protection they deserved as children of God. His two sons and daughter-in-law are now pastors as well.

South Korea, once a nation in desperate need, is now an economic powerhouse, a shining example of rebirth for the entire world. Korean children stopped receiving Compassion sponsorship in the 1990s. Then in 2004, in a surprising turn of events, the same Koreans whose relatives suffered through a catastrophic war became sponsors themselves for Compassion.

Currently, South Korea is a global support partner, second only to the United States in the number of children it sponsors beyond its own borders.

* * *

In 1965, when Everett Swanson crossed that celestial finish line into the arms of his heavenly Father, he completed the unlikely race from small-town farm boy to world-traveled evangelist. There is little doubt he heard the words: "Well done, good and faithful servant. . . . Enter into the joy of your Lord."

Hearing a question, he answered.

Seeing a need, he acted.

He was a foreigner with no funding and no knowledge of the language. He faced very real fears of getting shot or contracting disease. Nevertheless, he chose to take responsibility for the opportunity, and many others did the same. From Gi-sook and Doc Hemwall to Yo-hee and Miriam Swanson, men and women responded in monumental ways. They chose to alter their own lives, thus transforming the lives of millions.

Throp, throp, throp . . .

The question that once spun along with those airplane propellers still lingers today, six little words for any of us who are confronted with a need. Whether we are young or old, rich or poor, we can reach out with hearts of compassion, choosing to sacrifice and suffer with. We might be faced with a situation at work, on the street, or in another state. It could mean giving someone a smile and a bottle of water, or a hug and a pair of shoes. It could involve stopping instead of walking by, listening instead of talking.

Needs usually come at inopportune times, and they come in all shapes and sizes.

A bite of food.

An act of forgiveness.

A prayer, a song, or a phone call.

Throp, throp, throp . . .

Wherever and whenever we are faced with a need, we are given an opportunity. Everett Swanson found such an opportunity in an alleyway where orphans huddled beneath dirty rags. He didn't decide in that moment to change millions of lives. He simply fed a few children, then fed a few more.

His life was an exclamation point wrapped in a question.

And that question remains for each one of us:

What are you going to do?

ACKNOWLEDGMENTS

From Eric: This four-year writing project would not have happened without Matt Bronleewe's willingness to bring me onboard. What an honor to work together!

On the back end of the process, Kevin Mungons has given much-needed fresh eyes in the editorial process and saved me a load of embarrassment and backpedaling.

My wife, Carolyn Rose Wilson, has listened to multiple readings of my latest scenes and, as always, has given honest feedback and encouragement. After thirty-three years together, and twenty-one books completed, she deserves awards not yet created for patience and love.

Duane and Kathi Smith not only provided a month of quiet workspace in their home, but also painted a room and furnished a desk and chair. Thanks for many laughs and yummy meals together.

My father, Mark Wilson, provided office space when I needed to complete the final draft, which gave us time to revisit many of our own family missionary stories. What a rich heritage I have been given, and I pray some of it seeped into this project.

From Matt: First, I need to thank my wife, Karin, because if I hadn't married her almost thirty years ago, this story would never have seen the light of day! Her connection to Great-Uncle Everett provided the genesis for this entire adventure.

Her parents, George and Sandy Swanson, introduced me to so many wonderful stories that fueled the earliest embers of this project.

Over many years, the entire Bronleewe and Swanson families have been endlessly supportive, helping me through the inevitable dark moments life provides.

Eric Wilson was the first and only person I wanted to work with on this book, and I'm forever grateful to him for lending his time and formidable skills to this labor-intensive mission.

Mike Lenda connected me to all the right people at Compassion International, which opened many important doors in the early days of gathering research and interviews.

David Swartz read an early version of the manuscript and challenged many important aspects of it, leading to a deeper involvement with Compassion Korea, and bringing forth a more globally minded narrative.

Dave Steunebrink and Emily Kaiser of Showdown Management have gone above and beyond in supporting the creation of this book, and the film we hope will soon accompany it.

Don Pape has acted as my book agent over a decade (though I've provided him with a meager number of books to represent!) and I'm thankful for his unwavering encouragement, and for getting me the best deal possible!

Drew Dyck and the entire staff of Moody saw the vision for this book when few did, and I'm forever in their debt for giving this story a chance to reach audiences around the globe.

Thanks to God for whispering in my ear that the time had come to tell Everett's story. I've been inspired and challenged, and I know many of the people I've met along the way have felt that way too. Now, whenever I encounter a twist or wrinkle or valley or where-is-the-bottom pit along life's winding road, I hear the same question Everett did so many years ago: What Are You Going to Do? The answer for me has been life-changing.

NOTES AND SOURCES

In the tradition of our favorite missionary biographies, we wrote *What Are You Going to Do?* in story form, relying on hundreds of pages of research to craft scenes and render dialogue. We hoped to make it immensely readable, while also making every effort to get the details right.

This process took over three years.

You are holding the result.

Our research began with unprecedented access to Compassion International archives and culminated in interviews of Everett Swanson's surviving relatives. We leaned heavily on Compassion newsletters, sermons and correspondence from Everett himself, newspaper and magazine articles, reputable online sources, and books about Korea and the Korean War. Many narrative portions of historical events are drawn from standard reference works, generally without citation unless a contemporary account is quoted directly. Michelle Donahoe, executive director of the DeKalb County History Center in Illinois, gave us a tour of her facility and offered helpful facts about Sycamore Township.

We also benefited from telephone, online, and in-person interviews with Swanson family members and friends. David Swanson, oldest son of Everett, opened his home to us. He gave honest, poignant, and personal responses to the scenes in this book—and made sure we knew his dad gave up coffee for all the right reasons. Everett's niece and nephew, Sally Lee Swanson and George Swanson, were generous with their time and knowledge. Judith Hemwall provided insights about her father, Doc Hemwall, and Betty Edward shared her experiences as Miriam's younger sister in their Sycamore home.

A former Korean orphan, Cathy Carey—mentioned as Jung-won Lee in the book—and her daughter, Abbi Lee, allowed writers and a film crew to invade their home for insights into the work of Compassion, past and present. They could not have been more hospitable.

At Compassion USA, Lorie Lee, former employee, provided access to her excellent thesis on the origins of the ministry. Wess Stafford, former Compassion president, was kind enough to share his insights and memories. Special thanks to the entire staff for supporting and encouraging this project.

Compassion Korea, headed by Dr. Justin Suh, took a great deal of time reading and rereading drafts of this book to make suggestions and corrections, and ensure its merit to audiences on both sides of the world. Thanks also to Junyoung and the tireless staff in Seoul.

In our travels to conduct interviews for this project, Grant Howard and Kip Kubin served as an excellent film crew, as well as lively traveling companions.

We love accuracy and realize many readers will appreciate the high level of documentation included here. However, following the conventions of many modern biographies, we did not use footnote indicators in the main text. We turned to published sources such as newspapers and magazines, while also basing much of our work on unpublished sources such as interviews, corporate documents, and private journals. All of these are presented with quotation marks or block quotes, and are documented in the notes. Every page of this book was read, reread, vetted, and approved by the Swanson family, Compassion International, Compassion Korea, and Moody Publishers.

We used representative dialogue, without quotation marks, to indicate our creative license in setting historical scenes, which are well sourced from historical events. This dialogue was approved for contextual accuracy by Swanson family members and Compassion International. Some names were also changed for legal and privacy purposes.

If any mistakes remain, they are ours alone.

We trust you have enjoyed this journey!

Abbreviations Used in the Notes

BSC	Bob Swaney correspondence, Compassion USA Archives, October 22–November 15, 1965.
BSIT	Bob Swaney (assistant executive director, Compassion International), interview by Matt Bronleewe, 2018.
CCIT	Cathy Carey (Korean adoptee), interview by Matt Bronleewe and Eric Wilson, May 2019.
CMFS	"Media Fact Sheet," Compassion International, 2023.
CNL	*Compassion* newsletter, Compassion USA Archives, 1951–1965.
DLW	"Details in the Life and Work (gathered by Rev. Swanson)," Compassion USA Archives, n.d.
DSIT	David Swanson (son of Everett Swanson), interviews by Matt Bronleewe and Eric Wilson, 2018–2019.
EFSA	Everett F. Swanson accounts, Compassion USA Archives, 1951–1965.
EFSC	Everett F. Swanson correspondence, Compassion USA Archives, 1951–1965.
ESEAM	Everett Swanson Evangelistic Association materials, Compassion USA Archives, 1951–1965.
ESM	Everett Swanson Memorial Service (transcript of Lawrence Swanson), authors' collection, November 1965.
GPIK	*God's Parallel in Korea* (film script, narration by Everett Swanson), Compassion USA Archives, 1950s.
GSIT	George Swanson (nephew of Everett Swanson) interview, May 20, 2019.
KCPR	Korean Crusade Pictorial Report, 1959.
LFSA	Lawrence F. Swanson article, May 3, 1971.
LLIT	Lorie Lee (Compassion archivist) interview by Matt Bronleewe, 2018.
MOC	Jim Grant, screenwriter, *Man of Compassion*, executive produced by Byron Skalman, Compassion Incorporated.
MSC	Miriam Swanson correspondence, Compassion USA Archives, October 5, 1965–December 2, 1966.
NTYHS	Lorie Henry Lee, "'Now That You Have Seen': A Historical Look at Compassion. International 1952–2013" (PhD dissertation, Southeastern Baptist Theological Seminary, 2014).
RORS	Reflections on Rev. Swanson (by assorted orphanage directors), authors' collection, 1965.
ROOD	Everett Swanson, "The Responsibility of the Open Door to Me" (sermon transcript), Compassion USA Archives, 1952.
SSC	Sharon Swanson correspondence, December 2–29, 2011; October 17, 2018.
SSFH	The Stenstrom and Swanson Family History, Sycamore Public Library Collection, Illinois, June 19, 1994.
SSLT	Sally Swanson Lim interview by Matt Bronleewe and Eric Wilson, May 2019.
TWOG	*The Wrath of God* (film script, narration by Everett Swanson), Compassion USA Archives, 1953.
WSC	Wess Stafford communication, interview by Eric Wilson, 2019.

Notes

Part 1—Fall 1952: Seoul, Korea

13   *By invitation of Chaplain Hyung-do Kim:* EFSA, 1.

16   *American soldiers have shocked many:* GPIK, 1.

17   *Children have frozen:* Charles Townbridge, *American*, November 1, 1961, 1.

17   *"What are you going to do?":* Sylvia Shepherd, "Crusade Offers Compassion for Korean Orphans," *Chicago Tribune*, December 31, 1964, 38.

Chapter 1: A Nobody

18   *He had immigrated from Sweden:* SSFH, 1.

19   *They wanted to raise a family:* LFSA, 11.

21   *Highly regarded:* "Emil F. Swanson Dies During Major Surgery," *True Republican* (Sycamore, IL), May 4, 1948, 8.

21   *He trudged through the fields:* NTYHS, 20.

Chapter 2: Time to Grow

22   *Everett's feet were rooted:* NTYHS, 20.

22   *Let him borrow the shotgun:* GSIT.

23   *Would he still have to milk:* LFSA, 11.

Chapter 3: Just One Glimpse

23   *There was no greater joy:* LFSA, 11.

28   *The moment I opened my heart's door:* ROOD, 1.

Chapter 4: Defenseless

29   *"Fought to preserve the Union":* Phyllis Kelly, *Images of America: Sycamore,* 36.

30   *Private lives and public companies:* Bennett Lowenthal, "The Jumpers of '29," Washington Post, October 25, 1987.

31   *All He asks in return:* TWOG, 2–3.

32   *"Everett Swanson's excuses":* excerpt from "Senior Class Will," *Oracle,* 1931.

Chapter 5: The Spark

33   *He found inspiration:* Phyllis Kelly, *Images of America: Sycamore,* 99.

34   *Dr. O. L. Swanson had helped:* "Calvary Baptist Observance Ends," *True Republican* (Sycamore, IL), September 14, 1938, 1, 4.

34   *Dolder had recently run:* Phyllis Kelly, *Images of America: Sycamore,* 92.

35   *They attended the late-autumn corn pageant:* November Calendar, *Oracle,* 1930.

37   *The class motto:* Roberta S. Amrine, "Class of 1931," *Oracle,* 1931, 81.

37   *He had grown up thinking:* ROOD, 1–2.

38   *Class of 1931:* Roberta S. Amrine, "Class of 1931," *Oracle,* 1931, 81.

39   *The love of his life:* SSC, 2.

Part 2—Spring 1953: Daegu, South Korea

43   *"Waiting for the earth to spin":* Tucker Elliot, *The Day Before 9/11* (Amarillo, TX: Black Mesa Publishing, 2013), chap. 19, Kindle.

43   *Gi-sook and her father flee:* Gi-sook Story, as told to Junyoung Jang, 1–4, authors' collection.

44   *Gi-sook believes all hope is lost:* Ibid., 2.

Chapter 6: No Guarantees

48   *The Swansons barnstormed:* NTYHS, 21–22.

49   *Billed as the Singing Evangelist:* "Special Gospel Meetings" (display ad), May 16–30, 1937.

50   *Koreans who dared to resist:* Dolf-Alexander Neuhaus, "Awakening Asia: Korean Student Activists in Japan, the Asia Kunglun, and Asian Solidarity, 1910–1923," *Cross-Currents: East Asian History and Culture Review* 6:2 (2017).

Chapter 7: Taking a Toll

52   *Little Daver:* DSIT, 8.

53   *Eased his foot off:* DSIT, 10.

53   *Few places were hit harder:* Clifford R. Hope, Sr., "Kansas in the 1930s," *Kansas History* 36:1 and 2 (Spring 1970): 1–12.

54   *Everett Swanson has closed:* N. E. Wilson letter, Chautauqua, Kansas, November 21, 1937, Compassion USA Archives.

54   *A union evangelistic meeting:* C. H. Newton letter, Chetopa, Kansas, November 28, 1937, Compassion USA Archives.

Chapter 8: Very Little Hope

56   *Everett accepted an appointment:* NTYHS, 22.

59   *One of the greatest battles of his life:* MOC.

60   *Everett was never stingy:* Ray W. Johnson correspondence, January 18, 1967, 1–2, Compassion USA Archives.

60   *As Emmanuel Baptist grew:* NTYHS, 22.

Chapter 9: Worries of War

61   *A young man from Sycamore:* Thomas E. Woodstrup, *Sycamore, Illinois During World War II* (Sycamore, IL, self-published, 1991).

61   *An air force officer named:* GPIK, 5.

62   *"War is always a terrible thing":* TWOG, 1.

63   *The moment Everett said go:* DSIT, 19.

64   *"The moment some people":* ROOD, 3.

Chapter 10: Chicago Calling

67   *David clung to his father:* DSIT, 11.

68   *The responsibility of the opportunity:* ROOD, 1–4.

69   *Everett didn't even try to hide the tears:* NTYHS, 23.

70   *Grandpa later read:* SSLT, 15.

71   *We've got over two hundred:* Thomas E. Woodstrup, *Sycamore, Illinois During World War II*, 110.

Chapter 11: A Nest of Their Own

73   *Built in 1913:* Carl G. Ericson, *Harvest on the Prairies*, 75.

73   *He would spread his handwritten notes:* DSIT, 5.

74   *Sharon had the patio enclosure:* DSIT, 7.

Chapter 12: The Next Stage

74   *The snoring in the balcony:* DSIT, 21.

75   *Doc had hoped:* Judith Hemwall interview with authors, 1.

76   *Doc Hemwall attended to:* Ibid.

78   *The Swansons found cheaper activities:* DSIT, 18–20.

Chapter 13: Results

79   *It isn't fair, David whispered:* DSIT, 5.

81   *With no need to spice things up:* Ibid.

83   *Choosing publicly to follow Jesus:* Ibid.

83   *"There's a hallelujah meeting over there":* source unknown, public domain.

85   *The neighbor was plowing:* GSIT, 4.

Chapter 14: No Boundaries

86   *"Emil Frederick Swanson":* "Emil F. Swanson Dies During Major Surgery," *True Republican* (Sycamore, IL), May 4, 1948, 8.

87   *The five men sang:* DSIT, 9.

88   *As for the shotgun:* GSIT, 20.

Chapter 15: Cloth Over Plate

90   *When my father told me:* ROOD, 4.

91   *Everett's disappointment was real:* GSIT, 21–22.

92   *Everett and David sat side by side:* DSIT.

Chapter 16: The Envelope

99   *"While God is so good to us":* TWOG, 2.

94   *As he read aloud:* ESEAM, 3.

96   *A spinner, that's fine:* GSIT, 6.

97   *Admitted to being visibly shaken:* GSIT, 22.

98   *This money would get the Swansons:* SSC, 3.

Part 3—Winter 1957: Haksan, South Korea

101 *"The only clear, deep good":* Marguerite Higgins, *War in Korea: The Report of a Woman Combat Correspondent* (Borodino Books, 2017), chap. 7, Kindle.

101 *Meaning "to raise them in love":* Yo-hee Story, as told to Junyoung Jang, 1.

102 *Going another day without food:* Ibid., 2.

104 *The Lord has healed her husband:* Yo-hee Story, 1.

Chapter 17: This Evening Only

104 *His original plan:* SSC, 4.

105 *His response was adamant:* Ibid.

108 *As he stepped into the YMCA:* NTYHS, 25.

Chapter 18: Ambush

110 *Everett took photos:* ESEAM, 3–19.

110 *He found people uprooted:* MOC.

112 *The guerrillas poked around:* "Tent Campaign Will Open Here Sunday," *Suburbanite Economist*, July 9, 1952, 1.

113 *There were three types of POWs:* "Mass Suicide Predicted If POWs Forced to Return," *Ogden Standard-Examiner*, May 29, 1953, 7.

114 *My mother is in heaven:* GPIK, 5.

Chapter 19: Man on a Mission

115 *Women who had once joined the workforce:* Betty Friedan, *The Feminine Mystique* (New York: W. W. Norton, 1963), 3.

116 *You'll have to hold tight till Christmas:* DSIT, 17.

117 *Rev. Everett Swanson, who recently returned:* "Plan Series of Lectures for Calvary," *Daily Chronicle* (DeKalb, IL), May 16, 1952, 6.

117 *He will appear in native costume:* Ibid.

117 *"Our responsibility does not end":* ROOD, 3–4.

118 *Betty and my father:* Betty Edwards interview, 1, authors' collection.

119 *The most devout man she had ever met:* Ibid., 2.

Chapter 20: The Crucible

120 *Missionaries such as Horace Newton Allen:* "Early Missionaries and Martyrs in Korea," The Esther Project, February 27, 2017, http://theestherproject.com/early-missionaries-martyrs-korea/.

120 *"I realize much more my debt":* ROOD, 2.

121 *A meeting in a natural amphitheater:* "Evangelist Plans to Speak in City," *Ludington Daily News*, June 5, 1953, 3.

124 *Johnny "Cyclone" Thompson:* Phyllis Kelly, *Images of America: Sycamore*, 104.

124 *Spun round and round:* WSC.

Chapter 21: A Different Fight

125 *"We ought to get down on our knees":* TWOG, 2.

125 *A check for $50:* ESEAM, 2.

127 *They are everywhere, Miriam:* DSIT, 8.

128 *$1,000:* Sylvia Shepherd, "Crusade Offers Compassion for Korean Orphans," *Chicago Tribune*, December 31, 1964, 38.

Chapter 22: Twelve-Packs

129 *He made a handwritten list:* EFSA, 2.

130 *He wasn't interested in arranging adoptions:* NTYHS, 32.

131 *Meaning "faith and love":* Swanson Family article, 1960, 7.

131 *Churches and Sunday school groups:* "Lebanon Class Meets with Mrs. O'Bryan," *Linton Daily Citizen,* Linton, IN, October 17, 1963, 3.

Chapter 23: Shoveled Dirt

134 *"No one can eliminate prejudices":* B. William Sitcock et al., *Managing Television News* (New York: Routledge, 2006), 49 (quoting a December 31, 1955 television broadcast).

135 *US planes had dropped more explosives:* Charles K. Armstrong, "The Destruction and Reconstruction of North Korea, 1950–1960," *The Asia-Pacific Journal*, March 16, 2009.

135 *"Help these poor victims of war":* CNL, June–August 1959, 3.

136 *"My hands were empty when I began":* ESM, 3.

136 *Don't Miss These Meetings:* (display ad) *Des Moines Tribune*, March 14, 1953, 3.

136 *Evangelist Everett Swanson:* (display ad) *Ludington Daily News*, June 5, 1953, 3.

136 *You'll Know Why:* (display ad) *Ogden Standard-Examiner* (Ogden, UT), May 23, 1953, 3.

138 *Dear Mrs. W—:* Everett F. Swanson letter, December 10, 1953, Compassion USA Archives.

138 *Her life was fully and beautifully lived:* "Services Held on Monday for Mrs. Emma Swanson" *True Republican* (Sycamore, IL), October 20, 1953, 8.

Chapter 24: One at a Time

140 *I want to take this opportunity:* ESEA newsletter, December 1953.

141 *The mailing of the newsletter:* SSC, 7–10.

143 *"Directors and staff members are all Koreans":* ESEAM, 21.

143 *"By God's grace":* EFSC, March 1956.

144 *"It was wonderful to get the pictures":* CNL, January 1, 1959, 5.

144 *"I spend most of the day in prayer":* Ibid.

144 *Even got George signed up:* GSIT, 19.

144 *"I get more lickins":* GSIT, 8.

Chapter 25: Put Things Right

146 *"Although this war has cost America many lives":* TWOG, 2.

147 *Son, where'd you go?:* DSIT, 9.

148 *We lost it:* Ibid., 14–15.

Chapter 26: Round Three

151 *Gifts of traditional Korean clothing:* "Doing Something About It," *Today,* January 5, 1958, 8.

152 *What does a day:* CCIT, 1–4.

152 *The older kids learned vocational skills:* CCIT, 5–9.

153 *He had made the shift:* NTYHS, 32.

153 *Everett met a boy named Sung-dong:* "Look at This Boy" (display ad), World Relief Committee.

Chapter 27: Into the Trenches

155 *They grew from 17,000:* KCPR, 21.

156 *Come back soon!:* Ibid., 10.

157 *This DMZ was a reminder:* Ibid., 15–16.

158 *Drawing from this treasure trove:* Ibid., 2–21.

158 *Reasons to Praise God:* Ibid., 20.

Chapter 28: Doctor's Orders

160 *The first to bring concerns:* DSIT, 9.

161 *I offered to help him:* Ibid., 7.

165 *Boxes of clothing:* EFSC, November 1958, 2.

165 *The largest of its kind:* "Pastor Cited with Degree," *Suburbanite Economist,* January 1, 1964.

Part 4—Summer 1959: Masan, South Korea

169 *"All the classrooms were destroyed":* Korean War: A History from Beginning to End, (CreateSpace 2017), chap. 3, Kindle.

171 *He is a thief:* Ei-sun Story, as told to Junyoung Jang, 1, authors' collection.

173 *I would love for you to go:* Ei-sun Story, 1–2.

Chapter 29: Picking Up Speed

174 *"On April 19, 1956":* NTYHS, 34.

174 *Per state guidelines:* ESEAM, 2.

175 *"The End of the World":* "Evangelist to Conduct Services Here," *Great Falls Tribune,* May 28, 1956, 24.

176 *I'll spend the first hundred years:* SSC, 14.

177 *I want to express:* EFSC, Summer 1956.

177 *Everett created a new letterhead:* EFSC, Winter 1956.

Chapter 30: To Heal and Rebuild

180 *The letter translator, a Buddhist, was so moved:* RORS, 4.

182 *Operated with a minimal cost:* NTYHS, 38–39.

182 *Joining the National Guard:* Swanson Family article, 1960, 6, Compassion USA Archives.

182 *The story of Hillside Christian Children's Home:* Hillside Christian Story, 1.

183 *"I received your most welcome letter":* Yak-shin Lee to Elmer Rund, March 7, 1957, Compassion USA Archives.

Chapter 31: In the Rough

186 *I get it from all sides:* DSIT, 5.

188 *He'd been invited to preach:* NTYHS, 40.

Chapter 32: At Last

188 *My sense of responsibility:* ROOD, 1–4.

190 *I've come to see the children:* Yo-hee Story, as told to Junyoung Jang, 5, authors' collection.

191 *It means "beautiful life":* Gi-sook Story, as told to Junyoung Jang, 11–14, authors' collection.

191 *I will help you:* Ibid.

Chapter 33: You Must Take Care

192 *Rev. Swanson found his true compatriot:* NTYHS, 40.

196 *John was raised under enemy occupation:* CNL, August 1961, 1–2.

196 *I made a great mistake:* Ibid.

197 *Intestinal troubles were common:* NTYHS, 41.

Chapter 34: Photos and Records

198 *He was skin and bones:* CNL, June–August 1959, 1–3.

198 *"Then I prayed for you":* Ibid., 2.

200 *Admitted for a hysterectomy:* EFSC, November 1958, 2.

200 *Angel Orphanage, in Daegu:* Ibid., 1.

200 *It was of utmost importance:* Compassion Evangelistic Quarterly Report, 1959.

Chapter 35: Puzzle Pieces

201 *Even their pigs and ducks were dying:* NTYHS, 44.

201 *Dr. van Lierop informed him:* CNL, June–July–August 1959, 4.

202 *If we set up an ESEA office in Seoul:* BSIT, 3.

203 *Worried no one would come:* "A Korean Deacon Is Thankful," CNL, April–May 1959, 3.

Chapter 36: To Suffer With

206 *"I have compassion on the multitude":* CNL, April–May 1959, 1.

207 *Three more had already been added:* Ibid.

Chapter 37: No Inkling

208 *In the Swanson household:* Swanson Family article, 6.

208 *A traveling man for Jesus:* Ibid.

209 *The Swansons' expansive basement:* NTYHS, 45.

210 *Encounters with the beggar boys:* CNL, September–October 1959, 4–5.

Chapter 38: Surprises

212 *You have probably read in the papers of the typhoons:* CNL, November–December 1959, 1–2.

213 *Soon, projects were added:* CNL, September–October 1959, 5–6.

214 *"Enclosed is $15 . . . our orphanage has been changing":* "Out of the Mailbag," ibid., 6.

215 *"I am very well now":* "Older Orphan Boy in Korean Army," CNL, November–December 1959, 6.

Chapter 39: Fire and Steel

218 *Miriam strolled through:* SSLT, 18.

219 *Send out a letter immediately:* ESEAM, May 1, 1960, 1.

220 *Rev. Swanson visited our home:* RORS, 3.

220 *Political unrest:* Michael Breen, "Fall of Korea's First President Syngman Rhee in 1960," *Korea Times,* April 18, 2010, https://www.koreatimes.co.kr/www/nation/2023/09/113_64364.html.

222 *They received an unexpected blessing:* NTYHS, 47.

Part 5—Autumn 1960: Busan, South Korea

227 *"It is only through":* Ki-moon Ban, "Statement to the United Nations Framework Convention on Climate Change," December 6, 2011.

228 *The place is called Seoul Ae-Lyn-Won:* Myung-guen Story, as told to Junyoung Jang, 1, authors' collection.

228 *He even receives a grand award:* Ibid., 2.

230 *Doctors confirm the reverend's concerns:* Ibid.

Chapter 40: Reflections

231 *The board agreed to launch Operation Long Underwear:* EFSC, 15.

232 *I want to arrive emptyhanded:* Judith Hemwall interview with authors, 2.

233 *She attended Wheaton:* SSLT, 5.

234 *John Seong and his bride:* "ESEA Korean Secretary Marries," CNL, July–August 1961.

235 *He was comfortable with people:* Rev. Jun-gon Kim statement, Compassion USA Archives, September 25, 1963.

Chapter 41: At a Cost

236 *WARM met a familiar, yet vital need:* NTYHS, 50.

238 *Enroll in Korean language courses:* SSLT, 7–9.

238 *You'll need to apply:* Ibid., 6.

239 *Help newborns in Cabrini-Green:* Ibid.

Chapter 42: The Summons

240 *He carried over $100,000:* Charles Townbridge, "One Man Is Merciful, 10,000 Children Live!" *American,* November 1, 1961, 2.

243 *Office of the President:* ESEAM, 20.

244 *President Yun stepped toward him:* CNL, January–February 1962, 4.

244 *About the ministry's origins:* Charles Townbridge, "One Man Is Merciful," 2.

Chapter 43: Special Edition

245 *The building project launched:* NTYHS, 52.

246 *Sally's freighter embarked:* SSLT, 4.

246 *A little orphan girl:* Ibid., 7.

248 *Time for a change:* EFSC, 4–5.

250 *This special edition booklet:* ESEAM, 1–20.

250 *For ten years:* ESEAM, 6.

Chapter 44: Pack Your Bags

251 *A million-dollar ministry:* Progress Through the Years, 2.

251 *Canada was a major contributor:* NTYHS, 54.

251 *I have an idea for you:* "Minister 'Loses' Coat, Finds Career in Korea," *Chicago Tribune,* December 29, 1963, 13.

253 *Bob was a Chicagoan:* BSIT, 1.

255 *Six telephones in a line:* Ibid., 3.

256 *He also coordinated the 16mm film: The Runaway* (promotional flyer), April 1, 1965.

Chapter 45: About to Break

257 *One of the city's leading private institutions:* https://www.konkuk.ac.kr/eng.

257 *Receiving an honorary doctorate: The News,* Chicago, IL, November 25, 1965, 8.

258 *David cleaning Doc's medical office:* DSIT, 22–23.

258 *The ad ran immediately:* Ibid.

Chapter 46: Flying Arrows

259 *The release of a 16mm film:* "Pastor Cited with Degree," *Suburbanite Economist,* Chicago, IL, January 1, 1964, 10.

260 *The globe-trotting physician:* "Spiritual Life Crusade Opens at Bethel," *The News*, Chicago, IL, May 6, 1964, 2.

261 *A man named Kil-yong Choi:* Kil-yong Choi letter to sponsors, May 1, 1964, Compassion USA Archives.

262 *Called Director Kim to a meeting:* RORS, 1.

264 *Audits revealed discrepancies:* EFSC, June 2, 1964.

265 *A flash announcement:* BSC, June 9, 1964.

Chapter 47: Eagle Eye

266 *What about the orphan quartet:* "General Information for Those Holding Meetings with Reverend Swanson and Group," 1–2.

267 *He then sent letters:* EFSC, July 30, 1964.

267 *Things took another negative turn:* BSC, July 13, 1964.

269 *You have an eagle eye:* BSIT, 2.

270 *You'll meet someone square on:* Ibid., 3.

Chapter 48: No-Man's-Land

271 *In fact, I tried to warn you:* LLIT, 2.

271 *He's very sharp:* SSLT, 19.

272 *I saw barrels of vitamins:* EFSC, October 7, 1964.

274 *This had to end:* NTYHS, 58–59.

276 *Already asked me to step down:* NTYHS, 60.

277 *You no longer work for us:* BSIT, 3.

Chapter 49: Precious Jewels

278 *The Compassion board:* NTYHS, 35, 58.

278 *John was a real operator:* BSIT, 3.

279 *Then reached for the garage door:* SSLT, 17.

280 *"How do you do, everybody?":* Tom Newsom, "They Sing for Orphan Aid," *Quad-City Times* (Davenport, Iowa), September 26, 1966, 15.

281 *Already a fine success:* EFSC, October 7, 1964, 1.

281 *Miriam would sign up sponsors:* GSIT, 19.

281 *With over sixty scheduled venues:* "Korean Orphan Trio to Give Program Here," *Sioux City Journal*, October 28, 1964, 24.

281 *The incident even made it:* "Thief Robs Chicago Cleric," *Chicago Tribune*, September 5, 1964, 3.

Chapter 50: The Drive Home

284 *She met Jung-won Lee:* CCIT, 3, 10.

286 *It's just broken his heart:* DSIT, 9.

287 *One of his legs had locked:* Ibid., 12.

288 *Admitted to the Mayo Clinic:* BSIT, 5.

289 *At no time has your testimony been brighter:* ESM, 3.

290 *"We have been told":* MSC, October 29, 1965.

290 *He wouldn't be joining the tour:* NTYHS, 62.

Chapter 51: And Now This

293 *A cablegram from Bob Swaney:* BSC, 4.

294 *"He was . . . humble before anyone":* RORS, 3.

294 *Offering to help:* Ted W. Engstrom to Doc Hemwall, November 22, 1965, Compassion USA Archives.

294 *"Everett's not here":* ESM, 2.

295 *Standing at attention:* GSIT, 13.

295 *Answering to Rev. Harvey:* NTYHS, 64.

296 *"So much a part of my life":* "Beloved Husband," MSC, December 1965.

Today: An Exclamation Point

298 *One US president:* Mahita Gajanan, "A Filipino Boy Was 'Speechless' after Discovering George H. W. Bush Was His Pen Pal for Years," Time, December 19, 2018, https://time.com/5484261/george-hw-bush-pen-pal-filipino-boy.

299 *They were treated like celebrities:* DSIT, 39.

299 *Continued as a registered nurse:* SSLT, 28.

299 *He fulfilled his lifelong wish:* Judith Hemwall interview with authors, 1.

300 *Served the orphans for decades:* Gi-sook Story, 7–8.

300 *Amidst the hardships:* Yo-hee Story, 5–6.

300 *Founded the Swanson Memorial Foundation:* Ei-sun Story, 2–4.

300 *The boy who would have gone blind:* Myung-guen Story, 2.

BIBLIOGRAPHY

Brown, David G. *The White Hurricane*. Camden, ME: Ragged Mountain Press, 2004.

Buck, Pearl S. *The Living Reed*. New York: Day Company, 1963.

Cumings, Bruce. *Korea's Place in the Sun: A Modern History*. New York: W. W. Norton, 1997.

Davy, Harriet Wilson, ed. *From Oxen to Jets: A History of DeKalb County, 1835–1963*. Dixon, IL: Rogers Printing.

Elliot, Tucker. *The Day Before 9/11*. Amarillo, TX: Black Mesa Publishing, 2013. Kindle.

Ericson, Carl G. *Harvest on the Prairies: Centennial History of the Baptist Conference of Illinois, 1856–1956*. Chicago: Baptist Conference Press, 1956.

Everett Swanson in Ethiopia, produced by Everett F. Swanson (1951), 16mm film.

Feinstein, Stephen. *The 1950s: From the Korean War to Elvis*, Berkeley Heights, NJ: Enslow, 2006.

First Four Orphanages, produced by Everett F. Swanson, Everett Swanson Evangelistic Association (1953), 16mm film.

God's Parallel in Korea (film script), narration by Everett Swanson, (n.d., 1950s).

Gross, Lewis M. *Past and Present of DeKalb County, Illinois, Vol. 1*. Chicago: Pioneer Publishing, 1907.

Johnson, Paul. *History of the American People*. New York: Harper Perennial, 1999.

Kelly, Phyllis, et al. *Images of America: Sycamore*. Charleston, SC: Arcadia, 2007.

Langford, Donna, ed. *Historical Markers of DeKalb County*, DeKalb, IL: DeKalb Area Agricultural Heritage Association, 2018.

Lee, Lorie Henry. "'Now That You Have Seen': A Historical Look at Compassion International 1952–2013." PhD dissertation, Southeastern Baptist Theological Seminary, 2014.

Man of Compassion, written by Jim Grant, screenwriter, produced by Byron Skalman, Compassion International (n.d.), videotape.

McLagan, C. R. "Luke." *Sycamore (Illinois) According to Luke*, DeKalb, IL: DeKalb County Historical and Genealogical Society, 1994.

Paxton, Norbert. *Rough Guide to Korea*. London: Rough Guides, 2018.

Pembroke, Michael. *Korea: Where the American Century Began*. London: Oneworld Publications, 2018.

Perritano, John. *America at War—Korean War*. New York: Franklin Watts, 2010.

The Runaway, written and directed by Charles Davis, produced by Burt Martin, Compassion International (1963), 16mm film.

Sides, Hampton. *On Dangerous Ground: The Marines at the Reservoir, the Korean War's Greatest Battle*. New York: Doubleday, 2018.

Story of Compassion, Wess Stafford, Compassion International (2009), videotape.

Warren, James R. *The War Years: A Chronicle of Washington State in World War II*. Seattle: University of Washington Press, 2001.

The Wrath of God (film script), narration by Everett Swanson, Everett Swanson Evangelistic Association (1953).